Learning, Behavior, and Your Classroom

How to Create an Environment That Sets Students Up for Success

Staci M. Zolkoski

Solution Tree | Press

Copyright © 2025 by Solution Tree Press

Materials appearing here are copyrighted. With one exception, all rights are reserved. Readers may reproduce only those pages marked "Reproducible." Otherwise, no part of this book may be reproduced or transmitted in any form or by any means (electronic, photocopying, recording, or otherwise) without prior written permission of the publisher.

555 North Morton Street
Bloomington, IN 47404
800.733.6786 (toll free) / 812.336.7700
FAX: 812.336.7790

email: info@SolutionTree.com
SolutionTree.com

Visit **go.SolutionTree.com/behavior** to download the free reproducibles in this book.

Printed in the United States of America

Library of Congress Cataloging-in-Publication Data

Names: Zolkoski, Staci M., author.
Title: Learning, behavior, and your classroom : how to create an environment that sets students up for success / Staci M. Zolkoski.
Description: Bloomington, IN : Solution Tree Press, [2025] | Includes bibliographical references and index.
Identifiers: LCCN 2024049985 (print) | LCCN 2024049986 (ebook) | ISBN 9781958590690 (paperback) | ISBN 9781958590706 (ebook)
Subjects: LCSH: Classroom management. | Motivation in education. | Teachers--Job stress. | Learning, Psychology of. | Mental health.
Classification: LCC LB3013 .Z64 2025 (print) | LCC LB3013 (ebook) | DDC 371.102/4--dc23/eng/20250208
LC record available at https://lccn.loc.gov/2024049985
LC ebook record available at https://lccn.loc.gov/2024049986

Solution Tree
Jeffrey C. Jones, CEO
Edmund M. Ackerman, President

Solution Tree Press
President and Publisher: Douglas M. Rife
Associate Publishers: Todd Brakke and Kendra Slayton
Editorial Director: Laurel Hecker
Art Director: Rian Anderson
Copy Chief: Jessi Finn
Production Editor: Kate St. Ives
Proofreader: Sarah Ludwig
Cover and Text Designer: Fabiana Cochran
Acquisitions Editors: Carol Collins and Hilary Goff
Content Development Specialist: Amy Rubenstein
Associate Editors: Sarah Ludwig and Elijah Oates
Editorial Assistant: Madison Chartier

Acknowledgments

I would like to thank my Mr. Wonderful, Sean, for his love and support. Nothing I do would be possible without him and his unwavering support. I also want to thank my amazing kids, Colton and Zoe. They give me ideas, make me laugh, and are the best cheerleaders! I cannot thank my family and friends enough for listening and encouraging me along the way. I truly have the best support system.

Solution Tree Press would like to thank the following reviewers:

Tonya Alexander
English Teacher (NBCT)
Owego Free Academy
Owego, New York

Doug Crowley
Assistant Principal
DeForest Area High School
DeForest, Wisconsin

Kelly Hilliard
GATE Mathematics Instructor
  NBCT
Darrell C. Swope Middle School
Reno, Nevada

Teresa Kinley
Senior School English Teacher
Calgary, Alberta, Canada

Jennifer Renegar
Data & Assessment Specialist
Republic School District
Republic, Missouri

Visit **go.SolutionTree.com/behavior** to download the free reproducibles in this book.

Table of Contents

Reproducibles are in italics.

About the Author.. ix

Introduction.. 1
   Why This Book.. 3
   How to Use This Book... 4

Chapter 1

Understand Student Behavior and How They Think 7
   The Basics of Student Brain Development 8
   How Internal and External Factors Influence Students'
      Behavior and Brain Development........................... 13
   Understand Students' Needs 27
   How to Support Students With an Effective Management Plan...... 29
   Concluding Thoughts... 33
      Reflecting on Showing Empathy 34

Chapter 2

Cultivate a Positive Classroom Environment 35
    Research on the Classroom Environment and the Whole Child 36
    Strategies for Implementing a Positive Classroom Environment 38
    Concluding Thoughts 63
        Building a Positive Classroom Environment 64

Chapter 3

Communicate Expectations and Establish and Reinforce Boundaries 67
    Strategies for Communicating Expectations and Establishing and Reinforcing Boundaries 69
    Strategies for Engaging With Families 92
    Concluding Thoughts 97
        Classroom Expectations 98

Chapter 4

Provide Additional Support for Students Who Need More 101
    Strategies for Providing Students With Additional Support 102
    Supports for Students at Tier 3 123
    Concluding Thoughts 130
        Reflective Thinking About Bias 131

Chapter 5

Promote Student Independence and Learning 133
    Strategies for Implementing Best Practices for Teaching Academics 134
    Concluding Thoughts 151
        Thinking About Differentiating Instruction 153

Chapter 6
Practice Self-Care 157
    Tips to Remember for Taking Care of Yourself 158
    Strategies for Implementing Self-Care 159
    Concluding Thoughts 163

Epilogue 165
References and Resources 169
Index 185

About the Author

Staci M. Zolkoski, PhD, is an associate professor of special education and the director of the School of Education at the University of Texas at Tyler (UT Tyler). Prior to working at the collegiate level, Dr. Zolkoski taught kindergarten and fourth grade. She teaches classroom management at the undergraduate and graduate levels as well as courses in special education, behavior disorders, and educational strategies. She has won the White Fellowship for Teaching Excellence Award and Piper Professor Nominee for UT Tyler. She earned the Teaching Award for the UT Tyler College of Education and Psychology and Kappa Delta Pi International Honor Society Teacher of the Year Award.

Dr. Zolkoski is a member of the Council for Exceptional Children as well as an active member of the Division for Emotional and Behavioral Health (DEBH), where she served as the editor of the DEBH newsletter for six years. She is the treasurer of the DEBH Foundation. Dr. Zolkoski has presented and published her research on resilience and social-emotional learning at the national and international levels. She worked with local school districts to implement social-emotional learning and has trained teachers and schools in social-emotional learning and classroom management. Dr. Zolkoski has also presented for ElevateTXEd, which is a collaborative effort across the University of Texas System. She currently supports schools and school districts throughout the United States on classroom management and working with students with challenging behaviors.

Dr. Zolkoski earned her bachelor's degree in early childhood education from the University of Toledo in Ohio. She earned her master's degree and doctorate in special education with an emphasis on behavior disorders from the University of North Texas.

To book Staci M. Zolkoski for professional development, contact pd@SolutionTree.com.

Introduction

Today is Mrs. Cates's first day teaching. She has been dreaming of this day since she was young and playing school in her room with her stuffed animals. She went to college to prepare for her future as a classroom teacher.

Mr. Watts has his degree in kinesiology but hasn't found the right job fit for him. He thinks off and on about teaching but isn't sure if it's for him. After subbing a few times, he realizes he wants to participate in a program where he can earn his teacher certification while he teaches.

Mrs. Miller has never taught before, but after losing her job, she decides she wants to teach because there are a lot of job openings in her area. She goes to a school that is still suffering shortages brought on during the COVID-19 pandemic, and they offer her a job, telling her she can get her teacher certification later.

Mr. Thomas has been teaching for ten years and has always loved his job, but he is feeling frustrated and burned out. The system is challenging, and the needs of the students are higher now than they used to be.

Mrs. Favre has been teaching for five years and loves it. She is always eager to consider new ideas and learn new strategies so she can help her students as best she can.

You may or may not see yourself in one of the preceding scenarios, but I hope the diversity of experiences conveyed in these scenarios makes clear this book is for all K–12 teachers—new teachers, ambitious teachers such as those in pre-service training, veteran teachers, teachers who feel burned out, teachers who are on fire with a sense of meaningful purpose and possibility, and teachers who have or will fit all of these roles during the course of their career.

I believe there is nothing more rewarding than teaching, because you can make a huge positive impact on the lives of the students you have in your classroom each year. With that said, I also believe it is one of the most challenging jobs a person can have. Each teacher enters the classroom as one single person working to meet all the different needs of each student in the class while also working to meet the requirements of administrators, which can be demanding. We must also, as teachers, consider our students' families and both the challenges and the supports they offer to the students in our care. It can be a complex job to navigate those challenges as we work to give our students what they need to best learn and grow. Unanticipated difficulties, such as those presented by the COVID-19 pandemic, only exacerbate the pressures and stress inherent in the teaching profession. Teachers have a lot of irons in the fire, so to speak, and sometimes it feels and is overwhelming.

Classroom management is a particularly difficult part of teaching, perhaps because the need to develop and maintain a classroom environment that supports high-level learning underpins every other part of the teacher's responsibilities. Principals and school leaders always ask about classroom-management skills when hiring teachers, both veteran and new, yet often, teachers go into the classroom with little to no training on effective classroom-management skills. We all have the best intentions, but sometimes what we have planned in our minds doesn't meet with reality, or we find ourselves facing situations in the classroom that we simply aren't prepared to confront. Without effective classroom-management strategies, it is extremely challenging for teachers to deploy the amazing lessons they may have prepared for their students. Too often, teachers are left feeling defeated, stressed, and burned out, with all students missing out on vital instruction and those students who struggle with their behavior ending up with ever more challenging behaviors, which in turn is more exhausting for the teachers who work with them.

Such cycles inevitably feed on themselves to the detriment of all, and it's with the goal of preventing this from taking hold in your classroom, and many others, that I offer this book.

Why This Book

My motivation to write this book springs from several sources. First and foremost is my lifelong love of teaching. I always wanted to be a teacher. Like Mrs. Cates from the introductory scenario, I played teacher in my bedroom when I was young, and my stuffed animals were my students. When my mom went back to school while I was growing up, I loved it because I could be her teacher! I gave her quizzes and graded her work. As an adult, I remember having my first classroom and how excited (and terrified) I was. I remember thinking, "What am I supposed to do now? How am I possibly responsible for all these kindergarteners?" But I settled in and loved it. It was completely exhausting, and there were lots of struggles and tears along the way, but I discovered I was good at teaching and especially loved working with students who had challenging behaviors.

This led me to pursue my master's degree in special education with an emphasis on working with students who had emotional and behavioral disorders (EBDs). I wanted to learn more strategies to help them be successful. Later, I went back to school to earn my doctorate in special education, also with an emphasis on working with students with EBDs. I am currently the director of the School of Education and an associate professor at the University of Texas at Tyler. It is an honor to get to work with preservice and in-service teachers. The impact I always wanted to make is even bigger than I could have ever dreamed.

My second reason for writing this book comes from teaching a course on classroom management for the past eight years. Through teaching the course, I have learned there is so much more to classroom management than rules and procedures. Teachers need to understand why behaviors occur in the first place. When we know why behaviors occur, we can fix them. Each student's why is different, and we can't respond to their challenging behaviors in the same way. However, regardless of individual needs and challenges, all students have better behaviors when they feel like they belong and are cared for, and managing a class becomes much easier. Teachers need to understand why it's so important to build a positive environment and how to do it. I find it easier to support *all students* when I have a better understanding of why some students act the way they do and when I've created an environment where everyone wants to be. I want to give teachers tools they can use to truly support all students in this way.

Lastly, I want to further explore topics connected to those of my previous book, *Motivated to Learn: Decreasing Challenging Student Behaviors and Increasing Academic Engagement* (Zolkoski, Lewis Chiu, & Lusk, 2023), which I coauthored with my excellent colleagues Calli Lewis Chiu and Mandy E. Lusk. While

Motivated to Learn focuses specifically on teaching strategies to address challenging student behaviors, the intent of *Learning, Behavior, and Your Classroom* is to offer classroom-management strategies that encompass all student behaviors and classroom situations teachers may encounter in K–12 teaching.

Specifically, this book walks educators through how to set up a classroom, how to build a positive environment, how to create a positive management system, how to support students who need extra support, and how to effectively communicate with all stakeholders. This book is intended to be a strategy-packed practical guide to classroom management to help any K–12 teacher be and *feel* successful in the classroom.

To achieve this lofty goal, it's important to know how to be preventative and proactive rather than reactionary. Having a plan in place allows teachers to be proactive and support students by explicitly stating what expectations are. *Learning, Behavior, and Your Classroom* provides each step needed to create a plan for success. I am confident that as you read and apply the strategies this book offers, you will feel charged, or maybe even recharged, to continue making a positive difference in the lives of your students, both current and future.

How to Use This Book

My hope for you with this book is that you not only understand why you need a positive classroom-management plan but learn how to create one and implement it. In the book, I discuss such elements of management as the different teaching challenges from starting to teach a class at the beginning of the school year versus the middle of the school year and the reality and value of diverse teacher perspectives and experiences. I address these factors while acknowledging that what works for one teacher will not always work for another, and this is OK! You don't want to implement strategies that aren't a good fit for you because they won't work as effectively. I offer a variety of strategies and the rationale behind why the strategies work. The goal is for you to take the information and find what works best for you and your classroom.

The chapters build on one another, and each is part of an approach of best practices for effectively teaching. You will learn why behaviors occur and how to set up a positive learning environment. You will learn the elements needed for an effective classroom-management plan and what to do when students need more support with their behavior. Although I recommend reading the book in order to begin, you can easily refer to any chapter to familiarize yourself with it. Some of the concepts in each chapter may not come as naturally as others, which is completely OK. Where appropriate, you will find templates you can use to aid in your own classroom-management plan or to augment your work developing your classroom environment. The idea behind the book is to learn not only why the concepts are important but how to effectively implement them in your classroom.

This book contains six chapters, along with an introduction and epilogue. In chapter 1, I walk you through the basics of brain development and articulate how brain development influences student behavior. I also examine what internal and external factors affect brain development and behaviors. This chapter aims to help readers gain an understanding of students' needs and therefore develop compassion and the desire for efficacy in meeting those needs. Chapter 2 discusses why building a positive environment is the most important thing for student success. It goes on to describe how to build this kind of environment. Chapter 3 focuses on creating a positive classroom-management plan by learning how to effectively set up your room with rules, procedures, positive reinforcement, and consequences. You will engage most of your students with the plan you create in chapter 3; however, some students will still struggle. Chapter 4 provides my favorite strategies for supporting students who have challenging behaviors, including choice, a token economy, self-monitoring, positive peer reporting (PPR), and the Good Behavior Game, which is a game focusing on the positive behaviors you want to see from your students (for example, raising their hand to answer questions). This chapter also includes guidance on what to do when there are students in your classroom who continue to struggle despite receiving additional support with their behavior. In chapter 5, I share how to promote student independence and learning by providing effective tools for teaching the amazing lessons you plan. Finally, chapter 6 is about teacher self-care; this is arguably the most important chapter because the only way we can be our best selves for our students is by taking care of ourselves.

Each chapter begins with research-based support for the topics you will be learning about, but then you learn exactly how to implement the strategies. The book is intended to meet the needs of all teachers, including primary and secondary educators. You will also learn how to diversify strategies for all types of learners. Voices From the Field offer perspectives from administrators, teachers, and students. I believe it's important to hear the perspective of others, particularly students, because that is how we learn and can ensure we are truly meeting the needs of others. Chapters 1–5 also have a reproducible tool at the end, which is intended to support reflective thoughts about the chapter and how it can be used by the readers.

Now, let's get to it and begin with chapter 1, where you learn all about the links between brain development and behavior. As you read, remind yourself that behavior, no matter how disruptive, is a form of communication! Let's dive into what the brain is doing while our students work, play, and learn in their classrooms.

CHAPTER 1
Understand Student Behavior and How They Think

Have you ever looked at a student and thought, "Why? Why is this student acting this way?" Or, "Why did that student respond positively to the strategy I tried while this other student did not respond at all?" I think all teachers can say they've had these thoughts. Figuring out how to respond to student behavior is difficult and sometimes frustrating.

This is because the reasons for students' behaviors are often not visible or easily accessible, even to experienced teachers. Additionally, the reason for one student's behavior is likely going to be different than the reason for another student's behavior, while the behavior itself may be the same! You may have had a student in the past and figured out what to do, but when you have another similar student and try the same strategies, it doesn't work, and you're left wondering why.

The purpose of this chapter is to explore the reasons driving student behavior. There are both internal and external factors that influence student behaviors. I discuss brain development in children and adolescents, how student behavior is linked to processes and structures in the brain, and what teachers may actually see (that is, the visible, external results of these complicated internal processes). I then examine a multitude of factors that have an impact on behavior and brain development, including genetic components, teachers, peer influences, the home environment, stress, adverse childhood experiences, and other forms of trauma. Next, I look at the important ways in which understanding student behavior reflects an unmet need. Finally, I discuss how to support students with an effective classroom-management plan comprised of five critical components. It is important to begin with the foundation for how each component relies on the others. For example, if you don't understand why behaviors may occur, it makes it more difficult to relate to your students. I have found that explaining this process helps teachers come from a better place of understanding when working with students. Now, let's start with the basics of brain development in school-aged children.

The Basics of Student Brain Development

The most complex part of the human body is the brain. Knowledge of the brain helps us to better understand our students and their behavior. The brain controls our intelligence, interprets our senses and body movement, and controls our behavior (National Institute of Neurological Disorders and Stroke, 2023). All parts of the brain work together, and each part has its own unique responsibilities. Scientists used to think that the human brain formed entirely in early childhood; however, by using an MRI to scan children's brains year after year, they discovered the brain goes through fundamental changes in adolescence and isn't fully developed in humans until they reach their mid-twenties (Society for Neuroscience, 2018).

During early childhood there is significant brain development. Millions of neurons are formed, connections are formed, and there is continued growth of gray matter (Society for Neuroscience, 2018). The brain is 90 percent formed by the age of 5, leaving plenty of room for growth during childhood, adolescence, and early adulthood. During critical periods of development, the brain adapts to factors (for example, being helped by parents and getting basic needs met, including sleep and food) in the environment surrounding an individual, which means both the environment and a person's genes exert a strong influence on the brain. There is a correlation between high rates of learning and the critical periods of brain development (that is, the first few years of life, early childhood, adolescence, and early adulthood) when neural connections are changing (Society for Neuroscience, 2018).

Typical adolescent behavior can be impulsive, energy-filled, and frustrating to those who interact with adolescents. A favorite story in my family is when my early-teens-aged son was making pasta noodles with my mom, which he had done multiple times within the week he was visiting. My mom told him to slap the cup of flour on the counter. All he heard was slap the flour on the counter, so that's exactly what he did! Flour went literally everywhere! Of course, after the fact, he realized she didn't really want him to slap the flour—she was just using an expression; but in the moment, that's what she got . . . a giant slap of flour.

It's almost like you can see sparks coming out of adolescent students' ears from the wires trying to connect and things just not working right. However, there is often a reason behind these sometimes-confounding behaviors that has nothing to do with the adolescent's conscious intention. Puberty changes the brain (Vijayakumar, Op de Macks, Shirtcliff, & Pfeifer, 2018). The brain's capacity to learn during the teenage years is extraordinary, and all this learning happens while the brain is improving connections (Society for Neuroscience, 2018). While the adolescent brain is much like a ball of clay and is ready to be molded and changed by new experiences, the process is a mess. The brain changes and develops in set patterns, which leaves adolescents with a mix of immature and mature regions of the brain (DK Publishing, 2020).

Teens have a reputation for being emotional, rebellious, self-centered, and impulsive. For example, you may have a student who appears to overact to a situation you don't think is a big deal. It becomes a big deal to teens because the limbic system is highly reactive, causing heightened emotional responses and the experience of feeling things on a deeper level. Similarly, have you ever looked at teenage students around you and found that they are really clumsy or maybe more clumsy than usual? Clumsiness is due to rapid growth spurts, and the body maps in the brain cannot keep up, which causes the body and brain to be out of sync. Teenagers are experiencing all this all at once, and it's a lot!

During childhood and particularly adolescence, there are enhanced connections forming in the brain. Although this means your students have ever-enhanced learning abilities, it also contributes to increased risk taking. Increased risk taking occurs because the stage of brain development includes an inability to gauge risk accurately and the inability to control impulses. Scientists would argue that our brains are always changing (Society for Neuroscience, 2018), but as adults with fully formed brains, we need to remember our students' brains are actually different than ours. Students throughout the K–12 age range don't have the capacity to think in the same way we do because their brains are still developing. Let's take a closer look at how this all is reflected in the classroom and how you see and experience it all as a teacher.

HOW STUDENT BEHAVIOR IS LINKED TO BRAIN DEVELOPMENT

Now that we have looked at the basics of how the brain develops over time and how the childhood brain differs from the adulthood brain, let's consider a bit of how the brain impacts student behaviors in our classrooms. I find it is easier to understand students when I realize the behaviors they are exhibiting are linked to how their brain is developing. For example, a student may excitedly call out the answer to a question without raising their hand. This is frustrating if we have an expectation of students waiting to be called on. Impulsivity can be connected to brain development. Or, a student might stare at you as though you are speaking another language when you ask a simple question in class or refer to homework or some other task you previously discussed. How information is processed is also connected to brain development. For adults, it is difficult to remember or even comprehend how brain development is linked to certain behaviors. We are operating with our fully developed brains and probably don't remember what it was like not to have one. Table 1.1 provides a breakdown of the different parts of the brain, including the purpose of each part, how it functions for adults, and how it functions for adolescents.

TABLE 1.1: Comparing Adult and Adolescent Brains

Parts of the Brain	The Adult Brain . . .	The Adolescent Brain . . .
Prefrontal cortex: Includes planning and reasoning; matures around age 25	Is fully developed	Is immature and prone to high-risk behavior
Amygdala: Emotional core for passion, impulse, fear, aggression	Relies less on this; favors prefrontal cortex	Is more impulsive
Parietal lobe: Responsible for touch, sight, language; grows until one's early 20s	Is fully developed	Does not process information effectively
Ventral striatum: Reward center; not fully developed in teens	Is fully developed	Creates more excitement from reward than consequence
Hippocampus: Hub of memory and learning; grows in teens	Is fully functional; loses neurons with age	Has a tremendous learning curve

As you see, puberty encompasses major changes in the brain, particularly throughout the limbic system (Physiopedia, n.d.). The parietal lobe is responsible for touch, sight, and language, and because of this, teens do not process information effectively. We can get frustrated with teens because they may not do a task as quickly as we would like or they may look at us with a blank stare. In actuality, they are processing the information more slowly than we are providing it. The brain's reward center, the ventral striatum, in teens is not fully developed, and because of this, teens are more excited by rewards than consequences. Sometimes, we think we are providing a consequence for a misbehavior (for example, detention for missed work), and the behaviors are not changing. However, if we flip our response and provide a reward for task completion (for example, homework pass), students are more likely to do the work. Our students' brains are wired to be excited about the reward. The prefrontal cortex is responsible for planning and reasoning, but it develops into the mid-twenties (Society for Neuroscience, 2018). Adolescents are prone to more high-risk behaviors because their ability to reason, plan, and problem solve is not fully developed. The amygdala is a part of this process, too. The amygdala is considered the emotional core for passion, impulse, fear, and aggression, which makes teens more impulsive. Adults don't rely as much on the amygdala and use the prefrontal cortex more.

Teens tend to be impulsive and have big feelings. As adults, we may dismiss feelings students have. When something happens, teens can think the world is going to end. As adults, we know this isn't true, but it truly feels like it is for teens. For example, when a teen has their first romantic breakup or a fight with a best friend, it can feel like the entire world is ending. Our adult response to similar experiences occurs, in part, because we have a perspective that teens don't have, but it also has to do with brain development. As adults, we use our fully formed prefrontal cortex to counteract some of the strong feelings the amygdala produces in order to reason beyond the immediacy of an important experience. Again, this is something we need to remember so we can help our students as they learn how to process their emotions while their brains are developing. While the impulsivity in teenage students can create challenging situations in the classroom and be frustrating to adults (and sometimes to the teens themselves), it isn't necessarily a bad thing. Teens are more willing to try new things whereas we, as adults, may be more apprehensive and unwilling to try.

The hippocampus is a part of the temporal lobe and is near the amygdala. The hippocampus is where memory and learning occurs (Society for Neuroscience, 2018). There is tremendous growth in the teen years, causing a steep learning curve. As development occurs, there will be times when learning and memory click and other times when it doesn't, which is completely normal. In adulthood, the hippocampus is fully functional. Unfortunately, we lose neurons with age, which causes us to begin to forget things or makes it harder for us to learn new things.

Perhaps most important to remember when teaching K–12 students is that executive function skills, and their sweet frontal lobes, aren't fully developed, which causes children and teens to react and then think. The important executive function skills are forming, which makes planning and reasoning difficult (Society for Neuroscience, 2018). You may have a young student who cuts their clothes rather than the paper, telling you they wanted to see what would happen. It is obvious to us what will happen, but it's not so obvious to a child. I remember, as a child, I used my mom's hairbrush. I wasn't supposed to, and when it got stuck in my hair, the logical thing to do, according to my brain, was to cut it out of my hair. I didn't want to get in trouble for using the brush, and I didn't think about the fact I was cutting my hair. Thinking about that now makes me laugh because it really doesn't make any sense. Can you think of similar moments from your childhood? How does remembering experiencing moments like this yourself make you think differently about these kinds of behaviors in your students?

I love learning about the brain and thinking about students and how their brains work. It's fascinating and so much fun! Rather than being frustrated with students, it's fun to laugh about how normal their brains are. Celebrate those frontal-lobe moments! When you come from a place of understanding, it does ease some of the frustration. In the following section we'll look more closely at the student behaviors you might see in large part as a result of an immature brain processing challenges, decision making, and excitement—all part of learning and being in school. As you consider your students' behaviors, remember that we operate with our fully developed brains, but we cannot expect our students to be able to do the same thing because, as we have learned, that's just not how their brains work. Give students tools for problem solving; help them learn how to think and then react. Reassure them that they are in fact normal. Let them know there will be days they are frustrated with their own brain, and that's OK. Give students tools to be successful, and don't just expect them to do things we know they probably won't be successful doing. For example, problem solve out loud with students. Walk through the pluses and minuses of a situation. When a student looks at you with a blank stare, rather than getting frustrated, repeat the instructions in a different way or have another student explain the task. Slow down when explaining things or write them down. There are small things you can do like the examples just provided that will set you and your students up for success.

WHAT TEACHERS SEE

As educators, we don't always think about the fact that our students' brains don't work in the way that adult brains do, but we see behaviors that, when we understand the way brain development influences students' behavior, we can interpret as a form of communication—as our students communicating their needs.

What we see might be a lot of energy, curiosity, inattention, hyperactivity, talkativeness, getting out of the seat, being overly quiet, being what we might consider disrespectful, asking a lot of questions, and so much more. For example, excitement in a third-grade student may involve being talkative and full of energy. I picture a student who has the wiggles they cannot control. As an adult, we may wish for the student to control themselves. In a ninth-grade student, what we think should be excitement could look like aloofness, and we may see that as disrespect because we aren't getting the emotional response we were looking for. With that said, emotional responses look different in everyone, and age is only one piece of these differences.

Let's think about a few other illustrative examples of these behaviors in the school setting. Say, for example, you have a procedure in your classroom requiring students to raise their hand to answer a question. Students can be so excited when they know the answer that they just shout it out. Or maybe you have an expectation for your students to come to your class with all their materials, but some of the students forget a pencil or their assignment. You may expect your students to remember to study for a test or to have a form signed and returned the next day, but it doesn't happen. You probably even have students who seem to never be sitting down when you ask them to.

Encountering behaviors like these may lead to feelings of frustration or even feelings of being disrespected by a student. I want to encourage you to think about the root causes that might contribute to these behaviors. Rather than seeing a behavior itself, it's important to dig a little into why it is happening. Think back to brain development. Considering its role in your students' behaviors may give you a greater sense of understanding and empathy for your students. Of course, we can't just say, "Oh, their brain isn't developed," and then let it go; we must adopt strategies that are supportive to students to correct or redirect their behavior in a more productive way. Your students will learn because you've set them up for success, and doing so is what we'll explore throughout the rest of this book.

Now, with the understanding that typical student brain development creates a baseline form of influence for all students, we'll explore other mitigating factors, both internal and external, that may have an impact on brain development and drive student behaviors in school. In the following section, we take a look at some of those factors.

How Internal and External Factors Influence Students' Behavior and Brain Development

Internal and external factors influence students' behavior and brain development. Internal factors are biological, those involving genetics or heredity. External factors include everything within the surrounding environment, including teachers or the school, peers, the home environment, the community, and various sources of trauma and stress. Following, we will look at each of these factors in a little more detail.

BIOLOGICAL FACTORS

We have established the relationship between the developing brain and behavior. Now we need to look at other factors contributing to behavior. To start, we will look at how biological factors influence student behaviors. Emotions and behaviors can be influenced by biochemical, neurological, or genetic factors or even by combinations of these (Hallahan, Pullen, & Kauffman, 2023). For example, low birth weight and congenital defects are considered biological risk factors that can contribute to behaviors in students that are challenging. Additionally, prenatal exposure to drugs or alcohol can contribute to several types of disabilities, including EBDs, attention deficit hyperactivity disorder (ADHD), and learning disabilities. Daniel P. Hallahan, Paige C. Pullen, and James M. Kauffman (2023) note that although there is a relationship between specific biological factors and challenging behaviors, there is no real evidence demonstrating biological factors alone to be the cause of challenging behaviors.

Children are born with a predetermined temperament, although how children are brought up can impact temperament (Slagt, Dubas, Deković, & van Aken, 2016). For example, researchers have found through MRI that there are neurological differences among individuals with ADHD and those without (Hallahan et al., 2023). Brain chemicals or neurotransmitters such as dopamine and noradrenaline are abnormal in those with ADHD. Additionally, there are structural differences and other functional differences in individuals with learning disabilities and those without. Autism, dyslexia, epilepsy, depression, anxiety, and dyscalculia are some of the exceptionalities shown to correlate with neurological differences compared to individuals without (Hallahan, Pullen, Kauffman, & Badar, 2020). When working with students, we must consider characteristics of their exceptionalities and remember the physical makeup of these students' brains is different than that of a brain without exceptionalities. It is critical for us to come from a place of understanding when first responding to student behaviors. We must think about the behaviors as a form of communication and then work to figure out how to best meet students' needs.

TEACHERS AND SCHOOLS AS FACTORS

Children and adolescents who come into classrooms come with various needs or behaviors we may or may not be aware of, but behaviors can become better or worse depending on how the class is managed (Hallahan et al., 2023). Interactions between students' temperament and their social competence, when combined with behaviors of teachers and peers, can contribute to all behaviors you see in a classroom. For example, you will have some students who are naturally cheerful almost all the time. You will have others who have a natural tendency to be quiet, and you may have other students who have challenging behaviors. The risk for students who exhibit challenging behaviors is becoming stuck in a cycle of negative interactions where they become progressively frustrating to and frustrated by both teachers and peers. As students continue to have negative interactions in school, by the time they reach middle school and high school, they can have a negative view of their school climate, including their perceptions of the physical and social environments. It is important to note that, just like with other factors, while negative school experiences can become a self-perpetuating cycle, they are not the root cause of challenging behaviors.

Another challenge that can occur is *disproportionality* in education, meaning there is either a higher or lower representation of students than we would expect based on the representation in the general population of the students (Zolkoski et al., 2023). Identifying specific statistical demographic data is difficult, but we do know Black male students are more likely to be referred to school administrators for challenging behaviors than their White counterparts, even if the incidences are the same (Owens & McLanahan, 2020). Sometimes, often without realizing it, we act on biases. These biases may suggest some students' actions are acceptable while other students' behaviors may not be acceptable. Educators, families, and students are embedded in the cultures that influence them (Hallahan et al., 2023). Adults communicate their behavioral standards and values to students through a variety of cultural conditions, and the same can be said about the students in our classrooms, how they interact, and what they expect from the adults in their lives as well as from their peers. If students have had negative experiences with teachers or peers in the past, whom they connect in some way with current teachers or peers, they may be defensive, which can in turn have negative implications (for example, a student ends up in detention because of an attitude problem).

As educators, we need to remember how important it is to create a safe and nurturing environment so our students feel valued and respected in our classroom (Zolkoski et al., 2023). When our students feel valued, they are more likely to exhibit positive behaviors and are more successful academically.

Let's think about a few examples of how our behaviors can impact our students. We see a student who is standing and talking to the person sitting next to them during a class session. We see the talking part and get frustrated. One way to respond is by letting the frustration get the best of you (it happens to all of us from time to time) and snapping at the student, which causes the student to feel embarrassed. An alternative way to respond would be to walk up to the student and ask them to sit down. You can also provide the student with the opportunity to stand but stay within a certain area so the standing isn't a distraction to other students. You could give the student opportunities to move around the room by passing out papers or taking something to the office or another teacher's room.

Before responding to challenging behaviors, it's important to think about why the behaviors are happening. Further, the way we respond to our students' behaviors will impact the way they respond back to us and how they feel in our classroom. Our ultimate goal is for our students to feel safe in class so they can learn to their fullest potential. It is best to be teachable and proactive rather than punitive and reactive. When we are teachable and proactive, we have a positive learning environment; in turn, we positively impact not only the students but ourselves too. However, when we make assumptions without asking and are reactive to what we see in the classroom, we become punitive, which causes a negative feeling. Our students don't feel safe, they aren't learning to the extent they can, and we feel stressed out and drained.

PEER INFLUENCE

Navigating friends and peer groups can be tricky, particularly for students in middle and high school. Elementary-aged children rely on their parents as their main influence, but as children get older, peers become more influential. Throughout school, students are trying to figure out how they are valued by their peers and within peer groups (Farmer, Reinke, & Brooks, 2014). Students can be valued for being sporty, popular, or funny. Couple the need for a teen's peer acceptance with brain development, and teens become more likely to engage in risky behaviors (Society for Neuroscience, 2018). While some students are seen as defiant because of their misconduct, others are seen as popular for the same misconduct, which may cause them to rebel against authority figures such as parents or teachers to try to gain admiration from peers.

We have a responsibility to meet students' social and behavioral needs. I remember when I had my own kids. People often said, "When your kids get older, they don't need you as much." As my kids get older, I realize they need positive adults in their lives even more. Although they no longer need me for basic things, they need me more as they navigate school and friends. Teachers are placed in the same position, in a sense. I often had students in my classroom wanting to talk about friend problems. Colleagues teaching in middle school and high school talk about their students coming into their room during their free periods because they want to talk. Yes, peers are a strong influence on students, but we can still help our students problem solve and make decisions. Remember, the adult brain is developed. We have those decision-making skills that our students don't have.

Another issue that can cause great hardship to students is bullying. For behaviors to be considered bullying, they must display three key components: (1) there is a power grab (meaning the bully is higher in status, or at least trying to be, compared to the one being bullied), (2) the behavior is intentional, and (3) the behavior is repeated (U.S. Department of Health and Human Services, 2024). There is not a specific demographic of students or a single profile of individuals who are bullied more than others. R. Matthew Gladden, Alana M. Vivolo-Kantor, Merle E. Hamburger, and Corey D. Lumpkin (2014) find that all age groups are affected by bullying, but the most prominent age of bullying seems to occur between the ages of 12 and 18. Jenny Mischel and Anastasia Kitsantas (2020), researchers who explore bullying in schools, find that although bullying does not occur only at school, most bullying behavior does occur on school grounds. School climate—how you feel when you are at the school (connectedness, peer attachment, and so on) based on how the people (for example, staff, administrators, teachers, parents, and students) at school act—impacts the acceptance of bullying. Specifically, a negative school climate correlates with the acceptance of bullying. According to Mischel and Kitsantas (2020), a positive school environment reports less bullying. A positive school environment can include many things, but overall, the feeling is positive. Administrators are supportive of teachers, and teachers are supportive of the students and families. There is structure and consistency in expectations, which allows for a proactive environment because everyone knows what to expect. Teachers are welcoming to students, and students are welcoming to one another. Everyone treats each other with respect. In other words, when students feel a sense of belonging, there are fewer occurrences of bullying behaviors. Researchers Joie Acosta and colleagues (2019) conducted a study to better understand the relationship between perceived school climate and bullying. Out of the fourteen middle schools serving 2,834 students they studied, they found most students reported experiencing fewer physical, emotional, and cyberbullying behaviors in a positive school climate. They also reported higher levels of school connectedness, assertiveness, peer attachment, and empathy.

According to the U.S. Department of Health and Human Services (2021), students bully to attain power, fit in, exclude others, and control the behavior of their peers. They may also bully due to family factors such as coming from a family who bullies, having a lack of emotional support or communication, responding in an authoritarian or reactive way, or being too lenient. Emotional factors contributing to bullying behaviors include the student being bullied currently or in the past, having low self-esteem, lacking an understanding of others' emotions or even their own, or not having the skills to handle social situations in positive ways. The school can contribute to bullying behaviors by not properly addressing bullying behaviors, or the student may have been excluded or not accepted at school.

Students who are bullied can experience negative academic, emotional, social, mental health, and physical problems (U.S. Department of Health and Human Services, 2025). On the other hand, students who bully often engage in violent and other risky behaviors into adulthood. It is worth noting that although the media reports a link between bullying and suicide (National Association of People Against Bullying, n.d.), according to the U.S. Department of Health and Human Services (2025), bullying is not the only factor contributing to suicide in children and adolescents. Many other issues contribute to the risk of suicide, such as a history of trauma, challenges at home, and depression.

HOME ENVIRONMENT

Students' home lives play an important role in their success in school. Research shows a strong link between academic success and parental involvement in school (Benner, Boyle, & Sadler, 2016). Some of the parents of students you have in your classroom are easy to work with. They volunteer when they can, they sign and return papers when needed, they show up at events, and they ensure your students' homework is complete. However, not all parents are like this. Home environments are very diverse (families can be single-parent, two-parent, or multigenerational; socioeconomic status can vary, as can parenting style), just like the students who walk into our classrooms. It's easy to relate to families and students who are like us. It's much more difficult to understand families who don't support our students in a way we think they should. I have often heard school personnel say things like, "Well, that student comes from a bad home life," or "Their parents don't care." I would argue that while students may not come from the most ideal home environments, it is still the job of teachers to teach the students in the classroom and make those students and their families feel welcome.

Educators have students in their classrooms who have parents whose mode of relating to them ranges from supportive and responsive to rejecting and unresponsive (Zolkoski et al., 2023). Research shows parenting styles vary considerably, and parents' behaviors contribute as risk factors or protective factors for their child's behaviors (White & Renk, 2012). Children who live in adverse conditions, such as physical or emotional neglect, enter school at a disadvantage that *can* have a potential for school failure, which is particularly true for individuals with multiple risk factors over a long span of time. When families are dealing with conflict, have harsh or inconsistent discipline practices, struggle with addiction, have a history of mental illness, or are neglectful or abusive, children and adolescents have an increased risk for struggling academically, socially, or emotionally (Hallahan et al., 2023).

Brain development is also impacted by the type of environment students are exposed to (Society for Neuroscience, 2018). With all this in mind, it is important to point out again that it is not possible to find valid or consistent research findings specifically blaming parents for their students' behaviors (Hallahan et al., 2023).

COMMUNITY

When thinking about how the communities in which students live affect their development and behaviors, there are many things to consider. For example, is the community safe? Do your students' families have easy access to grocery stores? Do they have plenty of green space? Research consistently shows that students who have access to nature and green space, which is often found in more affluent neighborhoods, have lower levels of stress, reduced symptoms of ADHD, and fewer problem behaviors (McCormick, 2017). Additionally, students who live in neighborhoods with fewer resources encounter overwhelming challenges compared to their peers in more affluent neighborhoods. Thinking back to brain development, the environment students are a part of has an impact (Society for Neuroscience, 2018).

Additionally, school performance is directly impacted by the effects of class discrimination (Gorski, 2018). According to Paul C. Gorski (2018), for decades, there has been a discriminatory practice of stereotyping that has pointed against students living in poverty, wrongfully assumed to be lazy and uncaring about education. For example, low-income families who are not involved in their child's school are seen as not caring about their child or their child's education. On the other hand, a family who is considered more well-to-do but who does not attend school functions may be excused as having a work trip.

One important influence occurring more often in neighborhoods with lower socioeconomic status than in more affluent neighborhoods is violence. According to Emily Ozer, Iris Lavi, and Laura Douglas from the School of Public Health at the University of California, Berkeley, and Jennifer Price Wolf (2017) from the Prevention Research Center, there is a negative impact on student mental health and academic performance when students are exposed directly and indirectly to violence. Violence in school communities can have a ripple effect among students because students who live with high levels of violence make students and teachers feel less safe—there are lower levels of trust and more disciplinary issues (Burdick-Will, 2018).

When students live in neighborhoods with violence, they can display anxiety and aggression, particularly when they feel hypervigilant about perceived threats. Anxiety and aggression can become their default state, breeding even more aggression as they attempt to keep others from bothering them. Being in an environment such as this can be extremely stressful, which has a negative impact on brain development (National Institute of Mental Health [NIMH], 2022). It can lead to the feeling of fight or flight. Additionally, there may be times when students mistakenly interpret their classmates' actions as hostile because of their unconscious response to stress and fear from the anxiety and aggression they are feeling due to community violence.

While violence is often an overt influence that has a negative effect on developing students, less obvious elements of the community environment can also have an impact. One particularly clear way in which this environmental impact can be seen is in the impact of exposure to books. When children and youth are exposed to books and to a verbally rich environment, brain development occurs. Language and learning support executive functioning and social intelligence, in turn positively impacting school performance (Society for Neuroscience, 2018). Community centers, churches, and mentorship programs can have a positive impact on students' brain development and academic success because of the exposure to things such as language, social cues, and decision making, which all support a healthy brain (Society for Neuroscience, 2018).

Although access to resources is important, parental involvement, no matter the socioeconomic status, supports academic achievement. Many of the community risk factors we've examined are associated with lower socioeconomic backgrounds, but one cannot assume families from affluent backgrounds are involved in their children's lives and mitigating risks to healthy brain development and academic success (Benner et al., 2016). When trying to navigate pressures such as living up to the high expectations of families for achievement, youth are more likely to engage in higher levels of risk-taking behaviors, particularly youth from more affluent backgrounds (Romm, Barry, & Alvis, 2020). Additionally, students from more affluent communities are more likely to engage in sensation-seeking behavior, including alcohol use and substance abuse, and demonstrate externalizing and internalizing behaviors when compared to their peers in middle-class communities (Luthar, Barkin, & Crossman, 2013).

TRAUMA

There are major implications on behavior and brain development for children and adolescents who experience trauma. Childhood trauma is considered a serious and pervasive public health issue requiring a coordinated response from both health and mental health providers (Substance Abuse and Mental Health Services Administration [SAMHSA], 2022). *Trauma* refers to an event or circumstance an individual experiences that is physically or emotionally harmful or life threatening. The impact of the event or circumstance can have a lasting adverse impact on an individual's physical, mental, or emotional health; social well-being; or spiritual well-being. Trauma can happen to anyone regardless of age, gender, race, ethnicity, socioeconomic status, or sexual orientation.

When a person experiences trauma, a heavy burden is placed on the individual, family, and community. Many people who experience a traumatic event do not have lasting negative effects, but others have difficulties and experience traumatic stress reactions (SAMHSA, 2022). Immediately following the event to several weeks and even months after, responses may include feelings of sadness, anger, or anxiousness; difficulty sleeping or concentrating; or continuously thinking about what happened (NIMH, 2022).

For most people, symptoms generally lessen over time; however, in some cases, responses continue and interfere with the person's everyday life. Sometimes, for very young children (less than 6 years of age), forgetting how to talk, acting out the event during playtime, or being unusually clingy to an adult are some of the symptoms seen (NIMH, 2022). Children over the age of 6 typically show similar symptoms as those seen in adults, including developing disruptive, disrespectful, or destructive behaviors. According to NIMH (2022), they may also have feelings of guilt for not preventing the traumatic event from happening and may have thoughts of revenge.

Physical symptoms may include feeling tired; having a racing heart, headaches, stomach pain, or digestive issues; sweating; or being easily startled or jumpy. Research shows trauma can negatively impact school performance (Perfect, Turley, Carlson, Yohanna, & Saint Gilles, 2016). Students' ability to self-regulate, be organized, comprehend, or memorize material can be negatively impacted by trauma, in turn negatively impacting students both socially and academically (Thomas, Crosby, & Vanderhaar, 2019).

Adverse childhood experiences (ACEs) include anyone's experiences during the first eighteen years of life and include the following (Centers for Disease Control and Prevention [CDC], 2021).

- Major emotional abuse (recurrent humiliation)
- Major physical abuse
- Contact sexual abuse
- Major emotional neglect
- Major physical neglect
- Growing up during the first eighteen years of life in a home where one member of the household was an alcoholic or drug user
- Loss of a biological parent in any context, whether from death, abandonment, divorce, imprisonment, or others

- Growing up in a home where a member of the household was chronically depressed, mentally ill, suicidal, or in a state hospital
- Growing up in a home where the mother was treated violently
- Growing up in a home where one member of the home was imprisoned

Sixty-seven percent of the population have at least one ACE (National Congress of American Indians, 2016). One in eight of the population have more than four ACEs. Individuals who have four or more ACEs have three times the levels of lung disease and adult smoking, have eleven times the level of intravenous drug abuse, are four and a half times more likely to develop depression, have two times the level of liver disease, are four times as likely to have begun intercourse by age 15, and have fourteen times the number of suicide attempts. Individuals with six or more ACEs are more likely to die twenty years earlier than individuals who have none.

Figure 1.1 depicts what can occur when individuals experience childhood trauma. ACEs can lead to disrupted neurodevelopment, which leads to social, emotional, and cognitive impairments. This can lead to adopting health-risk behaviors and to disease, disability, or social difficulties, in turn causing early death.

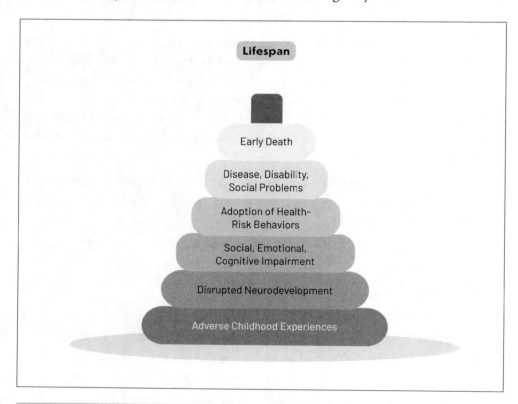

FIGURE 1.1: Childhood trauma repercussions.

The trauma caused by ACEs can have a major impact on brain development. The three parts of the brain impacted by trauma are the amygdala, hippocampus, and prefrontal cortex. If you remember from the previous discussion (page 8), the amygdala is considered the emotional control center and helps protect us from danger by acting as an alarm when stressful events occur (Society for Neuroscience, 2018). The hippocampus helps with long-term memory, motivation, emotion, and behavior. The hippocampus also helps calm the amygdala. The prefrontal cortex is known for executive function and controls behaviors and regulates emotional responses to events. However, trauma causes an increase in the amygdala activity, which then puts the brain in overactive mode and can create feelings of being in danger or feelings of anxiety (Thatcher, 2019). While the amygdala activity increases, the hippocampus shrinks, so those calming cues it provides the amygdala weaken. Trauma also causes the prefrontal cortex to weaken, which can allow signals to weaken, potentially leading to negative emotions from the traumatic event taking over the prefrontal cortex's ability to reason. See figure 1.2.

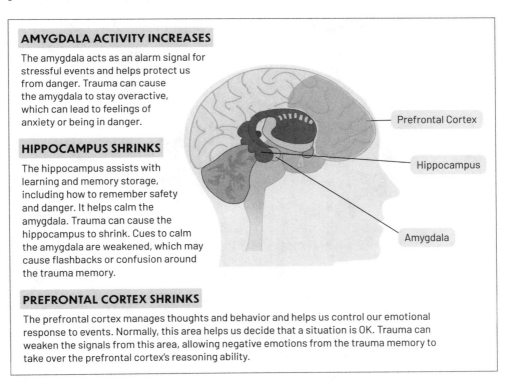

Source: © 2020 by EMDR International Association. Used with permission.

FIGURE 1.2: Brain affected by trauma.

As an educator, it is important to recognize that behaviors you are seeing in the classroom may be due to trauma students are currently experiencing or have experienced in the past. Often, students who are facing trauma cannot get to learning due to the impact trauma has on their brains. They are focused on simply trying to survive, emotionally, mentally, and quite often physically. Trauma can cause a feeling of "fight or flight." Individuals who experience trauma are in survival mode while a person going through typical development does not need to think about survival in the same way. In looking at figure 1.3, we see an image representation of how students who experience developmental trauma are not thinking about learning (cognition); they are thinking, primarily, about surviving. On the other hand, students who experience typical development are able to learn (cognition) and are not thinking about survival in the same way or to the same extent as students who have experienced trauma. Let's think about an example of what this looks like in the classroom. Students are asked to complete an independent task, and a loud noise occurs without warning. A student who has experienced trauma may have a feeling of being in danger and act out (for example, refuse to work or try to escape the room) while the other students in the room may be startled but can easily get back to work.

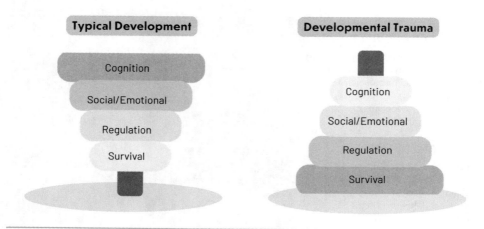

FIGURE 1.3: Typical versus traumatic development.

Another aspect of child and adolescent behavior deserving of attention is the idea of mental health. Although mental health can be affected by trauma, mental health issues can also occur without experiencing trauma. Child and adolescent mental health is a critical concern. Globally, mental health conditions have become a huge problem with almost 15 percent of children and youth ages 10–19 experiencing a mental health disorder (Agency for Healthcare Research and Quality [AHRQ], 2022). According to the AHRQ (2022), in the United States, about 20 percent of children and adolescents between the ages of 3 and 17 have a mental, emotional, development, or behavior disorder. Suicidal behaviors for high school students increased more than 40 percent in the decade before 2019 with mental health challenges becoming the leading cause of death in this age group. In the

United States in 2016, the AHRQ found almost 20 percent of children ages 2–8 years were diagnosed with a mental, behavioral, or developmental disorder. Around 15 percent of adolescents 12–17 years of age in 2018–2019 were diagnosed with a major depressive episode, 37 percent had feelings of persistent sadness or hopelessness, and about 20 percent of this age group reported serious thoughts of suicide. A study conducted by SAMHSA (2022) found the number of children and adolescents 3–17 years of age diagnosed with depression increased by 27 percent between 2016 and 2020. The COVID-19 pandemic only exacerbated these trends.

The number of adolescents between the ages of 12 and 17 receiving mental health services increased from 11.8 percent in 2002 to 16.7 percent in 2019 (AHRQ, 2022). Within the educational setting, there was an increase from 12.1 percent in 2009 to 15.4 percent in 2019. Although it is positive to see an increase in children and youth receiving mental health services, the number is still extremely low for the number of students who are facing mental health disorders. We need to work to increase mental health treatment for children and adolescents.

In 2020, suicide was the twelfth leading cause of death in the United States, the second leading cause of death among children between the ages of 10 and 14, and the third leading cause of death for individuals ages 15–24 (AHRQ, 2022). The number of instances of death by suicide among children aged 12 increased by 16 percent between 2008 and 2020. Depression is strongly associated with suicidal ideation and is also one of the characteristics increasing the risk of suicide among individuals with depression. The need for mental health treatment for children and adolescents is clearly not being met. Often, families face significant challenges trying to navigate mental health services.

Let's pause to process everything we have talked about up to this point. It can take a moment to process the information because it is heavy. We need to acknowledge the difficulty of what a classroom today looks like. We have learned a bit about brain development and the impact it has on our students' behaviors. We have also learned about trauma and how it can negatively impact our students' brains, which in turn can negatively impact their behavior. What does all of this mean for us as teachers? We still have to educate these students. This is where my positive self comes in. When I get overwhelmed with the thoughts of how to even begin to help and educate, I can be the change agent. I must show students that despite the things that have happened, they can be successful. My job as we move through the book is to show you the same thing. You can teach *all* your students, no matter where they come from. You can teach and support despite the challenges you may face. You can be the positive change agent for your students. You can show them they can learn despite what they have been through. You will learn how to create a classroom environment where students feel safe and are able to learn.

STRESS

Stress is something everyone, including the students in our classrooms, experience. Short-term stress can push students to study for an exam or train for a track meet rather than hang out with friends or spend time playing video games. However, chronic stress is much different and may include social unrest, violence, and pandemic- and post-pandemic-related pressures (American Psychological Association [APA], 2022). Chronic stress can be detrimental, causing high blood pressure, weakened immune system, and diseases such as heart disease and obesity. As the APA (2022) explains, mental health problems including anxiety and depression are also caused by prolonged stress and are becoming more common in children and adolescents.

In children, a common source of stress is tension at home due to things like loss, divorce, or family conflict (APA, 2022). Happy changes can also cause young children stress such as a new home or the arrival of a new baby. Another frequent stress for students is school itself, due to situations like making friends, getting along with teachers, understanding teacher expectations, making good grades, doing well on a test, and dealing with bullies.

Sources of stress as children get older expand because teens are more likely to become stressed over situations happening outside the home compared to younger children (APA, 2022). However, when the family environment is stressful, it impacts how adolescents respond to other stressful events in their lives (Coward, 2018). Although peers can act as a buffer for teens, they can also be a source of stress. Social relationships are extremely important for teens. They often worry about fitting in, have romantic relationships, and feel pressure from peers around sex and substance use. School is a major stressor for adolescents because there is constant pressure to perform well and there is competition with peers. Parents and teachers can put high or even unrealistic expectations on students, which can cause a significant amount of stress for teens. Feelings of potential failure or striving for perfection instead of excellence can cause stress. Often adolescents have increasingly hectic schedules with extracurricular activities and academic demands that can cause a disruption to self-care behaviors, like getting enough sleep, which can cause adverse effects on relationships with friends and family. Life events, like COVID-19 or a physical illness, can also contribute to stress.

Students who report being bullied have a more difficult time making friends and experience frequent feelings of loneliness; have higher levels of stress, insecurity, anxiety, and depression; and have lower self-esteem (Coward, 2018). Generally, students who are bullied have a drop in academic achievement and reduced motivation. Antisocial behaviors such as being quick-tempered, mean, or disobedient can impact relationships with others and school performance, which puts these students at great risk for developing a depressed mood and feelings of stress.

It is important for educators to recognize signs of stress. Young children may be irritable and easy to anger. Adolescents may be argumentative and short-tempered (APA, 2022). You may notice a change in a student in your classroom. Maybe you have a student who suddenly begins to act out or a normally active teen who no longer wants to do anything. Grades may begin to slip because of not completing assignments on time or at all. Sometimes children and adolescents have a hard time sleeping at night and then fall asleep in class or are irritable because they are tired. Every student can be different in how they exhibit signs of stress.

Chronic stress also impacts brain development. Chronic stress can impair development of the frontal lobes, amygdala, and hippocampus, and a hormone called cortisol floods the brain, which can become toxic and begin to destroy neurons (Society for Neuroscience, 2018). The impact on the brain can lead to problems with memory, regulating emotions, and learning. As educators, we often see the problem behaviors, but we must think about why the behaviors are occurring in the first place. Remember, all behavior is a form of communication.

Understand Students' Needs

Gaining an understanding of childhood brain development and of how the behaviors K–12 students may exhibit stem from stages in this development and from other internal and external factors allows teachers to have greater empathy for the students in their classroom. This understanding helps teachers ask, "How can I help?" Responding with empathy and a genuine commitment to help paired with knowledge can aid in developing research-supported strategies to meet students' needs. Abraham Maslow, a pioneer in humanistic psychology and one of the first to seek causes of behavior in the needs people have, offers insights to inform empathy for students. While Maslow's *hierarchy of needs* (Maslow, 1943, 1962, 1987) is very well known in education, many other fields, and popular culture, it can be helpful to review it when considering the needs students have and how to meet them.

Maslow (1987) theorized that human needs are arranged in a hierarchy as illustrated in figure 1.4 (page 28).

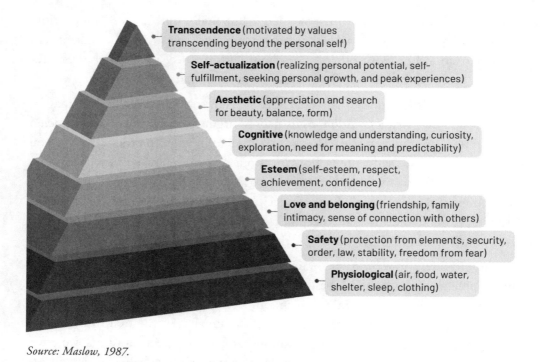

Source: Maslow, 1987.

FIGURE 1.4: Maslow's hierarchy of needs.

Maslow's model affirms how students' cognitive needs cannot be met until their basic physiological needs are met. While teachers face some limitations in meeting their students' needs—after all, teachers are not parents or guardians, and they spend a limited amount of time daily with their students within parameters that have specific boundaries in place to protect both students and teachers—there are actions they can take to meet needs from the most basic physiological through the higher-level psychological needs. For example, if a teacher discovers that a student's food or shelter needs are not being met, they can reach out to the family and talk to the counselor or administrators to see what resources can be provided to help the family.

However, one of the most powerful and actionable things teachers can do is maintain classrooms where students feel safe and accepted and to put in place expectations and boundaries that foster respect and build support for one another. We need to create an environment where all our students feel welcome and like they belong, and then our students will develop the resilience to move into meeting higher learning needs. We can offer our students this critical support by developing and following a classroom-management plan that is built on an understanding of the causes and triggers of behaviors, the cumulative nature of needs fulfillment, and the compassion that allows us to lead with a sense of inclusivity—meaning the belief that all of our students belong in our classroom and that all have an ability and a right to learn at high levels.

In the following pages, we'll look at specific ways to approach management of your classroom not only in terms of addressing challenging behaviors but also for cultivating acceptance and security.

How to Support Students With an Effective Management Plan

When thinking about classroom management, I want you to think about it as a multitiered framework in the same sense as you might think of response to intervention (RTI), positive behavioral interventions and supports (PBIS), or multitiered systems of support (MTSS). These approaches all refer to multiple levels of support for students academically and behaviorally. In this case, Tier 1 is support for all students and includes building a positive learning environment and having an effective classroom-management plan. I focus on Tier 1 in chapters 2 (page 35) and 3 (page 67). Chapter 5 (page 133) of the book is also focused on Tier 1; however, some instructional strategies are more specific and applicable as Tier 2 strategies. Tier 2 involves students who need additional support with their behavior beyond what they are already receiving. Typically speaking, when Tier 1 is implemented consistently, most students are successful. However, there may be a few students who need extra help. They receive support at Tier 1 and Tier 2. Tier 2 is more specific and targeted to support a small group of students. Chapter 4 (page 101) focuses on specific strategies to support students who need extra help with their behavior. I will also explain what happens when students are still not successful and need to move to Tier 3, which is designed for students who need the most targeted support. Although Tier 3 does not fall under the umbrella of general education teachers, it is important to understand the process, because you will be a part of it at some point.

Let's dig a little deeper. To start making intentional supports for students, we have to understand why behaviors occur in the first place, which is why chapter 1 starts with behavior development. Understanding behavior allows us to have more empathy for our students. Empathy doesn't mean we don't have expectations; it just means we have a proactive, understanding concern, and we can better set up our classrooms and interactions with students to be supportive. Tier 1 of MTSS involves creating a positive environment and establishing effective classroom-management practices. Creating a positive environment in your classroom is supportive to your students, and to you, helping both you and your students be your best. Additionally, we need to set students up for success by ensuring they understand what we expect of them. As described in this chapter (page 26), students thrive off of structure and consistency because it helps reduce their feelings of stress. Chapter 3 is still a part of Tier 1 because it involves establishing and reinforcing expectations. As we move forward, despite best practices, there will be students who need extra support with their behavior, and these students move to Tier 2. They still receive support of Tier 1 but need additional help learning how to get needs met in a more positive way. Chapter 4 (page 101) is where you learn specific strategies to support students at Tier 2 and also includes what happens when students need even more support and need to move to Tier 3 where a functional behavior assessment (FBA) is done. With solid classroom-management practices established, effective teaching strategies can be used to maximize academic achievement.

HOW A POSITIVE CLASSROOM ENVIRONMENT SUPPORTS STUDENTS

Students feeling safe in their environment is one of the critical aspects from Maslow's hierarchy of needs. Students need to feel safe in order to learn to the best of their ability. So far, we have looked at student behavior through the lens of *why*. As we have just learned, our students' environment impacts their brain development and behavior. We cannot change their environment outside of our classroom, but we do have control over our classroom environment. The first step in creating consistent management practices, or a management plan, is to get to know students to learn about them and the needs they may have. This knowledge will be key to our success in meeting their needs.

In chapter 2 (page 35), you will learn why creating a positive environment is important but also how to do it. The two key aspects of creating a positive environment include providing a space where everyone feels safe and ensuring *all* the students in your classroom feel cared for. We will talk about how to set students up for success both physically and emotionally through research-based practices to easily implement in the classroom.

HOW CLEAR COMMUNICATION OF EXPECTATIONS AND BOUNDARIES SUPPORTS STUDENTS

Now that you have a deeper understanding of the importance of having a positive learning environment, we need to add to it by establishing structure because students need structure to feel safe and learn. Students need to know what we expect. They have a lot of stress in their life, and things may not always be predictable. Structure, consistency, and predictability all help our students feel safe. It is important to set students up for success by creating clear expectations. Clear communication also helps families have a better understanding of your expectations and shows them how much you care about their child.

When we consider the structure of the classroom, we will look specifically at creating rules and procedures. Students need to understand what your expectations are, and the expectations need to be clear. No two classrooms are going to be the same, and that's OK! Some teachers will have rules and expectations that another teacher will not have. Keeping the *why* of behavior from what you learned earlier in this chapter, I will teach you why you need to have rules and procedures and how to do it to set you and your students up for success. Rules and procedures are important for success, but we also need to add positive reinforcement and consequences so that you see less of the behavior you don't want to see and more of the behavior you do want to see. A plan where expectations are created and reinforced with consistency provides a positive and safe, structured environment that ultimately sets students up for success and promotes academic achievement.

HOW ADDITIONAL STRATEGIES CAN BE USED TO SUPPORT STUDENTS WHO HAVE CHALLENGING BEHAVIORS

Despite having a positive and caring environment with a proactive plan for effectively communicating your classroom-management plan, the reality is that you may still have a student or two who need additional support. I think about this in the same way I think about academics. We can have amazing and engaging academic lessons, but there will still be some students who struggle. We don't think twice about offering those students extra academic support, but sometimes we see students who struggle with their behavior as "troublemakers" or "bad." I know it can be hard to respond to students with troubling behaviors in a positive way, but when we gain a better understanding of why behaviors may be occurring, and are consistent with communicating and seeing our expectations through while also providing a safe and caring environment, overall we are capturing more students academically. Some of my favorite research-supported strategies to support students with challenging behaviors include (1) *choice*, which is a strategy where students are given the opportunity to choose between two or more options equal in value; (2) *positive peer reporting*, which involves learning how to report the positive behaviors of classmates; (3) the *Good Behavior Game*, which is a game promoting behaviors you want to see your students do, like raise their hand; (4) a *token economy*, which is an individualized strategy focusing on two to three specific behaviors a student needs to work on; and (5) *self-monitoring*, which is much like the token economy but involves the student rating their own behavior rather than being rated by the teacher.

Within a MTSS, the strategies being discussed are considered Tier 2 strategies and can be used to positively support students who need extra support with their behavior. We will discuss students who need even more support and move to Tier 3 where a functional behavior assessment is completed. Within this framework, students are supported at all levels to support their success in school.

HOW TO SUPPORT STUDENTS' LEARNING AND INDEPENDENCE THROUGH BEST TEACHING PRACTICES

Within our framework, we have set the foundation and have an effective classroom-management plan where our students are able to get to the learning because of the safety of the structure we have put in place. Students learn best when they are the ones actively doing the work. Having structure and consistency with your classroom-management plan will allow you to be much more successful in implementing best practices to foster student learning and independence. Chapter 5 (page 133), which encompasses supporting students' learning and independence, provides specific strategies to best support students in their learning. To begin, we look at Bloom's taxonomy (Anderson & Krathwohl, 2001), which is a framework to ensure higher-order questions are asked of students. Classrooms are filled with many different types of learners, and it can be overwhelming when thinking about meeting every student's needs. Differentiated instruction is a way to ensure the academic needs of *all* students are met. We take a deep dive into all the ways instruction can be differentiated. Another way to support the academic needs of all students is through Universal Design for Learning (UDL). Each principle of UDL is discussed in detail to provide teachers with a plethora of ideas to use in the classroom to support academic achievement.

HOW TEACHER SELF-CARE SUPPORTS STUDENTS' NEEDS

When thinking about and taking care of the needs of others, it can be easy to forget ourselves. You are a critical piece of the puzzle to ensure student success, but you can't effectively do that without truly thinking about your needs and how to take care of yourself. Practicing self-care is an important way to build resilience against burnout and to ensure we are giving our best selves to others. Teaching is hard. It can feel like everyone is judging us or maybe even thinks they can do a better job. Our hearts are there for our students, and we feel all the emotions. I would agree that teaching is the most rewarding job out there, but that does not mean it is easy. It simply isn't. I believe it is one of the hardest jobs, too, which is why self-care is critical. Although self-care looks different for everyone, I will talk about a few of my favorite self-care strategies that also have research to support their effectiveness including exercise, mindfulness, and finding your joy. Teacher self-care is critical because it is difficult for a depleted and stressed teacher to create a positive classroom environment.

Concluding Thoughts

What are your thoughts now that you have learned more about the internal and external factors that influence student behaviors? Did you learn something new, or maybe it wasn't something new, but a refresher? I find the brain and brain development so fascinating. When we know a little bit more about our students' brains, we can engage with students more easily from a space of empathy and understanding. We can be educative and problem solve with our students. You will find me repeating myself when I say students are like puzzles; once you figure out the *why*, it's easier to help them be successful. The first question to ask yourself when you have a student who may be struggling is, "Are they getting their basic needs met?" Then we need to think about other things like trauma, mental health disorders, or disabilities like ADHD and determine if one or more of these things can potentially be causing some behaviors of concern. Students walk into our classrooms with their imaginary backpacks filled with bricks. Some have a few bricks, and some have more than we can comprehend. Sometimes we get too focused on the things we cannot control as teachers that we lose focus of what we can control. As teachers, we can control our response to our students. As we move through the rest of the book, we will focus on what we can do to support all learners, but first, consider using the following reproducible tool, "Reflecting on Showing Empathy" (page 34; also available online at **go.SolutionTree.com/behavior**), as you consider the role of empathy in your work with students.

Reflecting on Showing Empathy

Having empathy for our students is a critical part of teaching. We are better at working with our students when we understand their perspectives and where they are coming from. Let's consider some reflective questions to refer to as we work to ensure we are truly being empathetic toward our students.

What does empathy feel and look like for you?

How does your school foster a culture of empathy among staff and administrators?

In what ways can you enact empathetic kindness in your classroom?

Think about an example of a time when empathy helped you connect with a student: What did you do, and how did the student respond?

What impact can you imagine empathy having in the short and long term? What could the impact be on students who are challenging or on student learning and engagement?

How has empathy influenced, or can it influence, your teaching style now and over time?

What resources, training, and support would help you develop stronger empathy skills?

Learning, Behavior, and Your Classroom © 2025 Solution Tree Press • SolutionTree.com
Visit **go.SolutionTree.com/behavior** to download this free reproducible.

CHAPTER 2

Cultivate a Positive Classroom Environment

A positive classroom environment feels welcoming and inviting. When you walk into the room, you feel like you belong, and you want to be there. A positive learning environment in the classroom should be the first and primary focus area in your management plan because it is the foundation for all experiences students have in your class including all interactions they have with you. In this chapter, I share research on the impact cultivating a positive classroom environment has on student success and explore the notion of the "whole child" and what it means to teach to the whole child. Here, you'll find strategies for building a positive environment as well as strategies to show your students you care about them and their success. Finally, I examine social and emotional learning (SEL) and restorative practices that foster a true feeling of community in the classroom. The chapter ends with my concluding thoughts and a reproducible, "Building a Positive Classroom Environment" (page 64; for the online version, visit **go.SolutionTree.com/behavior**).

Research on the Classroom Environment and the Whole Child

Educators, parents, and policymakers agree that education needs to focus on supporting the fundamental abilities of children and youth to successfully navigate the world. When we think about the concept of the *whole child*, we realize students learn best when we focus not only on academics but also on students' physical, emotional, and social well-being—the student as a whole being. When we do that, academic achievement goes up. According to Mark T. Greenberg (2023), there are five broad focus areas to educate the whole child.

1. Develop and foster healthy relationships with others.
2. Treat other people with dignity and respect.
3. Develop and foster the mental aptitude to problem solve and think creatively.
4. Succeed in postsecondary education and beyond.
5. Contribute as a citizen in democracy.

To foster these capacities, classrooms need to be healthy and caring environments that convey a climate of support and equal routes for youth to accomplish their goals in both a dynamic and challenging environment. We need to get it out of our minds that our job as educators is to only teach the curriculum. We can't get to the learning without thinking about the whole child, because as we learned in chapter 1 (page 7), students' ability to learn is impacted by brain development, emotional well-being, and external factors, all of which are connected.

When thinking about how elements of life and learning are connected, consider mental health. It is as important a component to our students learning as academic support. According to the National Alliance on Mental Illness (NAMI, 2023), one in five adults in the United States experience mental illness each year, and one in twenty adults within the United States experience serious mental illness each year. Serious mental illness means that a person's life is being negatively impacted for two weeks or more. For example, a student who is normally bubbly and gets As and Bs begins to fall behind academically and doesn't engage like they used to—this change might represent a serious mental health issue the student is having. When we think about the students in our classrooms, we don't necessarily think they could possibly be experiencing a mental health disorder, but that may be the case. NAMI (2023) states one in six youth ages 6–17 experience a mental health disorder each year. It doesn't always look like the example I shared. It can also be that the student who gets along with everyone and does well in school has anxiety.

While focusing on the whole child, I believe it is important to mention what happens if we keep adopting an attitude focused on pressing on and attempting to ignore problems students may have while in our classrooms. Access to mental health care is not easy because of things like cost of services, access to services, time to talk to someone, cultural implications (some cultures do not believe in mental health care), and societal implications (needing mental health care can be seen as a weakness). As teachers, we have to remember what we learned from chapter 1 (page 7): it is difficult to learn when your mind and body are dealing with other things. Additionally, there can be detrimental implications for our students who don't learn coping strategies. Individuals who suffer from depression are at a 40 percent higher risk of developing metabolic and cardiovascular diseases when compared to the general population, and individuals with serious mental illness are almost twice as likely to develop these conditions (NAMI, 2023). Unemployment rates and substance use disorders are higher for individuals with mental health disorders when compared to those without. High school students who experience significant symptoms of depression are more than twice as likely to drop out of school compared to their peers, and students between the ages of 6 and 17 who experience mental, emotional, or behavioral concerns are three times more likely to repeat a grade in school. According to the CDC (2023a), in 2018–2019, among adolescents between the ages of 12 and 17:

- 15.1 percent experienced a major depressive episode
- 36.7 percent experienced persistent feelings of hopelessness or sadness
- 4.1 percent experienced a substance use disorder
- 1.6 percent experienced an alcohol use disorder
- 3.2 percent experienced an illicit drug use disorder (for example, heroin, cocaine, or meth)
- 18.8 percent experienced serious thoughts of attempting suicide
- 15.7 percent planned for suicide
- 8.9 percent attempted suicide
- 2.5 percent required medical treatment after making a suicide attempt

It is also important to discuss suicide because it is the second leading cause of death in youth and young adults ages 10–24 (CDC, 2023b). The statistics are mind-blowing and can feel overwhelming. However, when I get that feeling, I try to think, "How can I help?" You may be thinking, "I am just a classroom teacher, so how could I possibly help?" or "Educating the whole child is not my responsibility." I hear this. We need all aspects of care, which includes our administrators and counselors. It takes a village to support everyone in need. As educators, we are one piece of the puzzle, but we can be an important part, and there is always hope!

When we all work together, we can make a positive difference for our students. We have learned a lot of potential reasons for behavior. With this knowledge, we can work to honor the whole child by cultivating a positive environment that considers those reasons and how to respond to them. We can come from a place of empathy and support our students in learning what their emotional needs are and how to manage them. In a positive environment, our students are learning to think about others so we can all have empathy and support one another. Remember, when students feel safe and like they belong, they are able to better focus on learning.

Strategies for Implementing a Positive Classroom Environment

Before we dive into specific strategies for implementing a positive classroom environment, I want to share what research says about building a positive environment. Academic achievement goes up in a positive classroom environment (Daily, Mann, Kristjansson, Smith, & Zullig, 2019; Reyes, Brackett, Rivers, White, & Salovey, 2012). When thinking about the idea of building a positive learning environment, we get most of the way there by simply ensuring students know we are glad to have them in our classroom and by working to build positive relationships where *all* students *feel* like we care about them.

As teachers, we often think about what our students are bringing or not bringing to the table when they enter our rooms. They come to us with an imaginary backpack full of bricks, as we talked about in chapter 1 (page 7), with some students carrying heavier backpacks than others. We cannot control much of what is in their backpacks, but we can control how we handle ourselves and, ultimately, how we handle our students. Our students will only want to be in our classroom if we want to be there, too! We set the tone for our learning community. If we are enthusiastic, we inspire our students to be excited to be at school and learning, too (Smith, Fisher, & Frey, 2017).

Our enthusiasm to be at school and learning with our students comes across in how we communicate with our students. Communication includes both verbal (what we say and how we say it) and nonverbal (overall appearance, body language, and facial expressions).

According to Dominique Smith, Douglas Fisher, and Nancy Frey (2015), there are four types of teachers: (1) intentionally uninviting, (2) unintentionally uninviting, (3) unintentionally inviting, and (4) intentionally inviting.

- Teachers who are intentionally uninviting are harsh, vindictive, dismissive, and alienating. I would like to think there aren't many teachers like this in schools.
- Teachers who are unintentionally uninviting have low expectations and a low sense of efficacy. They tend to be negative and pessimistic.
- Teachers who are unintentionally inviting are positive but inconsistent, have an attitude that is hands-off, and are energetic but ultimately unaware. It may not sound all that bad because a teacher is ultimately being inviting, but the inconsistency can cause students to not feel secure in the environment, and when confronted with a difficult student, unintentionally inviting teachers don't know how to react and can then end up being reactionary rather than proactive.
- Teachers who are intentionally inviting toward students are purposeful, are consistently positive, are sensitive to the needs of their students, and have a growth mindset about their students and themselves as teachers.

To be intentionally inviting, we have to be careful of how we are speaking to others. For example, asking, "Why did you do that?" elicits feelings of defensiveness versus asking, "Can you talk to me about the situation?" Additionally, our clothes can help us be intentionally inviting. The clothes we choose to wear impact how we feel about ourselves and how others perceive us. Teachers are professionals and should dress the part. That doesn't mean wearing your fanciest clothes and shoes, but you should think about what your attire and overall appearance convey to colleagues, students, families, and your community. But also, what you wear should be authentic to you, because this will help you be your most authentic self to others.

I believe we all want to be and are capable of being intentionally inviting. If you feel you struggle in this regard, know that you will be able to use all the strategies in this section and across the book to execute a positive and proactive plan, and it will be intentionally inviting! In particular, I want to note that the specific strategies you find in the following sections will decrease any reliance you might have on *reactive management*, meaning you see a behavior and react to it. For example, a student shouts out the answer, and even though the teacher has a procedure where it is expected students raise their hands, the teacher isn't always consistent with following through with the procedure. The teacher acknowledges the student, but after it happens one too many times, the teacher shouts at the student and says they need to go to the hall. This is an instance of being reactive with the student. All the other times, the student is acknowledged, but then all of a sudden, the student is in trouble.

This is obviously not the outcome we want when we're trying to build a positive environment, so let's look at some things you *can* do by explicitly showing students that you care, arranging classrooms to better support learning, fostering students' social-emotional development, and using restorative practices.

SHOWING STUDENTS YOU CARE AND BUILDING POSITIVE RELATIONSHIPS

One strategy to build a positive environment that seems simple but isn't always as easy as it appears is showing students you care about them. It is very easy to show students you care about them when they are eager to please, want to be in school, and regularly do what you ask of them. It isn't as easy to show students in your classroom you care about them when they aren't eager to be there, present themselves in a way of being unmotivated and don't want to learn, and don't regularly listen to your directions. The reality is, when we come from a place of remembering what some of our students are dealing with, like we learned in chapter 1 (page 7), we can work to have empathy and learn to show those hard-to-reach students we care about them, too (even if we have to fake it). I once conducted a study where I was examining protective factors for students who had EBDs but were resilient. The goal was to learn, through interviews, what the protective factors were that helped these students be resilient. The number-one thing these students talked about was having a caring teacher. However, they felt very strongly about teachers on both sides of the spectrum, those they perceived as caring and those they perceived as not caring about them. They did not want to work for or respect the teachers they felt didn't care about them (Zolkoski, 2019). In a study dating back to 2009, Stephanie Mihalas, William C. Morse, David H. Allsopp, and Patricia Alvarez McHatton found students with EBDs achieved better outcomes when they had caring teacher-student relationships. Similarly, Christen Knowles, Christopher Murray, and Jeff Gau (2024) found students with perceived positive teacher-student relationships predicted their emotional, behavioral, and school adjustment. Despite data that support the tremendous importance of caring teachers, I think we can all admit it is easier to build connections with some students. It can be more difficult to show we care about students who have challenging behaviors such as defiance, physical or verbal aggression, or lack of motivation. There are many benefits to showing your students you care about them including an increase in academic achievement, as well as an increase in a positive classroom environment; in addition, the level of trust and respect increases, and students are more willing to do what they are supposed to do (Cook et al., 2017). Additionally, students with challenging behaviors are more supported in a positive classroom environment.

There are many ways to show your students you care about them. For example, smile at students, look at them in the eyes, and tell them you are glad they are in your classroom. Ask students how their day is going or what they did over the weekend. Find out what your students like and what they don't like. The most important thing to remember is to find ways that match your students' needs. The only way you can do that is by getting to know your students. Connecting with your students to get to know them will look different depending on the developmental stage of your students, on whether you begin working with them at the beginning of the year or partway through, and on whether they have specific challenges or learning needs.

Showing Care in Primary and Secondary Grades

Learn your students' names and the correct way to pronounce their names. It matters. In an elementary classroom, this can be a little bit easier because there are fewer students' names to learn. Learning names in middle and high school is a little trickier because there are more students, but it still can and should be done. For example, in a kindergarten class, you will have the same students all day long. Having assigned seats and name tags for students to wear the first few days will help you learn and remember their names. You can also play a game to learn everyone's names. A game may include having them say their name and their favorite animal or their favorite activity. In an upper elementary classroom such as fourth or fifth grade, you may switch classrooms. If you switch classrooms, you can have a seating chart where you have students' names and pictures from last year on it to help make the connection with their name and face. Playing a game where students introduce themselves and roll dice to determine the question they answer from a numbered list you've prepared is another way to learn their names. The same can be done in a secondary classroom. The trick is to find the easiest way for you to remember students' names. One way is to seat students in alphabetical order (although students don't always like this). You can also take pictures of groups of students at their tables. Pictures are simply for you to refer back to and are not shared beyond yourself in learning names. Secondary students may question the value of taking a name picture. These older students could play games, such as two truths and a lie, to learn names while starting to bond with one another. You can take the opportunity to talk to students about the importance of getting to know one another. I even do this in my college class, and my students appreciate my effort in learning their names and even often make comments about the fact they haven't had a college professor do that before. Before my class, I take a few minutes to look at the pictures so I can begin putting faces with names. In middle school and high school, or even elementary school, where students don't have a permanent seat, have the students bring their name tag to help you learn.

Greet your students by name at the door when they arrive each morning, with a smile on your face! If you can't stand at your door, you can still smile at your students while they are walking in and acknowledge them by name. A simple acknowledgment by name and a smile show your students you care that they are there. In a study conducted by researchers from universities across the United States, Clayton Cook and colleagues (2018) found positive greetings at the door to be a proactive classroom-management strategy because the positive greetings increased academic engagement and lowered disruptive behaviors in middle school students.

It doesn't matter the age or grade; it feels so much better to be greeted with a smile than to not be greeted at all. The greeting creates a sense of belonging and a sense of community, which ultimately creates a positive classroom environment. Greeting students at the door also allows you to get a quick check-in on how the students are doing. If you have a student who enters your classroom and their demeanor seems to be off (maybe they look tired or upset), you can immediately go and check on the student to see if they are doing OK and if there is anything you can do to help. Maybe you have an overly excited student who just had an amazing weekend adventure and wants to tell you everything! You can take a few minutes in the morning to talk with the excited student, which can help decrease disruptions from them. In elementary grades, a greeting may include a *feelings check-in* or the chance for the student to pick between a hug, a high five, a fist bump, or a wave.

I have seen countless videos of teachers and students at all grade levels creating their own moves (dancing, handshake) when students enter the room. Maybe your own specific comfort zone is simply the smile of acknowledgment and the greeting, which is fine! Really, what matters to students is the sense of belonging that occurs from being acknowledged when they walk in the door.

Students feel cared for when we take an interest in their interests. We can do something as simple as talking to them when they walk in the door. When we have our positive greeting, we can notice things students may be interested in. Maybe it is a type of book you see they always have or a certain color they are always wearing. The interactions don't have to be long, but the more students you have, the harder it is to keep students' interests straight. I recommend having a notebook or clipboard you can make a quick note on. It can even be divided by grade level and class period. I find writing things down helps me remember better and is also something I can refer to. Another way to learn your students' interests is to have them complete an interest inventory. There are many different types of interest inventories geared toward all grades. Younger grades will not be able to fill out an interest inventory independently. Often, classroom teachers do not have time to fill out a survey with all their students. In this case, consider getting the help of a parent. You can even partner with an older grade level and have the older students help fill out the survey for the younger students. Pairing an older student with a younger student will take some planning. It can be challenging if there are more students in one class than the other or students who may not be able to read or write. You will need to work with the corresponding teacher to plan how to best pair students so it stays organized and the goal of getting the surveys completed is accomplished.

Your students also need to learn about you. When your students know a little bit about you, they see you as more of a person than just their teacher. It adds a little bit of a personal connection students may be able to relate to. For example, share your love of animals or shoes. You should share stories about your life with your students because they will love hearing about it. When I taught elementary school, my students knew how much I loved shoes. I even had a student make me a quilt with shoes on it! They knew that I was getting married and even got invited to my wedding. My students were so excited when I was pregnant and got to see pictures of the baby. Now, as a college professor, I share pictures and videos of my family. My adult students talk about how much they love hearing stories. Even when they are no longer in my class, when I see them out and about, they will ask me about the kids. It matters to them. It helps our students make connections with us just as much as we need to make connections with them. You don't need to (and definitely shouldn't) tell your students everything about yourself. You need to find your happy medium, but small things you share can make a big difference in the connection you make with your students.

When you learn about your students' interests, you can find out if they are in extracurricular activities. When you are able, make it to those activities, because your students love seeing you there. You may not be able to attend the whole event, and that is OK. One year, I had a student who participated in Native American powwows. Going to those was something I will always treasure because I had never seen anything like it before, and seeing the look on my student's and her family's faces was priceless. In elementary school, there are so many different recreational leagues students participate in. Maybe it is an art festival or a dance recital you can attend. As students enter secondary school, it becomes a little easier because events happen at the school, and you can go to those. Anytime I was invited, I always tried my best to attend. If I said I was going to be there, I was there, because my students need to know that what I say is what I mean. If you aren't sure if your schedule will allow, say that to your students. Tell them you will try your best, but you may not make it. If you say you are going to attend an event, but something comes up, and you can't attend, try to get in contact with the family. If you can't get in contact with the family, when you see the student the next day, get down to their level and apologize. The apology will go a long way.

Another important way to show your students you care about them is making connections with family members. Parents and families like to hear about their student and what their student is doing in school. Sometimes we get in a habit of only contacting parents when there is a problem. When we do this, parents and the student feel like we do not care about them, which puts everyone on the defensive. Of course, communication also comes in written form, via email, text messaging, newsletter, social media, and so on. Across all media, it is important to ensure correct spelling and punctuation. It's also vital to know your audience, especially when professionalism is called for.

When communicating via email, always start the conversation using the person's name. Use complete sentences. If you are dealing with a sensitive problem, avoid addressing it in email, where it can be difficult to interpret tone. Such conversations are almost always better done in person. Social media posts come with their own rules. Apps like Remind, sportsYou, ClassDojo, BAND, and others are fantastic ways of communicating with parents and sharing pictures to show what is happening in the classroom and how students are engaged in their learning. However, it is also important to ensure you have family consent to post pictures of your students. And it's vital that you know what your school district's social media policy is and follow it. Newsletters can be shared via email, your school's learning management system, or an app like Smore.

In my experience, all caregivers and family members love communication, no matter the grade. Although communication seems to occur more in primary grades, it is still important in secondary grades. Think about time-efficient ways you can communicate with parents. Be careful with giving your actual cell phone number to others, particularly families, because you do need to protect your personal time. Instead, use apps that distribute text messages but don't require an actual exchange of your cell phone number such as Google Voice or the Sideline app.

Caring for others is important across all grade levels. Many of the strategies work for elementary and secondary students. For example, students of all ages respond in a more positive way to a smiling face and a teacher who knows their name. Ultimately, it comes down to you talking to your students to learn what they like and don't like, which in itself is caring because you are asking what they want and then doing the thing they said they like.

Starting at the Beginning of the Year Versus Starting Midyear

The start of a school year always brings about lots of feelings including excitement, worry, and everything in between. Some students will be excited to meet new friends and see old friends. It is important to remember there will be other students who struggle making friends and are terrified to talk to new people. School is easy for some students, but it isn't easy for everyone. Generally speaking, students in elementary school are more excited than students in secondary school. There is a lot more pressure (academically and socially) for students at the secondary level. We need to remember our students are coming from different places, and we must respond to them from a place of understanding and empathy. At the beginning of the school year, you are working to make a connection with your students, and you are learning everyone's names. Make sure you are thinking about the strategy that works for you to remember the names and how to pronounce them correctly. When students come in at the middle of the year, it's easier because it will be a few new names to learn at a time. If you are a teacher who has been teaching for a long time, and you realize you don't know all your students' names, that's OK! It's OK to explain to students you are having a hard time remembering everyone's name, but make sure they know it's important to you to learn their names. It's a great starting place! It can seem a little bit like you are putting yourself in a vulnerable position with your students, but they need to see you making an effort, and this one small thing shows them you are trying. Not only do our students need us to say we are going to do something, but they also need to see us actually do it.

At the beginning of the year, a procedure you can start with is greeting your students by name with a smile and hello. If you are starting your door greeting later in the year, that is OK, too. Greeting your students at the door can happen at any time. I look forward to the positive changes you see in your classroom by simply adding a positive greeting as they arrive in your room!

The wonderful thing about getting to know your students' interests is that it doesn't matter if it is the beginning of the year or the middle of the year. We can always learn something new about our students. Honestly, it is a good idea to have students fill out an interest inventory multiple times a year, or at least revise the already completed one, because students' interests change. It is important for us to know this information. A worry of some students is being able to fit in or find friends. When we do interest inventories, we may be able to find common interests between students and may be able to foster a friendship. Interest inventories can also help us learn our students' communication styles, which can help us as we navigate challenges (such as by asking, "How can I help you when you are upset?") as well as when designing lessons. Lessons can be designed based on students' interests and communication styles. We can also ask family members various questions about their child to learn likes and dislikes. It is a way to connect with parents while also learning how to best support their child.

At the beginning of the school year, you can complete an interest inventory you share with your students. If you are starting this later in the school year, you can do an interest inventory as an introduction to the students doing one, or maybe you begin by sharing small things you feel comfortable sharing with your students.

Just like with the other ways we have learned about so far, attending your students' extracurricular events can happen at any time. Finding out the extracurriculars your students participate in is something you can do at the beginning of the year. You can also ask for a schedule. However, if you are starting this practice at any other time, you can still ask your students what they are involved in and find out if you are able to attend. Going to students' extracurricular activities is a great way to talk with parents and family members. They also see you being at their child's event, which models you caring about their child because you wouldn't be there if you didn't care.

Diversifying Care for All Learners

Diversifying care for all learners starts with an awareness and appreciation of the many different learners in your classroom—that is, different backgrounds, different thinking styles, different knowledge, different challenges, and different gifts. When you have a student in special education who is in your room only some of the time, you need to make them feel like they belong by greeting them and acknowledging how excited you are when they arrive just as you would any other student in your class.

You may have a student who doesn't acknowledge your greeting, and that is OK. It then becomes your mission to learn why. Is the student shy and introverted? Is the student on the autism spectrum? Sometimes, students on the autism spectrum do not engage in social practices, such as a greeting. Maybe the student has been let down in the past and has a wall built up that you can tear down with those daily greetings. There may even be a cultural factor influencing behavior in this case.

With this said, the smile and positive interaction matter, perhaps more than ever. Mehrdad Sheybani (2019), whose work focuses on effective and reflective teaching, conducted a study and found nonverbal teacher behaviors (including smiling and eye contact) increased student motivation, attention, and academic achievement. Individuals with challenging behaviors are one of the biggest concerns educators have, and Cook and colleagues (2018) found a simple positive greeting at the door improved classroom behaviors.

It is much easier to build positive relationships with some students, but it is often extremely difficult to build positive relationships with students who are disruptive or have challenging behaviors. As educators, it becomes our most important job to build a connection with these students, as difficult as it may be. Greeting the students at the door is one strategy. Another strategy to build the connection is to learn what the students are interested in by noticing things about them. Jim Fay and Charles Fay (2016), authors of *Teaching With Love and Logic*, talk about the positive impact that noticing things about your students can have when building relationships. They describe a system called *one-sentence intervention*. The first step is to find six different and positive things a student values. Then, you write down the sentence, "I noticed that _____." Share these statements with a student, with the goal of providing the student with two of the statements per week for three weeks. After the three weeks are up, when asking the student to do something they may not prefer, because you have noticed things and are working to build a connection, the student is much more likely to do what you've asked. If it doesn't work, keep trying. The student needs to feel you are not giving up on them.

When thinking about an interest inventory for any type of student, it is important to accommodate as necessary. Does the form need to be in a different language? Can another teacher or even you talk with a student who hasn't gotten their interest inventory completed and help them complete it? It is important to adapt to the needs of all our students. If you send a survey home and it doesn't come back, avoid going straight to the thought, "That parent doesn't care." There may be so many different reasons for the form not being filled out. Helping the student is a great way to learn more about their life outside of school! Part of building positive relationships also involves being a bridge between school and home. Ask questions, and come from a place of "How can I help?" Listen and say positive things about their student. These are easy ways to build connections with families.

Another way to learn more about your students is to have them answer the question, "What do I wish my teacher knew?" This activity comes from third-grade teacher Kyle Schwartz, who taught in a school where 90 percent of the students lived in poverty. In her book, Schwartz (2016) talks about how overwhelming it was to think about the challenges her students faced. However, she thought about how important it was to focus on students' strengths and passions to help them feel motivated and become engaged in their learning.

One day, she decided to write on the board the phrase *I wish my teacher knew* and asked students to respond on a notecard they turned in to her. Schwartz (2016) explains that each student's response was unique. Some were funny, while others were honest and even vulnerable. After finishing the lesson, she felt she could connect with her students more. For example, learning one student didn't have a pencil at home to do homework deepened her understanding of the challenges that student faced and gave her a greater sense of how to meet those challenges while having empathy for the student. We need to think back to chapter 1 and Maslow's basic hierarchy of needs (page 27). If students are not getting their basic needs met, it is difficult for them to learn. We need to really listen to our students. When we do, they are more likely to feel heard and safe. When they feel safe, they are more willing to express their truth.

ARRANGING THE CLASSROOM TO SUPPORT STUDENT LEARNING

Another important aspect in cultivating a positive classroom environment is considering how your room is arranged. We communicate how much we care, in part, by the level of organization and cleanliness of our classroom. A classroom that is clean, organized, and decorated provides a perception of caring for ourselves and our students. I know this can be a difficult thought for my friends who struggle with organization. Like all things, there will be times when it is easier said than done, but it is something important to actively work on.

When students talk to me about a classroom they like to be in, they will say things like, "It feels like home" or "It feels cozy." These students associate cozy and home with feeling safe and welcome. We know from chapter 1 (page 7) that students are better able to learn when they feel safe. Simply having a room that is clean and inviting can support a student feeling safe. Students need to feel welcome when they enter our classrooms.

We need to come prepared each day and know exactly what we are doing. Materials need to be out and ready to go. If you are using markers, are there markers for everyone, and do they all work? Students will not be excited about the learning if they know we aren't prepared to teach them. When materials are not prepared, you are losing instructional time, and students have more downtime to do things you may not want them to do. For example, if you have a lesson where you need to pull something up on the computer for students to view on the SMART Board and it isn't ready to go, students are more likely to talk to each other or get up and wander around the room. You are then likely to get frustrated because the students are no longer on task. Similarly, if students need some sort of materials (for example, Expo markers) and they don't have them or the ones they have aren't working, students are more likely to talk to each other than get a working set of materials, or they will just sit and not do anything. Other students may get up and look for their materials. When you are prepared with all materials and have a place in the room for students to access additional materials, you are able to get to the lesson, and students are less likely to engage in the behavior you don't want them to. In this sense, you are being proactive. When you are proactive, you are automatically being more positive because you are preventing problems before they begin by simply being prepared.

We need to actively engage the students in their learning. Whoever is doing the most work is the one learning the most. For students to be actively engaged in their learning, you need to be prepared by understanding what the lesson you are teaching is about. There will be lessons you teach where you know the material, but there will be lessons where you don't know the material as well. Students expect you to know what you are teaching. We lose the feeling of having a positive learning environment when students feel we don't know what we are talking about. To that point, when we are prepared with wonderful and engaging lessons, our students are so engaged in what they are doing that the environment is positive and there is an automatic decrease in potential problem behaviors.

As we work to create a positive classroom learning environment, arranging your classroom for success is vital, but how do you make it happen? As we move through the rest of this section, I will share strategies to help you get organized and stay organized at the primary and secondary levels as well as when you are starting the year out from day one or you are beginning sometime after the school year has begun.

Arranging the Classroom in Primary and Secondary Grades

A supportive room arrangement will look a little different in primary school from what it looks like in secondary grades. Elementary teachers are typically more artsy, with ABCs hanging and some type of theme around the room. Remember, don't let a teacher store explode in your classroom with too many things. It can be overstimulating for students when there are too many things on the walls and filling all the spaces. Some students may have ADHD, making it difficult to concentrate with so many things going on. Other students may have sensory disorders, also making it difficult to concentrate on learning. Overstimulation can present itself as negative behaviors (for example, defiance). When there are too many things, it can also feel cluttered, and it is difficult for a cluttered space to feel inviting. Moreover, it can be difficult to find the materials needed for lessons when there are too many things everywhere in the room. The same challenges for students can occur in a classroom with few things. When walls and space are bare, it can feel uninviting, and students are less able to learn. Students with sensory integration disorders may find it difficult to be in what feels like a sterile room with white walls and fluorescent lights.

Teachers of secondary students typically have less impetus to decorate their classrooms, and secondary students are less likely to expect this embellishment. However, it is important to ensure the walls aren't bare in secondary classrooms. Blank walls aren't welcoming, and we want students to want to be there. In an elementary classroom, it is easy to ensure your students' work is on the walls because of the nature of the work being asked of them (for example, Martin Luther King projects, 100th day of school, or what will you do with $100?). In secondary classrooms, student artwork may not be as readily available, but what can be added? Can you take some time at the beginning of the year or even in the middle of the year and do a project in which students create something? There is a sense of pride when walls have student work on them. Students feel it, and parents do, too! This is more challenging in a secondary classroom because you have multiple periods, but it isn't impossible. Have a spot in the room to celebrate your students (for example, by displaying an award or a good grade on an assignment). Students can bring in something that means something to them. It can be used as a way to get to know students. Maybe it is sports related, a picture of family members, a picture of a family dog, or a student's artwork. The goal is for there to be meaning for the students so they feel like something in the room belongs to them. Make sure you have your diploma and your celebrations on the wall, too! No matter the grade, students comment about enjoying being part of a classroom that feels like home and feels safe. When a classroom is more personalized (with your things and theirs), it can help students feel like they are a part of a community they belong to.

When thinking about your classroom arrangement, you need to consider the seating. Students need to be active in their learning, and one way to do it is by having students work in groups or with partners. It is also beneficial to have tables or desks in group arrangements to allow for partner work. When creating those arrangements, make sure all students can see the board or screen. Everyone should easily be able to walk around the room. Traffic should be able to flow without obstructions. Also, think about your classroom and how you want your students to access materials. We will not always have students who bring materials from home. Some may have materials at home and forget to bring them to school. It is important to have spare materials for students to access so they are effectively able to learn. How things flow and how students access materials will change based on the type of room you have. If you have a smaller classroom, you will have to be more creative with your space and how you arrange desks and extra supplies. Do you have cabinets to put things in? Can you get access to some storage containers that can hold materials but don't take up a lot of space? Where will students receive whole-group instruction? Will this happen at their desks, or is your room big enough to allow for students to sit on the floor? Each person is different in what they like, and that is completely OK! The important thing is students feel welcome, there is a place to sit where they can easily see instruction, and there's an easy way to access materials. Materials for the lessons you are teaching should be readily available and organized so you can easily access them. We lose valuable instruction time when we do not have materials prepared or we are trying to figure out how to teach a lesson. Preparation is key.

Starting at the Beginning of the Year Versus Midyear

Getting organized is critical to support a positive learning environment. The key to organization is planning and preparing before the school year even begins. Before school starts, you will know what your classroom looks like and what subjects you will be teaching. You will be able to decorate and arrange your room prior to the first day of school. However, not everyone is so lucky. Some of us have to make sudden changes due to being needed in a different grade or school or being hired late. If you fall into this category, don't worry; you can still take time to get organized. Hopefully you will have a weekend to begin planning and preparing. Some of you may be reading this and don't fit into any of these categories, but you may realize you need to make some adjustments to how your classroom is arranged. It's perfectly OK to make adjustments midyear. You may be a person who had time to get organized prior to school starting, but things are not flowing in a way that actually works. The key is self-reflection. It's OK to make changes if you realize you are not comfortable in the classroom or you notice your students aren't comfortable. Sometimes we have great plans and realize in the middle of executing them that what we planned in our mind isn't working as well as we thought. The most important thing to remember is to make changes when you see a problem.

The task of arranging your classroom may feel extremely overwhelming whether starting at the beginning of the year or realizing adjustments need to be made in the middle of the year. I recommend starting small. Start with how the desks or tables are arranged. Once you get students settled on where they are going to sit, think about how materials will be organized so you and your students can easily access them. From there, you can think about getting walls decorated or taking things off the walls. No matter what grade you teach, you will have students ready and willing to help, which automatically promotes a positive environment because when students help, they have buy-in. If you teach a younger grade where it is difficult for students to be able to help, I bet a parent would be willing to help. Sometimes we can be afraid to ask for help, but it's worth a shot to ask others.

No matter when you are starting with finding the best way to arrange your classroom, remember the benefits it has. You are moving from being reactive to being proactive. Being reactive means something happens and then you react to it, which becomes exhausting. When we are exhausted, we are less tolerant of student behaviors, and our environment is in danger of becoming negative. A negative environment then becomes a place where we don't feel comfortable and neither do our students. When we aren't comfortable, we are less likely to be able to learn effectively. Planning and preparation allow for organization, which helps us be proactive. Being proactive is positive. You want to be there, and so do your students!

Diversifying for All Learners

When thinking about diversifying for all learners, my mind goes to students who have ADHD, or any other type of disability where they can easily get overwhelmed. A room with too many things in it can be sensory overload to some students. It probably won't happen every year, but there may be years when you have a student who requires physical accommodations. You may need to adjust your room to ensure the student can easily access materials in the classroom. When you have an active student, you may need to consider different types of flexible seating arrangements. Some students may need a wobble chair or a type of seat cushion that allows for movement. There are even bands that can be put on a chair that allows students to move their feet to focus more. Ultimately, it is important to find options that work for the student. Some students may do better standing in the back of the room. As long as they aren't bothering anyone, a student who stands may be able to focus better. One easy thing to do is ask your student, "What do you need to be successful?" You will find that they will answer honestly.

When thinking about diversifying for all learners, it is, once again, important to think about the seating arrangements. You will have to think of the size of your students and the size of the chairs and tables. For example, when you are teaching a lower elementary age group, you typically have small chairs and tables. However, you will have students who are larger for their age. Do they fit in the chair? Is there a way to access slightly bigger chairs and a table to help make these students more comfortable? The same can be said about smaller students in grades where the tables and chairs are larger. It may be more comfortable for these students to sit in a different style of chair. It is important to talk to your students about what makes them comfortable regarding the physical use of space and equipment in the classroom as well. We don't want to assume and unintentionally put students in positions they aren't comfortable in.

When preparing lessons with all learners in mind, it is important to truly think about all learners. Are there accommodations that need to be made (for example, making a notes page for a student with a disability)? Do you need to prepare different types of materials to meet accommodations? Have you thought about the interests of your students and what your students may need? Have you thought about your room arrangement and what works best? Will you have to move things around to ensure everyone has equal access to what you are doing? Again, preparation is important to ensuring everyone feels comfortable in the environment. This planning helps foster an optimal learning environment.

FOSTERING SOCIAL AND EMOTIONAL LEARNING TO SUPPORT STUDENT LEARNING

The Collaborative for Academic, Social, and Emotional Learning (CASEL) is a multidisciplinary network of researchers, practitioners, educators, and child advocates across the country who are committed to social and emotional learning for all students. CASEL (n.d.b) defines *social and emotional learning* as the process through which all young people and adults acquire and apply the knowledge, skills, and attitudes to develop healthy identities, manage emotions, achieve personal and collective goals, feel and show empathy for others, establish and maintain supportive relationships, and make responsible caring decisions. According to CASEL (n.d.e), "SEL is an integral part of education and human development." Research shows SEL promotes positive outcomes for students and the school community (Greenberg, 2023). CASEL (n.d.b) has developed an SEL framework that includes five core social and emotional competencies: (1) self-awareness, (2) self-management, (3) social awareness, (4) relationships skills, and (5) responsible decision making. In figure 2.1, see how the five competencies of the CASEL framework are ensconced by the four key settings in which they can be developed where students live and grow: (1) classrooms, (2) schools, (3) families and caregivers, and (4) communities.

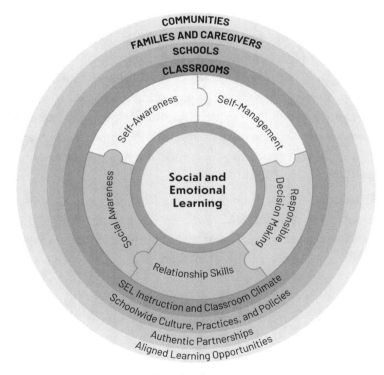

Source: ©2021 CASEL. All Rights Reserved. Used with permission.

FIGURE 2.1: Social and emotional learning.

Integrating SEL into your classroom is a wonderful strategy to support a positive classroom environment. Learning self-awareness is not always easy for our students. Moreover, it's one thing to be aware of your emotions, but it is another to be able to manage them. Students need to learn social awareness skills as well as responsible decision-making and relationship skills. Each of these skills is important to learn in the classroom and in life. When we are more aware of our own emotions and those of others, we are better equipped to have empathy for ourselves and others. This provides a sense of safety, love, and belonging, which leads to a positive environment. As you remember from chapter 1 and Maslow's hierarchy of needs (page 27), students are better able to learn when they feel safe, loved, and like they belong.

Joseph Durlak, Joseph Mahoney, and Alaina Boyle (2022) conducted a meta-analysis of universal (designed for all students), school-based SEL programs for students in early childhood education through high school. A meta-analysis involves reviewing previous research about a specific topic. In the case of the meta-analysis conducted by Durlak and colleagues (2022), the topic involved reviewing studies involving universal SEL programs for all grades. The study involved over a million students worldwide, and findings consistently showed SEL having a broad range of positive impacts on students. Specifically, student outcomes included increased SEL skills, attitudes, prosocial behaviors, and academic achievement while also showing a decrease in emotional distress and conduct problems.

SEL embodies the idea of educating the whole child. Research shows the positive impact SEL can have on students both academically and socially (Cohen, Opatosky, Savage, Stevens, & Darrah, 2021; Durlak et al., 2022). The idea of educating the whole child helps us ensure we are truly supporting the students in our classrooms by supporting students' abilities to develop healthy personal relationships, treat others with respect, develop the capacity to critically think and problem solve, succeed in postsecondary education as well as the job force, and contribute as a citizen in democracy (Greenberg, 2023).

In the sections that follow, I will be sharing how SEL can be implemented for primary and secondary grade levels. I will also share strategies for implementing SEL from the start of a school year or in the middle of the year. It is also important to share how SEL can be diversified for all types of learners.

Fostering Social and Emotional Learning to Support Student Learning in Primary and Secondary Grades

When talking to your students about the various components of SEL, it is important to ensure you are matching what you are sharing with the grade level you are teaching. It has to be relevant to your students, or it will not connect with them.

For example, an SEL topic may include perspective taking. For students in elementary school, you may find a children's book about perspective taking and then talk about different "what if" scenarios, for example, "What if you lost your favorite toy?" Or you could share a picture of a scenario and a person's response to it and then have students come up with different possibilities of response the person may have. In a secondary classroom, perspective taking may include having students watch a video and analyze it to identify different interpretations of events. Students may also role-play complex scenarios (for example, having a difficult conversation with a friend) or create a "walk a mile in their shoes" scenario where students have to imagine themselves in the shoes of someone from a different background than their own and imagine the challenges they may face.

Age-appropriate scenarios and language are important when deciding on lessons to teach your students. It is also important to set the stage by emphasizing the importance of listening to others' viewpoints and expressing opinions respectfully. Typically speaking, students in elementary school are much better at being accepting than students in secondary school. It is important to foster the respect from everyone. It is part of building your positive classroom environment. Students should also be encouraged to be reflective and self-aware. How can we encourage students to reflect on their perspective and potentially make adjustments to their thinking based on new information? Creating real-world connections will help link perspectives to real-life situations that are relevant to the grade level you are teaching.

SEL can be taught using a specific program that has a specially designed curriculum, but it can also be taught by teaching and modeling the basic skills SEL embodies: self-awareness, self-management, social awareness, problem-solving skills, and relationship skills. Some schools have an SEL program already in place while other schools may not. Some programs are free while others have a cost. Whether you work at a school with a curriculum in place or not, it is your job as the teacher to keep it as an important element to focus on in your classroom. In the following paragraphs, I want to share a little bit of information about a few of my favorite SEL resources you can go to when choosing an SEL program or if you are simply looking for ideas. SEL has been shown to be effective across all grade levels (Cohen et al., 2021; Durlak et al., 2022).

One of the resources to look at is the CASEL website (https://casel.org). On the website, you can view all the CASEL-approved programs and can filter by developmental state, grade level, and setting (that is, classroom or school). When viewing programs, you can click on the program website to learn more information about the program. Although CASEL has a lot of information about the importance of implementing SEL and shares specific program information, it is used more as a resource where you find a curriculum.

Conscious Discipline received the designation of a SELect CASEL program (https://consciousdiscipline.com). The website is full of amazing resources and information to use in the classroom, school, and home. What I like is the fact some of the resources and professional development opportunities are free. Others are included with a paid membership. There are four components of Conscious Discipline.

1. **Brain State Model:** Learn about safety, connection, and problem solving by looking at the brain stem (survival state), limbic system (emotional state), and prefrontal lobes (executive state; Conscious Discipline, n.d.a).
2. **Seven Powers for Conscious Adults:** Learn about the seven powers— perception, unity, attention, free will, acceptance, love, and intention (Conscious Discipline, n.d.d).
3. **Creating the School Family:** Learn how important the school family is and how to build a healthy family model to support the goal of fostering optimum development of all members (Conscious Discipline, n.d.c).
4. **Seven Skills of Discipline:** Learn about the foundation of problem solving— composure, encouragement, assertiveness, choices, empathy, positive intent, and consequences (Conscious Discipline, n.d.e).

The final program I would like to highlight, the Jesse Lewis Choose Love Movement, is CASEL aligned (https://chooselovemovement.org); this program is for classrooms, schools, families, and the community (Choose Love Movement, n.d.). There is information on the website about online trainings, resources, and events. What is amazing about this program is the fact that it is free. You can go to the website and create your own account. There are specific lessons designed for preK through twelfth grade based on the idea of Courage + Gratitude + Forgiveness + Compassion = the Choose Love Formula. Units are based on the Choose Love Formula and include lessons within each unit. Each lesson includes student outcomes and character and social-emotional development (CSED) model standards. There are links to videos and read-aloud slides as well as the things you need to prepare (for example, print out the monthly calendar to send home or write the Choose Love Formula on the board). Then, the lesson begins and can easily be followed. At the end of the lessons are ways to transfer the learning by using the language throughout the day so it becomes natural and for how to connect the learning at home.

The biggest challenge in implementing SEL in the classroom, no matter the grade level, is finding the time to do it. There is so much content needing to be taught, and adding SEL is just one more thing to do. To this point, I will remind you of the importance of educating the whole child and that, by doing so, academic achievement goes up (Cohen et al., 2021; Durlak et al., 2022). Whether you are implementing SEL in a first-grade classroom or in an eleventh-grade classroom, the most important thing to remember is consistency. When working with teachers, I find the most success when teachers implement their SEL lesson at the beginning of their day or period. It is a wonderful way for teachers and students to start out their day and helps get them ready to learn the designated subject area. Often, lessons are taught one time per week and can last anywhere from 10 minutes to about 20 minutes. Many times, programs in middle and high school grades are designed to be shorter but delivered more frequently because of the duration of classes. The main topic of the week can be taught in one lesson but should be reinforced throughout the week. For example, you may have a lesson on perspective taking, which can be tailored for any grade level. Throughout the day or week, when working with your students, you can use the language of perspective taking. There will be times when your students will have to understand and learn the perspective of others in the classroom or you as the teacher. You can also use the same language to understand the perspective of your students. It is important to note that lessons will be different depending on the program being used. The program materials will show you what you need to do, much like your mathematics book (or any other subject area) explains what to do.

Another challenge, particularly for students at the secondary level, can be having students take SEL seriously as well as understanding one another's viewpoints. You have to set ground rules for students. Also, it is OK if not everyone wants to actively participate by answering questions. Certain topics may be more difficult than others for some students (for example, dealing with loss). You may also want to consider beginning with topics that are easier (for example, gratitude). Reluctant students will begin to buy in as time goes on, and as students become more comfortable, they will be more willing to share.

Starting at the Beginning of the Year Versus Midyear

The wonderful thing about implementing SEL is the fact you can start implementing it at any time! If you are able to start implementing SEL from the beginning of the year, you will want to make a plan and prepare. For example, what lessons will you teach? Will the lessons come from a curriculum you have been given or from the resources you have found (maybe even from what I have shared so far in this book)? What is the topic, and how long will you take to teach it? How can the topic be incorporated throughout the week? When will you teach it? As I said earlier, the best way to ensure the lesson gets done is to start off at the beginning of the week with SEL as the first thing you do when you get to your class. In elementary school, it can be first thing in the morning. In a secondary classroom, you may not have the students daily and won't have them first thing in the morning, but you can teach the lesson at the beginning of the period. Just like in any lesson you teach, you will want to ensure your materials are prepared.

If you are starting SEL lessons midyear, you will want to do the same as you would at the beginning of the year by answering the questions posed in the previous paragraph. The challenge starting midyear is there will have to be a shift from what you were doing to adding SEL. Change can be a little difficult for some students. Another challenge can be trust. Do students feel comfortable sharing?

No matter when you begin implementing SEL, you will also want to set expectations for your students to follow. What are some classroom rules you want to establish as a group? You will want students to help create the rules to help with buy-in. You also want to use the language daily, whether you are doing a lesson or not.

Diversifying for All Learners

The essence of SEL is not only knowing and being able to express your own emotions but also being able to understand others' emotions and work to problem solve. This makes SEL inherently a powerful tool to create healthy, inclusive, and caring classrooms and schools for all students. Equity and excellence, as part of the CASEL definition, refer to all students across race, ethnicity, learning ability, family income level, home language, immigration status, sexual orientation, gender identity, and other factors to engage in high-quality educational environments where students receive the opportunity to promote their healthy social, emotional, and academic development (CASEL, n.d.c). When choosing and implementing an SEL program, it is important to keep the needs of your student population in mind. When thinking about a program, think about what SEL is supposed to do, according to CASEL—advance educational equity and excellence by doing the following.

1. **Supporting authentic school-family-community partnerships:** Support partnerships with community partners, families, and educators to ensure collaboration across diverse perspectives and backgrounds.

2. **Fostering collaborative and trusting relationships:** As educators, we need to appreciate the unique strengths and needs of our students by developing a deeper awareness of our students' backgrounds and cultures. When we do this, we create an environment that is inclusive of all learners. Through SEL, we can learn and practice empathy, active listening, and perspective taking to develop deeper connections with each other.

3. **Promoting meaningful and rigorous curriculum and instruction:** We need to set high expectations for our students and actively engage

them in developing social, emotional, and academic skills to help them not only achieve their goals but also contribute to their community.

4. **Applying ongoing evaluations of practices, outcomes, and policies:** This is an important step because it ensures we are treating all students fairly and they all have access to high-quality educational opportunities in supportive learning environments.

SEL is a wonderful way for students to be in a trusting and safe environment where they feel motivated and feel like they belong while learning with their peers and their teachers. Ultimately, an environment that feels safe is positive and fosters a sense of community and in turn promotes academic achievement.

An example lesson for supporting diversity could be based on celebrating differences in the classroom. At the primary level, a discussion could be had about what it means to be different, and a book such as *The Colors of Us* (Katz, 1999) could complement the lesson. Students can do an activity where they reflect on their own uniqueness. A diversity wall can be created where each student and their uniqueness is highlighted and celebrated. The emphasis is showing empathy and respect for others. A similar lesson could be done in a secondary classroom. Rather than reading a book, students could watch a video or TED Talk (for example, "The Danger of a Single Story," Adichie, 2009). Students can have a discussion on differences. Students can write on a sticky note or index card something that makes them unique. Students can be given the opportunity to share with the class or keep it private. The notecards or sticky notes can be collected, and the teacher can share with the class as a discussion, keeping stories anonymous. During the discussion, students can be encouraged to consider visible and invisible aspects of diversity.

When engaging in SEL lessons where an inclusive classroom is promoted, it is important to celebrate diverse perspectives. We also want to establish and reiterate the importance of respect as we work to learn how to acknowledge and validate differences we have. Active listening can be taught while we work to self-reflect and understand ourselves and others in a more meaningful way.

USING RESTORATIVE PRACTICES TO BUILD A CLASSROOM COMMUNITY

Restorative practices are a classroom-management approach where we proactively build a classroom community to prevent problem behaviors, and when challenging behaviors do arise, we use dialogue rather than punishment alone (Smith et al., 2017). Restorative practices are designed to support a respectful classroom, establish expectations for positive student behavior, develop a positive rapport with students, and effectively manage conflicts. There can be a misconception that restorative practices involve not giving consequences. However, this isn't the case. Rather than punishment alone, restorative practices equip teachers with necessary tools to ensure students are learning from their mistakes and relationships are restored. Let's look at some ways you can use these practices in your classroom.

Using Restorative Practices in Primary and Secondary Grades

Restorative practices can be used for any grade. Class meetings are a great way to check in with your students. The purpose of a class meeting is to provide a space where students feel connected and are able to problem solve. Class meetings foster a sense of community and belonging in your classroom. What is brought up during the class meeting will look different depending on the grade level. Class meetings can help solve problems and raise awareness and are truly a time for students to openly discuss things that are happening (Smith et al., 2017). The teacher serves as the facilitator by posing questions, and then the group discusses. Questions can be as simple as, "We are going on a field trip to the zoo tomorrow, so what do we need to make sure we are doing?" It is a wonderful way for students to practice positive behaviors. Be on the lookout for students who could act as leaders for the meetings. Other class meetings can be more informal and can include various topics such as, "We are taking our final exam next week. How is everyone feeling about it? Can we do anything to support one another and improve our confidence?"

All students benefit from restorative practices because the focus is on relationship building, empathy, and personal responsibility. Methods are adapted to meet the developmental needs of the different age groups. For example, the complexity of conversations will be different. Primary grades focus on simple conflict resolution and emotional support, but secondary grades will have more nuanced and deeper conversations about intentions and long-term implications. Additionally, in primary grades, students need more guidance from the teacher. In secondary grades, students are better able to take more ownership and have a higher level of autonomy and responsibility for their actions. Students are better at creating solutions to different problems together.

When there are circle meetings, there are responsibilities and expectations. In a primary grade, students may be given the option to sit in a circle on the carpet. They may choose to sit in their chair. At the secondary level, there may not be space in the classroom for students to sit on the floor, but students should be able to form a circle with their chairs. No matter the grade, you will want to set expectations for who is talking and who is listening. You will want to discuss what it looks like to listen to others (for example, look at the person talking or keep your voice off). Some teachers like to use some type of tool to signify the person who is talking (for example, a talking stick). The talking tool can be created by the students so they have ownership of it. Each student should have the opportunity to share if they'd like to. Also, students should be talking to one another during these meetings.

There should always be a purpose to the class meeting, which will take planning for the teacher. As the teacher, it is important to ensure everyone has an opportunity to talk if they'd like. When students are called for the meeting, expectations are set, and the purpose of the meeting is stated. An agenda may be helpful to use and follow. An example format for any grade may include the following.

- Review rules and expectations.
- State the purpose of the meeting.
- Give each student an opportunity to share what they notice or how something makes them feel. They can say "pass" if they choose not to share.
- Discuss potential solutions.
- Reach an agreement as a group.
- Summarize the outcome and provide feedback on collaboration skills.

The following are some topic ideas for the primary grades.

- Creating kindness in the classroom: What are small acts of kindness we can do in our classroom? How can we make others feel welcome?
- Peacefully resolving conflict: What can we do when we have an argument with a friend? How can we apologize and forgive our friend?
- Respecting differences: What makes each of us unique? What is bullying? How can we stop it from happening?

And the following are some topic ideas for secondary grades.

- Managing stress and mental health: What stresses you out the most? How can we help one another? What are healthy coping strategies we can use when we feel overwhelmed?
- Handling peer pressure: What does peer pressure look like? How do we say no when we feel pressured to do something we know we shouldn't do or don't want to do?
- Procrastination and time management: Why do we procrastinate, and how can we stop? What are some strategies to effectively manage time and stay on top of assignments and tests?

Starting at the Beginning of the Year Versus Midyear

Much like with SEL, restorative practices can be implemented at any time! Implementing restorative practices from the beginning of the school year begins with a plan and preparation. At the beginning of the year, topics can be more about establishing the expectations and routine while also getting to know one another. Implementing restorative practices from the beginning of the year can support a sense of belonging and community quickly. Students need to understand the purpose of restorative practices and what expectations are. Your first meeting may be creating a class contract everyone signs.

If you want to begin restorative practices midyear, you should plan and prepare accordingly. You will know your students better than you would if you began this practice during the first few days of the school year. You will be able to plan and prepare for different personalities, and you will probably have a better idea of a topic to begin with, although the first meeting will need to include information on the purpose and expectations (much like starting on the first day).

A challenge you may face, whether it's the beginning of the year or the middle of the year, is buy-in, particularly with secondary students. You may need to begin by asking a lot of probing questions. It will be important to foster empathy and understanding with your students. Not everyone is used to sharing thoughts and feelings in a meaningful way. It is OK if students choose to pass. Give your students time and space to see the value and buy in to the idea.

Diversifying for All Learners

Restorative practices can easily be diversified for all learners. To start, there will be some students who are open to sharing their thoughts and feelings, but others will not be so open. Giving space for all students to share, or pass, ensures everyone has an opportunity but no one is forced. There may also be opportunities where students can write their thoughts down rather than saying them out loud. Some students may feel more comfortable writing anonymously than speaking publicly.

Topics discussed can be varied based on topics students are interested in. There may be times when a topic needs to be serious (for example, bullying), but there will be times when the topic can be more fun (for example, two truths and a lie). Questions can also be based on things you, as the teacher, notice about what is going on in the classroom or even within the school. There may also be opportunities to have discussions based on topics happening in the world. Because of the nature of using class meetings, students learn to understand perspectives that are different than their own. Restorative practices can be a powerful way to truly understand others, where empathy is cultivated and students feel they have a community of people they have a connection and belong to.

Concluding Thoughts

As we reach the end of the chapter, I hope you realize the importance of building a positive learning environment and feel empowered with the ability to do it. Research shows the detrimental impact a negative environment can have (Huang & Cornell, 2021). Learning the statistics of the students who walk into our classrooms can be overwhelming, but it is important information and helps us understand the importance of educating the whole child. Now that we understand why it is important, we need to figure out how to do it. Please consider the following reproducible tool, "Building a Positive Classroom Environment" (page 64; also available online at **go.SolutionTree.com/behavior**), as you work to develop an environment that is positive for all learners. A positive learning environment means we are showing *all* our students we care about them in a way they feel cared for. Students don't need a grand gesture; a simple smile and showing up for them daily shows them we care. Room arrangement is another easy thing that fosters a positive environment because we are taking our students into consideration. We arrange the room by thinking about the layout, what's on the walls, and where to put materials. When we implement SEL and restorative practices, we are fostering a positive learning environment. Research continually shows that a positive environment creates a sense of belonging and increases academic achievement (Cook et al., 2017). We go to work excited to be there, and our students show up excited to learn. We are less stressed and less burned out, which means we are more likely to stay in the field of education. Not every day is going to be a great day. Teaching is hard. On the hard days, we must remember why we became teachers in the first place. I know I became a teacher because I wanted to make a positive impact on my students. What is your why?

Building a Positive Classroom Environment

We can sometimes get into a negative space where we are focusing on what our students are *not* doing or what they are doing *wrong*. We can sometimes lose sight and focus on our students who are the most challenging. I have created a checklist for you to help foster ideas and to ensure you are working to build a positive connection and environment for *all* your students.

☐ I have shown genuine interest in *all* my students.

☐ I have had check-ins with students.

☐ I have listened to my students' concerns.

☐ I am using positive reinforcement to celebrate successes.

☐ I am focusing on *all* my students' successes (big and small).

☐ I am teaching and modeling empathy to address conflicts.

☐ I am avoiding showing favoritism to ensure *all* students feel included and valued.

☐ My classroom is arranged in a way that meets *all* my students' needs.

☐ My walls and room have engaging decorations and reflect my students' work and interests.

☐ I have created flexible seating options to support various learning styles and comfort.

☐ I have regular morning meetings and check-ins with students.

Voices From the Field

What do you like about your teacher?

"My reading teacher was my favorite because her classroom felt like home."

—*A sixth-grade student*

"I loved my math teacher because he was funny, smart, and so chill. He made all the lessons fun, and he always told funny math jokes."

—*A sixth-grade student*

"I loved my science teacher because she had a great vibe. She told us stories about her kids and would show us videos. I really loved her laugh."

—*A sixth-grade student*

"My [social studies] teacher always took topics that were really hard and made them fun. We got to do debates in her class, and she had a wrestling ring and all the gear to go along with it."

—*An eighth-grade student*

"Kindness and patience make a good teacher. Mrs. Thompson was my favorite teacher because she gave us more freedom, and she was funny, and she was really kind."

—*A seventh-grade student*

"They have to be fun, and chill—basically just be Mrs. Constante."

—*A ninth-grade student*

"Obviously they need to be smart and learn that some kids don't know. You can't get frustrated when they don't know the answer, and you have to be kind. My favorite teacher is Ms. Clancy because she is nice and made really funny jokes that helped us learn."

—*A second-grade student*

"Teachers who are funny make the work more fun. It takes some of the pressure off when it's a difficult subject. My favorite teachers let us have a little more freedom and trust us unless we break that trust."

—*A ninth-grade student*

"My favorite teacher makes everything fun and is excited to be teaching us. She makes an effort to get to know you, and even when she isn't your teacher, she still is so excited to see you. She made sure we knew how much she cares about us and how important we are to her."

—*A student*

"Mr. Dupree because he talked to us, not at us."

—*A ninth-grade student*

"Mr. Miller because if we listened and did our work, he'd let us do whatever. He's cool and chill."

—*A middle school theater student*

"Good teachers are patient and answer your questions without making you feel inadequate, and they are always willing to listen."

—*A seventh-grade student*

"Good teachers are good people. By the way they come into the classroom every day prepared, stand up for the most silent in the class, know the material, and teach it so that everyone can understand but also make it clear that it's their job and pleasure to explain if someone doesn't understand. They are role models."

—*A high school graduate*

"Mr. Ingram is my fav because he makes class fun. If we ever had a project, it wouldn't be a normal project. It was like have a partner and make a 3-D model of the earth. He was the best science teacher ever. He would tell us stories about stuff he did when he was little in funny voices. He would tell us jokes every day. He would hold companionships between classes. We would have days off where we would do nothing in his class. We would watch videos about space or play games on our Chromebooks. When we had a problem with another teacher, he said that we could talk to him about it, and he would take care of the situation. He was the best teacher overall, and the best person in the world."

—*A seventh-grade student*

"Patience and being a great listener. Also, not making students feel stupid for asking questions. They need to be approachable and encouraging."

—*A twelfth-grade student*

CHAPTER 3
Communicate Expectations and Establish and Reinforce Boundaries

You understand how brain development impacts behavior and the *why* of students' behaviors. Given we don't control our students' genetics, their home life, or even the influence peers have over them, we must focus on what we can control. Influencing students through the classroom environment is one way to address behavior, but also consider that a significant source of student stress is having a lack of understanding of expectations, a lack of structure, and a lack of consistency. As teachers, these are things we can control! We can support our students by making sure they understand our expectations. We can create structure by having a plan in place that can help us be consistent.

Effective classroom management is the most important thing to grasp as an educator, but it is also the most difficult thing to do (Sprick, Sprick, Edwards, & Coughlin, 2021). When classroom-management practices are implemented correctly and consistently, we increase the likelihood of our students' academic success and improved behavior outcomes (Myers, Freeman, Simonsen, & Sugai, 2017).

Having a plan is one thing; putting that plan into action is the hard part (Sprick et al., 2021). What we talk about in this chapter may seem simple on paper, but when you are in a room with twenty to thirty students who are all different from one another, the plan starts to become more difficult to sustain, and we can become increasingly reactionary and punitive as lessons and interactions inevitably don't go quite the way we envisioned them. Here, you'll learn how to proactively implement and teach students to adhere to rules and procedures supported through preventative and positive reinforcements and consequences in your classroom. Accomplishing this means gearing your words and actions toward the level of students you are working with. For example, you will teach rules and procedures to any grade. However, how you explain the information to a kindergartener will be different than how you explain the information to students in a secondary classroom.

Figure 3.1 represents one of my favorite pictures of what an effective classroom looks like. Recall our initial discussion of RTI, MTSS, and PBIS in the section How to Support Students With an Effective Management Plan (chapter 1, page 29). I have seen all these systems used in support of behavior and academics with each of them structured around well-defined tiers characterizing levels of support, as illustrated in figure 3.1. When you are effectively implementing a positive classroom-management plan, you are capturing the needs of most of your students in a similar way. This is what being preventative and proactive looks like.

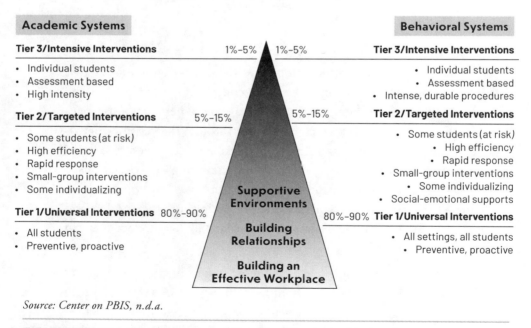

Source: Center on PBIS, n.d.a.

FIGURE 3.1: Tiered intervention across academic and behavioral systems.

Notice how building positive relationships in a supportive environment (see chapter 2, page 35) is part of Tier 1. Wonderful and engaging lessons are also a part of Tier 1 and must be accessible to all students. However, just as with academics, not all students will be successful. When students are struggling academically, we provide additional resources where they are pulled for small-group lessons on top of getting the engaging lessons. These are the students who move to Tier 2.

When thinking about behavior, students who struggle are often punished. Our classroom expectations and boundaries need to come in a form that is teachable with these students in much the same ways as are students who are struggling academically. Notice that we only have up to 15 percent of students who fall under the Tier 2 category. By effectively managing your class, you will only have a few students who need this additional support!

Some students are still not successful with Tier 2 support and need even more support. These students move to Tier 3 reflecting a need for more intensive one-to-one support. At the school level, Tier 3 can look a lot different from building to building, and it typically involves dedicated specialists or even special education referrals. Ultimately, you should find that only up to 5 percent of students need access to this tier *after* you have an effective classroom-management plan in place. But it still all starts with that first tier and the baseline structures all students need to get from you.

Through the rest of this chapter, you'll access strategies that communicate clear expectations and boundaries for your students that specifically address how you can maintain rules, use procedures, and support students through positive feedback. We will learn more about strategies to support students who move to Tier 2 and Tier 3 in the next chapter!

Strategies for Communicating Expectations and Establishing and Reinforcing Boundaries

Clear expectations and established boundaries in the classroom are both preventative and proactive and are the basis of Tier 1 interventions. By having a plan in place, you are preventing problems before they even happen. The essence of an effective classroom-management plan is having clear expectations through rules and procedures. To be most effective, those rules and procedures must be reinforced with positive reinforcement and consequences. When expectations are communicated to students, you are better able to reach most of your students and only have a few who need additional support. We will talk about students who need extra support in the next chapter. Our classroom-management plan is for all our students, but the reality is some students don't need it. They will do what is asked of them or do the correct thing without even being told. Our plan isn't for those students. Our plan is to support the diversity of students in our classroom. We need to support *all* our students.

When you tell students what your expectations are, you set them up for success, and you are being proactive rather than reactive. The more detailed and specific your expectations and boundaries are, the easier it is to put them into practice. Once you have them in place, you need to consistently apply them (Sprick et al., 2021). Consistency is key to all aspects of effective classroom management regardless of student age, knowledge, learning needs, style, or anything else.

It doesn't matter how amazing our lessons or activities with our students are; if we aren't implementing expectations with consistency, they will not be effective. Our students pick up on inconsistency, which can take away from the positive connections you've made with your students. We have worked hard to create positive connections with our students, and inconsistency and lack of structure can bring on stress for some of our students. If you remember from chapter 1 (page 7), lack of structure and inconsistency can cause students stress. When students feel stressed, they may begin to feel like they do not belong. Students are also much more likely to act out if your expectations aren't consistent or if your boundaries keep changing. For example, there may be a time when a student is allowed to eat in the classroom, but the same student may get in trouble when trying to eat in the classroom another time. There can also be times when a teacher acknowledges a student who hasn't raised their hand to answer a question, but there will be other times when the student gets in trouble for talking out. When a teacher is consistent, students are told if they can or cannot eat in the classroom, and when a student gets a snack out in a classroom where this is not permitted, they are told to put it away. If there is an expectation of students raising their hand to answer a question, then as a teacher, we can only call on students who raise their hand. The consistency of expectations will ensure students are following our expectations. There will not be feelings of favoritism for a student who gets away with something while another does not.

Remember, our students need consistency and structure to feel less stressed in our classrooms. An ineffective and inconsistent plan is stressful for us as teachers as much as it is stressful for the students. It causes reactive management rather than proactive management (refer to Strategies for Implementing a Positive Classroom Environment in chapter 2, page 38). We can't get to the learning, which means our students' academic achievement isn't where it could be, and we become burned out.

Strategies for communicating expectations and establishing boundaries include (1) maintaining rules (supports clear expectations), (2) using procedures (supports clear expectations), (3) using positive reinforcement (supports boundaries), and (4) maintaining consequences (supports boundaries). In what follows, we walk through each strategy area for communicating expectations and establishing boundaries, examining each at both elementary and secondary grade levels, starting on the first day or in the middle of the school year, and with the aim to diversify the strategy to work for all students.

MAINTAINING RULES TO SUPPORT CLEAR EXPECTATIONS

Rules are important to have in the classroom because they tell us what we can and cannot do. They are the important standards of conduct in our classroom. Rules are based on how we want the students to act, no matter what they are doing or where they are at. Establishing and teaching rules is a foundational practice for classroom management, and evidence is strong in showing the effectiveness of having rules (Myers et al., 2017). When thinking about rules to have in your classroom, there are a few things to remember (Wong & Wong, 2018). First, rules should be few, meaning you should have between three and five rules in your classroom. Another important thing to remember is you want the rules to be positively stated. Rules that have the word *no* in them are like dares to some students. If I say, "No running in the hall," some students hear, "Run in the hall!" It is more effective to tell students what you want rather than what you don't want. For example, you might say, "I need you to walk in the hall." You also want to be specific with your rules and avoid complicated jargon. Keep every rule in student-friendly language. You should ask yourself, "Will the students have a general idea of what my rule is without me having to explain it?" Let's break it down a little more by thinking of rules in terms of primary versus secondary grades.

Maintaining Rules in Primary and Secondary Grades

No matter the age of students, there should be basic rules set in place, and students should be told exactly what the rules are. Sharing rules with your students can happen in one of two ways: (1) You can have the rules already in mind and posted. The rules are reviewed with the students. (2) You have an idea of what the rules are but create specific elements as a class. Generally speaking, no matter how old students are, they can state basic rules. For example, a kindergartener will tell you they should not hit or kick their friends. A middle school or high school student will tell you they can't get into a fight or they can't use profanity.

When your students say things like, "No hitting" or "No fighting," flip it and turn it into a positive. "You're right! We don't want to hit others. We will create a rule where we need to keep our hands and feet to ourselves," or "You're right! We don't want to fight or use profanity. We will create a rule where we respect ourselves and others by keeping our body to ourselves." In this way, we provide students with examples of what things like following directions, being respectful, and listening to others look like.

Here are some examples of must-have rules—no matter the grade level.

- Respect yourself and others.
- Keep your hands, feet, and other objects to yourself.
- Follow directions.

Examples of adaptable rules are provided as follows—these could change depending on the grade level.

- **Technology use:** Some schools have computers for students to use, and other schools do not. Elementary grades may have access to some while secondary grades may have a Chromebook or similar device students can use for the school year. Using cell phones will vary depending on the grade, school, or classroom.
- **Homework and late work policies:** This also depends on the grade level, teacher, and school. Not every teacher will give homework, particularly at the elementary level. Some teachers will provide homework but have no policy for getting it submitted or submitted on time. Some teachers take points off for late work while others do not. It is a preference, but no matter what your preference is, you need to be consistent in following it.

We are trying to set our students up for success, and we need to do that by being as specific as possible as to what our standards are and what will happen if the standards are not met.

How you word your rules (still stated positively) will depend on where you are teaching and what grade you are teaching. It is important to remember that students need to understand what we are expecting of them. We cannot assume they know what respect looks like to us or what following directions looks like to us.

The rules should be posted on the wall in your classroom. The rules can be on a poster already, or they can be written down on chart paper or a poster as you create them with your class. The rules become a part of your class behavior contract that is signed by you and the students. The contract can even be sent home for parents to sign. It is important to know everyone is on the same page. Examples and non-examples should be shared with the students when discussing the rules.

Starting at the Beginning of the Year Versus Midyear

Rules should be gone over on the first day of school and reinforced throughout the school year. If you have already started the year and you realize you need to make adjustments to your rules, that is perfectly OK. No one says that just because you started something in one way means you have to finish it in that way. It is perfectly acceptable to push the reset button. When you push the reset button, you are modeling to your students how to handle situations where adjustments need to be made, thus creating a teachable moment! When we realize something isn't working the way we intended it to, we need to make adjustments. Ask students for their suggestions and talk to them about your intentions. Doing so can enhance the classroom environment by providing ownership and modeling what to do when something needs to be fixed. You are also promoting a growth mindset by modeling for students it is OK to make improvements when a challenge arises.

In a primary grade, I always like to read a book on rules to introduce the topic of conversation, but a song or a video can be played as well. Whatever you choose, make sure it is fun and engaging to capture your students from the very beginning. Secondary students probably don't need you to read them a book or play a video or song. However, I will say you know the students at your school best, and maybe it is something they would enjoy. That said, be authentic about how you present your rules. It is important to not force a "creative" presentation that isn't natural for you.

Following are some examples of rules you might adopt for your elementary-level class. From this list, and maybe others I have not included, you will find the rules you believe are non-negotiable. What one person thinks is non-negotiable another won't. It's OK to have differences. It is how you implement and follow through with your rules that makes the difference.

1. Be respectful of others.
    a. We will listen to others while they are talking.
    b. We will keep our hands and feet to ourselves.
    c. We will show kindness to others by helping them out when they need it!
2. Follow directions.
    a. We will listen to our teachers.
    b. We will do what our teachers tell us to do.
3. Keep your hands and feet to yourself.
    a. We will stay in our own personal space and respect other students' personal space.
    b. We will not kick, hit, punch, or throw things at others.

4. We will use listening ears.
    a. We will listen to our classmates and teachers when they are talking.
    b. We will be at a level zero when others are talking.
    c. When our teachers ask us to do something, we will do it.
5. We will treat others the way we want to be treated.
    a. We will listen when others are talking.
    b. We will keep our hands and feet to ourselves.
    c. We will be kind to one another.
6. We will try our best!
    a. We will work hard on our assignments.
    b. We will ask questions when we have them.
    c. We will listen to our teachers when they are teaching.
    d. We will participate in class discussions.

If you are cocreating rules with your students, you will write what they are telling you, but make sure to take any negative rules and turn them into positive rules (meaning they state what students should be doing rather than what they should not be doing).

Following are some examples tailored more to the secondary grades. As you can see, many of these are similar to each other; they are just phrased in slightly different ways. Rules in elementary school will be similar to rules at the secondary level. The biggest difference is the word choice.

1. Follow directions.
    a. I will do what my teachers ask me to do.
2. Keep your body to yourself.
    a. I need to stay in my personal space.
    b. I will keep my hands and feet to myself.
3. Show respect.
    a. I will listen to my classmates and teachers.
    b. I will do what my teachers ask me to do.
    c. I will be kind to myself, my teachers, and my classmates.
4. Do your best!
    a. I will participate in class and actively engage in learning.
    b. I will complete class assignments and homework.
    c. I will be prepared for class.
    d. I will ask for help.
5. Listen.

a. I will listen when the teacher is talking.

   b. I will listen when classmates are talking.

   c. I will listen when announcements are being made.

6. Treat others the way you want to be treated.

   a. I will respect others.

   b. I will listen to others.

   c. I will respect others even if their opinions are different than mine.

   d. I will keep my body to myself.

Again, these rules are examples. As the teacher, you know what wording works and what rules are most important to you and the environment you are in. You may be thinking, "Where are the cell phone rules or the bathroom rules?" They are important things to consider; however, they are not rules but procedures! Rules are standards of conduct and apply to any setting, whether in your classroom, the lunchroom, or another teacher's classroom. Procedures, on the other hand, are expectations that change depending on the activity being done, and we'll address these later in this chapter.

Diversifying for All Learners

Rules are a necessity, but we have to think about all the learners we have in our classroom when creating and communicating rules. For example, are multiple languages spoken in the classroom, and is there a language barrier between the teacher and one or more students? If so, it will be important to ensure the students truly understand your expectations. One way to do that is to have the rules translated into the student's primary language. You also need to constantly ask yourself, "Is the student breaking the rule to break the rule, or are they breaking the rule because they truly don't understand?" However, honestly, that question applies to any student! We also need to ensure we are meeting the needs of our students who are served under special education. For example, one characteristic of students with ADHD is having a hard time focusing. Listening or following multistep directions may be difficult. We must keep this in mind. Rather than being punitive, we need to come from a mindset of "How can I help?" Maybe we need to provide a student with a checklist that is easier to follow. The student may need for us to provide frequent reminders or even frequent breaks. Each student will be different. Remember brain development. Our students' brains are different than ours. We need to ask them what they need and how they learn best. Some students will know, but others will need you to help them problem solve and figure it out, but the point is, you figure it out together. We must really look at our students and come from a place of helpfulness even when considering our classroom rules. Rather than assuming negative intent, let's come from a place of truly evaluating to determine the *why* when a student breaks a rule.

USING PROCEDURES TO SUPPORT CLEAR EXPECTATIONS

I often hear teachers say, "Well, students should just know how to act." Oh, if it could just be that simple! Most of our students do know how to act, but maybe they don't know how to act based on our expectations. The expectations in your room may be different than another teacher's expectations. Home is going to look very different than school, and expectations are not even close to being the same. One grade level or one teacher will have different expectations than another, and that is completely OK!

It isn't OK when we don't explain what our expectations actually are. As I stated in the previous section, procedures are the specific expectations we have during the day. While we should only have three to five rules, there should be a procedure for everything. Students should know what you expect of them from the moment they enter the room until the moment they leave the room (Wong & Wong, 2018). We need to teach our behavioral expectations much like we teach academic subjects. We cannot make assumptions about what students will know or not know, no matter their age. Teaching procedures in an explicit way with opportunities to practice is another foundational component for establishing effective classroom management. Students need specific and thorough feedback on what they are doing correctly and on what they need more support for or practice on.

Using Procedures in Primary and Secondary Grades

Whether you are teaching primary grades or secondary grades, you will teach your procedures in the same way. According to Harry K. Wong and Rosemary T. Wong (2018), there are three basic steps to the process. We'll address how you differentiate them for school level next.

1. **Tell students what the procedure is and then model it:** This helps students who connect auditorily and also helps students who connect visually.
2. **Rehearse the procedure:** Have the students practice the procedure before actually doing the procedure.
3. **Reinforce the procedure:** Make sure you are telling the students they are doing the procedure correctly. You are focusing on the positive.

Where things differ in primary grades versus secondary grades will be the extent to which you need to teach the procedure. With that being said, just because a student is older doesn't mean they are just going to "get it." You will hear me say this a lot: Brain development is a real thing. What seems obvious to us as adults isn't always obvious to even our high school seniors. Make adjustments to your procedures as needed. In younger grades (primary, particularly kindergarten and first), you will have to be very detailed with your expectations and provide a lot of opportunities for modeling and practicing. As students get older, especially as they move into the secondary grades, they need to know what your expectations are, but they will not need as much ongoing guidance. When you explicitly teach your procedural expectation, students are set up for success, you decrease the likelihood of behavior errors, and you spend less time in the long run reminding students of what you want them to do (Myers et al., 2017).

When thinking about your procedures, let's think about what you will need to include.

- **Attention getter:** This prevents yelling. Have your attention getter and teach your students to stop what they are doing, look at you, and wait for further instructions.
    + I say, "Class, class," and students say, "Yes, yes."
    + I say, "Waterfall, waterfall," and students say, "Sshhhh, sshhh."
    + Count down from five.
    + Show five fingers and wait for students to stop talking.
- **Restroom procedures:** This is something I have a hard time not allowing a student to do. What are your expectations for when students can use the restroom? This should not be used as a punishment.
- **Arrival procedure (primary):** This ensures students come into the classroom and get settled doing their morning tasks.
    + Walk into the classroom.
    + Put your backpack and supplies away.
    + Sit down at your table and begin morning work—morning work can be either on the board or already on the tables.
    + If you finish your morning work early, you may get a book to read.
    + Some teachers have fidget bins that they like to let their students use. Offer students the chance to choose a fidget for the day or a portion of the day. The point here is students should always have something to do because they will find something to do if we don't help them with this process.
- **Arrival procedure (secondary):** This ensures students are on task as soon as they walk into the classroom.
    + Walk into the classroom.

- + Sit down and get your things out for the class based on what is written on the board.
- + Begin the assigned activity written on the board.
- **Dismissal procedure (primary):** Organization when students are leaving is important. You want to ensure students clean up, have their things, and go to the correct place at the correct time.
  - + Put your supplies away.
  - + Clean up your area.
  - + Wait for your group to be called.
  - + Walk to get in line when your group is called.
  - + Have a great night!
- **Dismissal procedure (secondary):** Students need to understand what is expected of them when the bell rings.
  - + The bell does not dismiss you; I do.
  - + Clean up your area.
  - + Quietly walk out of the classroom.
- **Participating in class discussions:** Are students allowed to answer questions without raising their hand, or do you want them to raise their hand to participate? How exactly do you want classroom discussions to go?
  - + I will call on students who raise their hand.
  - + Now you can only call on students who raise their hand!
- **Cell phone (primary):** Students (and parents) need to understand cell phone expectations. Often schools have a policy.
  - + Typically, cell phones are not allowed. If they are, cell phones stay in students' backpacks, turned off, at all times. If you see a student's phone, it becomes yours until the end of the day.
- **Cell phone (secondary):** Cell phones are a hot button issue. It is important to have a specific procedure and ensure you follow it. Often schools have a policy—be sure you are following it.
  - + There are a lot of differing opinions on this one. If you do not want cell phones with your students, the easiest thing to do is to have a shoe holder on the back of your door. Students turn their cell phones in at the beginning of class and get them at the end of class.
- **Completing seat work:** The questions presented as follows are questions you need to plan for whether you are teaching a primary grade or a secondary grade.

COMMUNICATE EXPECTATIONS AND ESTABLISH AND REINFORCE BOUNDARIES

+ Consider how students need to complete their work. Is there a specific order? Are students expected to sit at their own desk, or can they sit anywhere? Can students work together, or does it need to be done independently? When students are done, where is the work submitted? Do students submit online, or is there a spot in the room for them to put their work? What happens when they finish their work early?

- **Asking for help:** Students need to know what your expectations are when they have a question.
    + Are students expected to raise their hand?
    + What do you want students to do when you are working with other students? Should they wait, or should they ask a classmate? If a classmate doesn't know the answer, what should the student do?
- **Sharpening a pencil:** Students need to understand what to do if they need to sharpen a pencil or if they don't have one.
    + Will you have a spot in your room with sharpened pencils students can use?
    + Is there a specific time students are able to sharpen their pencil if there aren't pencils readily available?
- **What to do when work is finished:** Students tend to find things to do (not always what we'd like) when there is downtime. It is important to have expectations for when work is completed early.

Let's look at a few of these procedures in more detail.

First, let's think about restroom procedures. In primary grades, there are usually multiple opportunities for group restroom breaks. Sometimes, there are even restrooms in a classroom. However, you may still have a student who needs to use the restroom at other times. When is it best for you to let them go? I would avoid allowing a student to use the restroom during whole-group instruction, but sometimes an emergency happens, and it can't be avoided. How do you want your students to ask? Is there a restroom pass? Will you have a finger sign they can show to let you know they have to go?

For students in secondary classes, the expectation is for students to go during their passing period. However, sometimes there isn't enough time for a student to get from one class to another and use the restroom. Sometimes, students are afraid to use the restroom during passing periods because of what is happening in the restroom during those times. In a secondary classroom, I think a hall pass is appropriate or a sign-out sheet with the expectation to not go (unless it is an emergency) when whole-group instruction is occurring. We don't want to assume negative intent. We need to allow our students to use the restroom as necessary until we believe it does become a problem. At that point, the student loses the opportunity to go independently. A restroom procedure may include students asking permission (however works for you), quietly and quickly going to the restroom, taking care of their business, washing their hands, quietly walking back to class, and getting back to work.

For pencil sharpening, my favorite is having a cup with sharpened pencils and nonsharpened pencils. Rather than sharpening a pencil during class, it's easy to grab one from the cup. A great job for an early-arriving student is to sharpen pencils. Even in a secondary classroom, there will be a student who would like to sharpen pencils for you.

For supplies, I like to have a spot with extra supplies. In a primary grade, there are generally supplies readily available. Will you have your students have their own supply box, or will you have a communal space on each table or in a special spot in your classroom? In secondary classrooms, supplies are generally supplied by individual students.

When it comes to missing supplies, I am an advocate of having supplies in my classroom for students to use. There could be a financial reason why a student does not have supplies. Students can easily forget or lose things from one moment to the next. You can have a procedure in your classroom where they have to give you something in order to get something (such as a shoe or a backpack).

Other procedures may include expectations for completing seatwork, passing in or out papers and other materials, asking for help, completing work when absent, or what to do when work is finished early. What you want your students to do will depend on the classroom and you as the teacher. The most important thing to remember is the fact students need to explicitly be taught what your expectations are. I think about it like steps to cooking. Write your procedures down and have someone look at them to ensure they make sense. What makes sense in our head may not necessarily make sense to others.

Starting at the Beginning of the Year Versus Midyear

Typically, procedures are taught during the first few weeks of the school year. You will teach the procedures you have in your classroom as they come up. With that being said, it's never too late to start or to even make adjustments to what you are already doing. Also, you may realize one or more of your procedures are not working like you thought they would. It's OK to adjust what you are doing. Sometimes, what works in our mind doesn't actually work when we put it into practice. Additionally, you may find that something works great for one group of your students but doesn't for another group. Be flexible and make changes as necessary.

The academic teaching process of teach, rehearse, and reinforce will also be the process for all your procedures. If things aren't working, you can ask yourself, "Am I being consistent? Have I really taught the procedure thoroughly? Am I pointing out the students who are doing the procedure correctly?"

Whether you are starting on day one or in the middle of the year, there will be times you have to go back to reteaching or reinforcing. It is OK to stop, take a step back, and begin again. Having the reset will help everyone in the long run. Spending time focusing on how you want your classroom to run will help you as the year continues. The idea behind your procedures is that they will become a routine to your students, and you become the facilitator while they are busy doing what you expect from them.

Diversifying for All Learners

The more specific you are with your procedures, the better off all your students are. When students know what you expect of them, their behaviors are automatically improved. Most students will pick up on your expectations quickly, especially when you are implementing them correctly and consistently. However, we do need to consider all types of learners. When you have a student who is neurodivergent, has a disability, or has any form of unique need or perspective, ask them what they need to be successful.

You may need to make a few changes to procedures for individual students based on their needs. You want to come from a place of positive intentions rather than assuming the worst. We need to find out if our students truly understand our expectations. If they don't, then we adjust. When we have built positive relationships with our students, it is much easier for them to feel comfortable sharing and for us to see when we need to make a change. The power we give to our students when we ask them how we can help or what they feel they need to be successful is wonderful. They are much more likely to do what we expect because we ask in this way rather than assuming they don't care and just want to do the wrong thing.

PROVIDING POSITIVE REINFORCEMENT TO SUPPORT CLEAR EXPECTATIONS

There are differing beliefs on the idea of positive reinforcement. Some believe students don't need extrinsic motivation to do what they are supposed to do (Wong & Wong, 2018). Many teachers have this belief, too, particularly teachers in secondary grades. However, research shows that, when implemented correctly, extrinsic motivation for good behavior increases academic achievement and school climate for all grade levels (Bear, Yang, Mantz, & Harris, 2017).

Conversely, punitive consequences are associated with negative school climate. We'll get to those in the next section. Here, consider how we tend to spend more time interacting with students when they are doing something wrong than we do when they are doing something right. You will notice that you will see more of whatever it is you are pointing out. If you are pointing out more negative things, you will see more negative things. If you point out the positive things your students are doing, you will see more of the positives.

When delivering positive reinforcement, we have to be consistent just like when we are working through other parts of our classroom-management plan. In order for positive reinforcement to work effectively, you have to be authentic and specific with your praise. The reinforcement needs to mean something to the students. If there is no meaning behind what you are doing, it will quickly stop working.

Providing Positive Reinforcement in Primary and Secondary Grades

In all classrooms, there are multiple ways to build in positive reinforcement. The first thing is to tell your students when they are doing something good and be specific with it. For example, think of the following.

- "Thank you for sitting in your chair like I asked you to."
- "Thank you for lining up so quietly."
- "Wow, you did an amazing job completing your assignment. I hope you feel proud of yourself!"
- "Thank you for working so hard on that assignment."

In these examples, you are not just saying, "Good job!" Good job for what? A "good job" is positive reinforcement of a sort, but without specificity, it lacks meaning. The student may not even know what you are referring to when you say, "Good job."

It may seem easier to provide specific positive praise to students in primary grades, but secondary students like to hear positive praise, too. Even adults like to be told when they are doing something well. It makes us feel good about ourselves when someone notices something about what we are doing and says something about it. Remember from previous chapters that the brain operates better off of rewards than punishment and that students are more likely to do what we are asking of them when they feel a sense of belonging, and when you verbally reinforce the behaviors you want to see, you support them in feeling a sense of belonging.

In primary grades, consider having students earn tickets (in paper form) or some type of electronic ticket they can exchange for some type of prize. There are different ways of doing this. Some teachers have a menu where items are worth different amounts. Other teachers have a treasure box. The menu allows students to work for things. A treasure box may be a little simpler. Once students earn a certain number of tickets or points, they can earn an item from the treasure box.

In secondary classrooms, tickets and an app can also work, but you'll likely need to be more creative with your rewards (as we'll explore next). It can feel overwhelming when working with multiple classes, so my suggestion is to keep it simple.

Whether you do a menu of items or a treasure box, it is important to include items your students like. Teachers do not make a lot of money to spend on rewards, but rewards don't have to cost a lot of money or any money at all. Table 3.1 provides a list of ideas that do and do not cost money. Your students may have different ideas. What is current one year may not be current the next year. The most important thing you can do is ask your students what they like.

TABLE 3.1: Ideas for Student Rewards

Primary Grades	Secondary Grades
Line leader	Pencils or pens
Stickers	Homework pass
Hat day	Bonus points on a test or homework assignment
Special seat for the day	Leave class early
Pencil	Free answer for a test question
Lunch with a friend or teacher	VIP for the day
Game time or electronic device time	Teacher for the day
Opportunity to read to another class	Drink or snack pass
Open seating in class	Open seating in class

I like the idea of using tickets and menus because it fits students who need a prize immediately (use fewer tickets for a reward) and those who don't (save tickets for a "bigger" reward). For example, you might set up a menu where a bouncy ball or sticker costs five tickets, but time in a special chair costs twenty.

You might also choose to do a class reward rather than individual rewards. Class rewards can be based on a collective number of tickets or points that students pool together, or perhaps you add marbles to a jar when you point out positive behaviors that, when the jar is full, unlock a whole-class reward, like a pajama day, movie with the teacher, or taking the class outside on a beautiful day.

These are, of course, all just examples. It is important to ask your students what they want as this gives them more investment in reaching goals.

Starting at the Beginning of the Year Versus Midyear

When beginning on the first day of school, share your rewards plan while going over your overall classroom-management plan. During this time, you can also ask your students to help you create the menu of items they would like to earn. This gets them excited about earning different things. This plan is also something you can send home to parents as part of the contract everyone signs. Everyone has ownership of it, which creates a sense of belonging and promotes a positive classroom climate.

If you are starting your plan in the middle of the year, that is OK! It will be something fun to introduce to your students to shake up day-to-day routines. They will be excited about the possibility of earning different rewards.

Whether you are starting at the beginning of the year or the middle of the year, continue to check in with your students to see if there are other things they would like to earn. Some may say this is just bribery, and students should do what we want them to do because that is the expectation. I choose to see it as helping motivate our students. We are creating a space for them to feel excited about the good things they are doing.

Diversifying for All Learners

As recommended in the previous section, we continually need to check in with our students to see what they like and do not like. We need to find out from our students what they are capable of and where their struggles come from. When we have students who struggle, we need to be extra focused on what need those struggles are intended to communicate and how to better support that need, providing positive reinforcement for every success that follows. When students feel successful, they will be increasingly willing to try. Meet your students where they are and adapt as necessary. It is the only way your students will truly be successful.

ENSURING CONSEQUENCES TO SUPPORT CLEAR EXPECTATIONS

As much as we want to focus on reinforcing the positive, that doesn't mean we can ignore when students don't follow our classroom rules and procedures. Consequences are important, and students need to know that with every cause, there is an effect.

This said, there are important things to consider to effectively deliver consequences. As teachers, we are often quick to make assumptions, and our assumptions are not always right. We are one person surrounded by a classroom of students. Rather than making an assumption about a situation or about what a student has done or not done, we need to investigate by asking questions that create clarity. When we ask a student, "Can you tell me what happened?" they are much more likely to give us an answer because we are asking and not assuming. Assumptions, whether right or wrong, often put students on the defensive, which is a mindset you want to avoid. When asking for clarification, our tone must be even, not condescending or rude. Tone is everything. Think about how you might ask a student about their day. As teachers, we want our students to talk to us in a respectful tone, and students will know they belong in your classroom when you return that same level of respect.

The first question you need to ask yourself when delivering consequences is, "Does this consequence decrease the problem behavior of the specific student?" If the answer to the question is no, then it isn't an effective consequence. How your students react to a consequence will not be the same for every student. For some, a consequence might seem like a punishment to you but serve as a source of unintended reinforcement to the student. For example, you have a student in your classroom who continually talks out even when you have asked the student to stop. You send the student to the hallway. The student enjoys being in the hallway because that is where the action is! The student continues to disrupt the class in order to go to the hallway where they enjoy being. Your goal is for your consequences to do what you are wanting. Positive behavior should be reinforced so it will increase. Negative behavior should be punished so the undesired behavior decreases (IRIS Center, 2025).

It can be confusing thinking of positive reinforcements or punishments as giving something because we often think positive ends with a type of good result. However, it only means something is being added. For example, with *positive reinforcement*, when a student does something correct, the student gets extra recess (primary) or gets ten extra points on an assignment (secondary). The student will continue to make the correct choice because they receive something positive for it.

Positive punishment involves adding something to decrease a behavior. For example, a student quickly completes an assignment to be finished early but does the assignment wrong. The teacher gives the student another assignment to complete and returns the original assignment to be done again. The student doesn't want to do extra work, so the student finishes the work correctly. The teacher has decreased the student's behavior of turning work in quickly and incorrectly by adding additional work.

Let's contrast this with negative reinforcement and negative punishment. Just like we often see positive events as ending with something good, we think of negative events as ending with something bad. *Negative reinforcement* means something is being taken away in order to increase a behavior. For example, a student completes an assignment correctly and on time. The student doesn't have to complete a homework assignment. I have taken away (negative) an assignment to increase (reinforcement) a behavior. Leaving a class early or taking away assigned seating are examples of negative reinforcement. Sometimes, we can accidently increase a behavior we are trying to eliminate. For example, a student is disruptive in class by continually getting out of their seat rather than completing the assignment given. We remove the student from the class (negative), but the student gets out of completing the work they didn't want to complete in the first place, so the student continues to be disruptive in the future in order to avoid the work. In this instance, we have negatively reinforced the behavior.

Negative punishment, on the other hand, takes something away (negative) to decrease a behavior (IRIS Center, 2025). For example, a student has their cell phone out. After providing a warning, you take the cell phone from the student until the end of the class (negative). The student does not want to lose their cell phone again, so they stop getting it out when they shouldn't. Because the behavior decreases, it is considered a punishment. Taking away materials not being used correctly and moving a student from their location in the classroom are examples of negative punishment.

I will say I am not a fan of the word *punishment* because it has a negative and harsh connotation. Rather, there are consequences for all the choices we make. When we make good choices, there are good consequences, but when we make bad choices, there are bad consequences. I know it's all word semantics, but I do believe it is important to put the choice on our students. If we had our choice, they would always do what we asked of them. However, they have a choice, so they choose what happens. I am not doing anything to them; they are making the choice for themselves. This allows students to have ownership over the decisions they make.

The details in this section may be a little bit confusing, but I want to share them with you because it is important to really understand how the consequences students are getting impact them. To be considered a punishment, or what we as teachers view as a consequence, it has to decrease the behavior. If the behaviors are not decreasing, the consequence is not effective. Also, if we are intending to decrease a behavior, but the behavior is increasing, we need to evaluate to see if what we are doing is contributing to our students' behaviors.

There are also small things we can do before we have to get to an actual consequence. One powerful and easy thing to do is to employ the power of proximity.

As we are teaching, we can simply move closer to students who may not be on task. Most often, the behavior stops. Nothing else needs to be said, and instruction need not stop. Now, if you have to return to those same students, you may whisper to them about staying on task, or you may just tap them on the shoulder. Simple and easy.

When having a discussion with a student about their behavior, we need to use a soft but firm voice. We need to make direct eye contact with the student when talking with them. When we do this, we show that respect needs to go both ways. This does not mean we should expect students to look us back in the eyes, however. The student is going to be upset, defensive, or embarrassed about what they have done. Students often show this by looking away or looking down, and that is OK. It could also be cultural response where it is seen as disrespectful to look at an adult in the eye.

We also need to show our students empathy. Remember, consequences are not up to us; they are up to our students. We can be sorry for the choice they made. For example, "I am so sorry you made that choice. What are we going to do to fix it?" Responding to a student with empathy goes a very long way (Fay & Fay, 2016). Often, our students are used to being yelled at for messing up. Because they are used to being yelled at, they tune us out when we are yelling. However, when we respond with true empathy about the decision they made, the problem remains theirs, and we are likely to find them more willing to talk with us and work to solve the problem. Responding with empathy doesn't always come naturally, but you will be positively reinforced to show empathy when you get the response you are looking for from your student.

Ensuring Consequences in Primary and Secondary Grades

No matter if you are in a primary or secondary classroom, the way consequences are delivered will be the same. All students, no matter their age, deserve the level of respect we are seeking from them. When we are at our most frustrated with the choices our students are making, think back to brain development. Whether the students are in primary or secondary grades, their brains are developing. They are learning what it looks like to be in school and what it looks like to follow the expectations of all the different adults they encounter.

For the secondary grades, it is important to remember that although they may be older, they are still learning. Their brain development is ongoing, and they are constantly navigating school demands (teacher expectations, academics, friends). Your students will be forgetful. They will take longer to process what you say. They will mess up. Sometimes I think we are harder on our students than we are on ourselves. Giving grace and supporting students by providing logical consequences helps students learn and grow. As teachers, isn't that what we are in the business of doing—helping our students learn and grow into great humans and ultimately productive adults?

To support you in these efforts, ask yourself the following questions: "Is the behavior something I can ignore, or does it need to be addressed? Can I make a small investment to redirect the behavior, like providing the power of proximity or simply making eye contact?" Maybe a student is talking to their neighbor. You can still walk over to them and stand there while you continue teaching. Maybe you are working with another student and can't use power of proximity. You can simply say the student's name with eye contact and a patient expression that also conveys your desire for them to get back on track. Sometimes just simple acknowledgments are all that is needed. You can always have a chat with the student during a free moment.

The following is a sequence of steps I find effective.

1. **Ask the student what they should be doing:** Asking the student allows you to find out if they actually know what they are supposed to be doing. It also allows them to process what they should be doing because they have had to tell you. It can make a connection for some students (remember brain development).

2. **Provide a verbal warning:** Providing a verbal warning is proactive because you are letting the student know what is going to happen if they continue. You are setting the student up for success while also providing some grace.

3. **Deliver the consequence:** The consequence has to be natural and logical in order to be effective. We are trying to decrease the undesired behavior while increasing the desired behavior.

4. **Remind the student that mistakes happen:** Remember, we are in the business of teaching. We need to support our students and let them know that just because they made a mistake doesn't mean they can't make it right.

5. **Talk to the student about how to fix it:** When talking with the student about what happened, problem solve together. For example, try asking the student, "What can we do better next time? How can I help you learn best? When I accidently hurt my friend's feelings, I apologize. What do you think you should do? If this happened to you, what would you like a friend to say to you?" They may have an idea, and they may not. You can guide them through the thought process. As teachers, we want to be fixers, and we sometimes get into the habit of telling.

When we tell, our words can sometimes go through one ear and out the other. However, when we ask questions and guide students to solve their problems, we are giving them the independence to learn how to solve problems when we aren't around. We are teaching.

Let's look at some basic behaviors often seen in a classroom.

First-grade student Sean is touching Colton while sitting on the carpet.

1. Ask the student what he should be doing.

    Sean, what should you be doing right now?

    + Hopefully Sean will tell you he needs to keep his hands to himself. If he doesn't, then you can remind him to keep his hands to himself.

2. Hopefully Sean stops, but if he doesn't, your next step is to provide the verbal reminder.

    Sean, if you don't stop touching Colton, you are going to have to move [next to me, to a different spot on the carpet, or to another location].

    + Once natural consequences become a regular part of your classroom plan, you can also ask the student what will happen if they don't stop.

3. Again, hopefully Sean will stop, but if he doesn't, you have to be consistent by providing the consequence you said would happen.

    Sean, I'm really sorry you did not stop touching Colton. Now what happens?

    + Or you can say the following.

    I am going to need you to move to this spot. [You decide what is best for the student.]

4. It is important to allow the student to move back if they show you appropriate behaviors. Students need to know that it isn't the end of the world when they mess up. They can earn the right to move back.

    I understand you are upset, Sean. It's OK to be upset. You will have an opportunity to sit next to Colton again.

5. Now we get to problem solve!

   What do you think you can do to earn back the opportunity to sit next to Colton?

   + Hopefully, he says he will keep his hands to himself, and he will keep his listening ears on and stay on track. You can agree on the amount of time and the expectations you have for the student.

Students in the early grades (K–2) will need to earn back time sooner than a student who is a little bit older (grades 3–5). Each student will be a little different, too. As you get to know them, you will know what works and what doesn't. We need our students to feel successful. It doesn't work if we don't make an expectation attainable, based on their level, not ours. Next, let's look at a secondary example.

Tenth-grade student Zoe is talking to her neighbor during a whole-group lesson.

1. Power of proximity! Continue teaching while you walk over to where Zoe is and stand there. Hopefully the behavior stops. After class you can have a chat with Zoe about expectations during a whole-group lesson.
2. With power of proximity, you may need to tap Zoe on the shoulder or put your hand on her desk. This is another easy signal for Zoe.
3. If the behavior doesn't stop, either you can quietly ask Zoe what she should be doing, or if you feel the power of proximity and the quiet tap was enough, you can let Zoe know if she continues to talk, she will need to move.
4. At this point, she should have stopped, but if she hasn't, have Zoe move to a different location in the classroom.

When bigger problems happen (fighting, bullying, and so on), you will need bigger consequences and may need to contact parents, the counselor, or the administrators. Big things need administration. The hope is that with the procedures you have set in place, you won't need administration because students will be doing what they need to be doing, which is learning and growing.

There are positives and negatives to teaching and delivering consequences to students in primary versus secondary. For example, kindergarteners have little school experience. Not all of them will have gone to preschool or have experience in school, so they truly don't know what school expectations are. In the beginning of the school year, teaching kindergarten is much like trying to herd cats! There needs to be a lot of those teachable, problem-solving lessons. On the other hand, generally speaking, younger students love being in school and are eager to please their teacher. We still need to keep in mind their age and our expectations for their behavior.

As students navigate into the later primary grades, they are still often eager to please, but there will be students who haven't had the best school experiences. They will be the ones who will be the most challenging. Many of these students have built up a wall to not be hurt. Behavior is a form of communication, so some students will act like they don't care. They may look unmotivated and don't want to try.

As our students go through the secondary grades, they have more experiences, both good and bad. You can break the cycle for the bad ones and reinforce the positive. We will talk more in the next chapter about raising your level of intervention when it comes to the challenging behaviors.

Starting at the Beginning of the Year Versus Midyear

It is easy to fall into old ways. We tend to gravitate toward negatives rather than positives. Remember, what you point out is what you will see. Make adjustments to how you are handling student situations as you need to, always focusing on the consistency of your plan. When starting at the beginning of the school year, you introduce your consequences the first day when you talk about your classroom-management plan. You will share your rules and introduce the relevant procedures, your reinforcement plan, and your consequences plan. Sharing your plan for consequences is another way you are ensuring your students know what your expectations will be. They know exactly what to expect when they do things correctly and when they make mistakes. Consistency is key during all parts of a classroom-management plan. Consistency also makes it easier on us as teachers because our students aren't having to guess. They know exactly what will happen. After you have shared your plan with your students, have them sign a contract you create together. The class signs, you sign, and parents sign, too. Everyone is on the same page.

If you are reading this book and the school year has already started, you may think it's too late, but again, it's never too late! All you need to do is sit down with your students and explain what you are going to be doing differently. Consider having a class meeting to discuss with students that you want to make some changes to how things are done in the class. Share that you've learned some new things and want to try those things with them, explaining why.

I cannot emphasize enough how important consistency will be when delivering your consequences whether it is the first day of school or the middle of the year. You will continually need to have self-checks and evaluate whether you are being consistent.

Diversifying for All Learners

When thinking about delivering consequences, we do need to think about the different types of learners we are working with. The age of your students matters. We need to think back to chapter 1 (page 7) with what we learned about brain development and all the things that happen in the brain throughout childhood. We also must think about what our students may have been through. Questions to ask include, "Are they getting their needs met?" "Do they feel like they belong?" "Do they feel safe?" and "Do they feel loved?" A student may be neurodiverse, and their less common perspective may impact their behavior, for example. What accommodations can we make? Maybe a student needs to be able to stand rather than sit, or the student may need to get up and move. Maybe the student needs a checklist to help remember things to do or a buddy to help keep them on track. It isn't to say that your expectations will be lower, but you can come from a place of understanding and with the thought of "How can I help?" We can also ask the student, "What do you need to be successful?" or "How do you learn best?" It is also important to think about cultural differences. We need to ask questions and learn. Maybe what we think of as disrespect isn't intended to be that way. When we stop making assumptions and ask, we learn a whole lot about our students' intentions.

In the following, I would like to share the importance of engaging parents and families. Parents and families are a critical part of their child's education and ensuring our classroom-management plan is successful. Families come from all walks of life. Some may be similar to our own, and others will not be. Let's look a little deeper into how families can be involved in our plan.

Strategies for Engaging With Families

Engaging with parents and families is critical to the success of students. As educators, we have to work to include parents and families as much as possible. Research shows family involvement increases student achievement and academic success (Zolkoski, Sayman, & Lewis-Chiu, 2018). Encouraging positive relationships between the school and families promotes academic, social, and emotional success for youth throughout their lives. As educators, we need to come from a place of understanding and encouraging the positive relationships rather than judging families for not being or acting how we think they should.

There are levels of involvement, from parents who volunteer at school and are regularly at the school to parents who, for many different reasons, are not involved at the school level. Generally, elementary school parents are more involved than families of students in secondary school. As students get older, the level of parent participation in the school decreases dramatically because there aren't as many activities for them to be involved with, and as students get older, families are often unable to help their child with school (Zolkoski et al., 2018). It is important to remember that just because a family may not be involved at the school physically, they may be involved at home. Families may not know how to talk with their child. Sharing what is happening at school can give families an opportunity to talk to their child at home. Provide families with ways to engage their students by explaining what their child is doing in class. Awareness and understanding of different levels of involvement can make a positive impact on families and, in turn, positively impact students. When we get to know families, we can have a better understanding of where they are coming from.

Families from low socioeconomic areas, those with low levels of education, and single parents are often perceived by educators as less involved in their child's education (Zolkoski et al., 2018). Pragmatic issues including limited transportation, job requirements that conflict with school schedules, or lack of childcare can prevent families from being involved. When students are having a difficult time in school, families may feel a sense of being disconnected from the school or have repeated negative interactions. Families will often be less likely to want to engage in communication because of repeated negative interactions. Families' response to school personnel may come across as aggressive due to feelings of frustration. These circumstances can result in educators and other school personnel feeling like families are unwilling to work collaboratively.

Cultural and ethnic differences can impact levels of family involvement. A lack of understanding of cultural differences can impede participation and communication of families and educators. In some cultures, families may appear uninvolved because their culture believes they need to allow school personnel to perform educational duties without interference (Gonzalez, Borders, Hines, Villalba, & Henderson, 2013). It is important to develop cultural self-awareness (Friend & Cook, 2012). It is important to learn values, traditions, and customs of the families in your classroom. Particularly, it is important to understand families' cultural views of school involvement. There is not a single best way to engage families (Sawyer, 2015). However, building relationships and encouraging family involvement while actively providing ways to engage families will make a positive difference. Table 3.2 (page 94) provides strategies for engaging parents and families in the classroom and school (Zolkoski et al., 2018).

Parents need to know who you are. It doesn't matter the grade you are teaching; the first interaction needs to be positive. Whether it's the first day of school or middle of the year, you must work to have positive interactions. In elementary school, there is generally a "meet the teacher" night prior to the school year starting.

TABLE 3.2: Strategies to Engage Families

Strategy	Activities
Respect and understand cultural differences.	• Incorporate cultural and home experiences into learning. • Develop cultural awareness of students in the classroom. • Allow students and their families to share things about their culture or holidays.
Help families learn how to work with their child at home.	• Have mathematics, science, or language arts nights and provide food and childcare. • Provide opportunities in middle school and high school for families to be involved. • Provide opportunities for families to use computer labs to learn technology skills.
Establish trust and work to sustain collaborative family-school partnerships.	• Create a judgment-free space for parents to voice concerns or receive support. • Ensure communication with families occurs in a way that works best for them. • Treat families with respect and ensure consistent and relevant communication.
Include families at all levels in various ways to meet their needs.	• Distribute newsletters weekly in families' native language, including information about classroom events, lesson topics, student progress, and missing assignments. • Make personal phone calls inviting families to attend or participate in classroom or school events. • Create home learning activities to actively engage families in their child's academic development. • Ensure the native language of the family is included.
Recognize the value of families and include them on decisions made for their child.	• Create a proactive approach to discipline. • Provide opportunities for families to be involved in making decisions. • Ensure families are provided with all information and options available to their child.

In secondary school, there can also be a "meet the teacher" evening. As the teacher, you need to be there with a welcoming smile on your face. Your room should be inviting. Of course, not all families will come to a "meet the teacher" event, particularly in secondary grades, but as the teacher, you should come with your A game. If you are arriving in the middle of the year, you need to make an effort to show parents who you are. Whether you teach elementary or secondary, you should send a welcome email where you let parents know who you are, your expectations, and topics you will be teaching. The note should feel welcoming and positive. Weekly, information should be going out to families to let them know what's going on in the classroom and about upcoming events. Apps can be used as a form of communication (for example, Remind or GroupMe). Pictures can be posted on social media or within the app to share what is happening in the classroom. Social media can be a classroom page or the district page. It is important to be careful of students who are not allowed to have their face posted (put a smiley face over their face). Families like to see students actively engaged in learning. Communication must be positive. Consistent positive communication shows families you care about their student and makes a big difference when having to discuss a difficult situation.

I wish I could say dealing with difficult family situations never happens, but that just isn't the case. I will say fostering positive relationships with families makes all the difference when having to approach them with a difficult situation. Often, difficult situations occur because the students are challenging, although that isn't always the case. Much of what has been discussed in this chapter can help mitigate difficulties. I would like to spend a little time talking about the *why* of family behaviors, which begins with what was discussed in chapter 1 (page 7).

First, we need to get the idea of parents not caring out of our minds. Families care, but they may not care in the way we think they should. There are many reasons why families are not involved in a way we think they should. Mental health could be one of the reasons why there is a lack of involvement. Sometimes families are doing everything they can to stay afloat, and they can't begin to think about their child and school. Another reason why parents may not be as involved as we would like them to be is because of their own job. There can also be a cultural factor that causes a lack of participation. A family may feel too embarrassed to ask questions for fear of being seen as less than because they don't know how to help. As educators, it may seem simple, but we are trained in a way most parents aren't, and we need to remember that.

I think about trauma and what we learned in chapter 1 about trauma (page 20). Many people who have been through trauma have not gotten help in dealing with the traumatic events in their lives. We also learned what trauma can do to the brain. I also think about SEL and the importance of self-awareness, self-management, and social awareness. Not everyone has appropriate coping skills. Individuals who have been through trauma may not have gotten the self-regulation and coping skills needed. Parenting is not an easy feat. I often say it is the best or worst thing you can possibly do to yourself. I say that with all the love in my heart for my own kids. Babies don't come home with a book on how to best handle them. For every book you find, there's another book that tells you the opposite of what the first book says. If we don't have the best skills for handling our own emotions, how can we help our own children? Parents may not know how to respond to difficult situations appropriately. Additionally, parents' lack of involvement could be what is causing the difficult situation. Building a positive relationship, or at least doing everything you can to develop a relationship, will help you learn more about students' families and the intricacies of each family.

It is important for me to say that just because mental health or trauma may be a factor in a family's life, that does not mean a difficult situation will occur or a lack of involvement will be automatic. Just as our students' behaviors have different *whys*, families do, too. I will say this repeatedly: we must learn about our students and their families to truly know what is going on. Whatever is happening in our students' lives, we need to remove judgment and come from a place of "How can I help?" Whether it is true or not, families feel judgment.

After everything discussed in this chapter, particularly the family section, remember that positive communication from the very beginning (or when you start) is critical. Just like our students, parents need a higher ratio of positive communication to negative communication about their student and what is happening in the classroom. Learn about your students and their families and be sure you are doing everything in your power to make sure families know it's a judgment-free zone. The following are steps you can take when having a difficult conversation with a family.

As teachers, we see things in different ways. We want parents to do what we want when we want them to. We can forget about their feelings. We must remember, for some parents, there is a death of a dream. As parents, we have a dream of who our kids will be, and sometimes, our dream is completely wrong. It is much like a death. There are stages of grief and loss parents go through including denial, anger, bargaining, depression, and acceptance (Fay & Fay, 2016).

Fay and Fay (2016) talk about a win-win process when dealing with difficult families. The first step is to lead with empathy and collect information. Remember, we are trying to come from a place of helping and a lack of judgment. Sincere empathy goes a long way and soaks up emotions. According to Fay and Fay (2016), empathy changes the brain's functioning, moving the "lion's" portion of neurological activities to the prefrontal cortex (self-control and complex reasoning) rather than the limbic system, which is where the idea of fight or flight originates. Leading with empathy allows parents to feel more comfortable sharing their emotions. As educators, we can say something like, "I understand you are very upset about this."

Step two of the win-win process is slowing things down (Fay & Fay, 2016). As parents are talking, one thing to do is ask to take notes. Explain that you want to ensure you are hearing correctly. Write down exactly what the parents are saying. You may need to say, "I'm sorry. Can you repeat that so I understand?" Step three involves proving you have listened. You have taken notes during the meeting, which will allow you the opportunity to ask if you can repeat back what was said and ask if anything was missed. Typically, parents' second version is much more rational and less sarcastic or defensive. Step four of the process involves checking for entry into the thinking state. Hopefully, the previous steps have moved the parents from the limbic system (emotional state) to the prefrontal cortex (thinking state).

When parents are in the thinking state, you can ask if they would like to hear your thoughts. The last step in the process is beginning to problem solve, but don't be surprised if previous steps need to be revisited.

Remember, when communicating with parents about a problem, you need to contact them via phone and preferably face-to-face. Email and text messages are great for scheduling meetings or sharing positive events. I cannot emphasize enough the importance of building relationships before problems develop. Parents and families need to see and feel how much you care about their student.

Concluding Thoughts

There is a lot of information in this chapter on how to create an effective classroom-management plan. Having a plan is an important step in the process. The next step is implementing the plan with consistency. It isn't going to be easy. After all, classroom management is the hardest thing for teachers to master. There will be days you mess up, and things won't always go the way you planned. It is important for you to give yourself some grace, too. You will have days when you start to focus on the negative and feel worn down. It's OK. All you need to do is reset. When you feel like things are off with you or your students, ask yourself some questions: "Do my students feel welcome? Am I focusing on the positive? Do my consequences match the behaviors? Am I being consistent?" It can be easy, especially when making significant changes, to revert to ways that are not effective. When we continually self-check, it becomes easier and easier to stay consistent. You will be positively reinforced by how well your students respond with their behavior and with their academic achievement! Now, please consider the following reproducible tool, "Classroom Expectations" (page 98; also available at **go.SolutionTree.com /behavior**), as you develop your classroom management approach.

Classroom Expectations

The following is an outline of key behaviors that we will follow to help our classroom run smoothly.

Expectation	What It Looks Like (Provide examples of behaviors.)

Problem-Solving When Expectations Are Not Met
Gentle Reminder: "What should you be doing right now?"
Warning: "If you don't stop _____, then _____ will happen."
Positive Reinforcement

Menu Examples

- 10 tickets/points
    + Pencil, sticker, small pack of candy
- 25 tickets/points
    + Soda pass, hat day, no shoes in class (cozy toes), preferential seating
- 50 tickets/points
    + Homework pass, lunch with teacher, special chair, create a music playlist, read to another class
- 75 tickets/points
    + Lunch with teacher and a friend, cut assignment in half, sit in teacher's chair, create a seating chart
- 100 tickets/points
    + Lunch with the teacher and two friends, free test question answer, skip an assignment, switch roles with the teacher for 10 minutes

Natural Consequence Examples
• **Talking:** Move locations (closer to teacher, away from other students)
• **Bothering students around you:** Move location (closer to teacher, away from other students)
• **Improper use of materials:** Lose materials
• **Improper use of computer:** Lose computer privileges
• **Not completing work:** Complete work as homework or during free time (not recess)
Student and Teacher Agreement
As members of this class, we agree to maintain the expectations we created to support a positive learning environment.   Student Signature: _____   Teacher Signature: _____
Reflection Questions
• Am I consistent with my rules and procedures?   • Am I consistently providing reward opportunities (tickets/points) to *all* students?   • Am I consistently providing natural consequences?   • Are consequences decreasing behaviors like I want them to?   • Are there any students who need additional support? What are ways I can support these students?   • Are positive reinforcement ideas working for students? Do they want to earn different things?

Voices From the Field

Are expectations enforced in positive or negative ways?

"I don't understand why teachers take away recess. It's the same kids who sit out all the time. It doesn't help."

—*A third-grade student*

"I get so mad when teachers blame kids for stuff they didn't even do. Why can't they just ask?"

—*An eighth-grade student*

"It's embarrassing when teachers yell at you in front of the whole class."

—*A fifth-grade student*

"My students worked to earn best class. Whoever won best class earned lunch. It was so much fun seeing them all work together."

—*A high school Spanish teacher*

"My students love to earn candies. They also will work for stickers and other things you don't think older kids will like. They get excited."

—*An eleventh-grade teacher*

"Middle school students love to earn stuff like students in elementary school. When we focus on the good students rather than the ones who struggle, we see more of the good. We have VIP lunch for our students who have good grades and behavior. Students can choose to eat outside or inside. They love to play music, football, volleyball, and just hang out."

—*A middle school principal*

CHAPTER 4
Provide Additional Support for Students Who Need More

This chapter is all about supporting students who need extra help with their behavior. The strategies we talk about in this chapter can be very effective and are easy to implement. The strategies here are great for all students, but similar to the approach in my previous book, *Motivated to Learn* (Zolkoski et al., 2023), they truly support the needs of students who need them most.

Before we begin, let's look at our multitiered framework from previous chapters. We talked a lot about Tier 1 in chapters 2 (page 35) and 3 (page 67) where the focus was on the importance of building a supportive environment and building positive connections with students as part of an effective classroom-management plan. As you can see from referring to figure 3.1 (page 68), consistently implementing the Tier 1 strategies captures most of your students. Behavior is much like academics; you can have an effective system in place and still have students who need more support by moving them to Tier 2. Academically, we provide small-group support and provide extra help to hopefully get the students back on track. Behaviorally, instead of doing the same things we do to support academics, we tend to be more punitive rather than educative and supportive. Instead, we need to provide behavior support with the goal of supporting students to get back on track. When we are effective in our Tier 2 strategies, we are likely to find that very few, if any, students rise to the level of needing Tier 3 supports. We'll get into this step a little more at the end of this chapter, but first, let's run through some strategies for supporting students at Tier 2. Each strategy in this chapter has research to support the effectiveness of the strategy. I have chosen to discuss the strategies I believe are the most beneficial and easiest to implement because I have used them myself and have seen just how effective they are. We will specifically learn about (1) choice, (2) positive peer reporting, (3) the Good Behavior Game, (4) a token economy, and (5) self-monitoring. After delineating how to implement each of the aforementioned strategies, I will share what happens at Tier 3 and the implementation of a functional behavior assessment. One thing different in this chapter compared to the others is it does not include a section on beginning-of-year versus midyear implementation because Tier 2 strategies are only implemented after Tier 1 strategies are not working. It takes time to establish Tier 1 strategies and determine they are not as effective as they could be for some students. The chapter closes with a Concluding Thoughts section and a reproducible tool.

Strategies for Providing Students With Additional Support

Before we dive into looking at specific strategies, I want to look more closely at what can be done to make a positive connection with students. We have already spent time thinking about building positive relationships with students and why it is important to do so. This tends to be easy to do with students who don't exhibit challenging behaviors, but I'll provide a friendly reminder here about how critical it is for our students who struggle with their behavior to still feel like they are cared about in your classroom.

With our students who are difficult, we sometimes feel they are doing things *to us*, like they are out to get us and deliberately challenging us at every turn. However, generally speaking, students' behavior *is not about us*. Yes, we can absolutely cause a student's behavior to escalate because of how we handle a situation, something I see often. It's not surprising. These students are hard to manage; they are frustrating and exhausting. It's easy to feel like if they were just not in the room, we could teach effectively.

Consider, however, that students tend to live up to the expectations we set for them. If students believe we don't care about them and think they are bad, then they will be bad (Cook et al., 2017). They will show us what we believe about them. Sure, some might instead seek to prove our perceived assumptions wrong, but that's generally not how students of any age work. As teachers, sometimes we have to be the best actors because our students can *never* feel like we don't care or we don't like them.

I find it is easier to come from a place of understanding when looking for the *why* of a student's behavior. Make sure you're asking the questions we've outlined throughout this book:

- **Is the student getting their basic needs met?** Remember, sometimes students' behaviors can be extreme or difficult because they aren't getting their basic needs met (see chapter 1, page 7).
- **Are there external (home environment, peers, trauma) or internal factors (neurodivergent conditions) contributing to the behaviors?** As explained in chapter 1, we can expect to see challenging behaviors when the answer to the question is yes.
- **Does the student feel cared for by their teacher or their peers?** As we explored in both chapter 1 and chapter 2 (page 35), research shows students with challenging behaviors respond more positively when they are in a positive environment and they feel cared for (Zolkoski, Bullock, & Gable, 2016).

In chapter 2 and even in chapter 3 (page 67), we talked about how to build a positive environment. Chapter 3 discusses not only a positive environment but the structure and consistency all students, but particularly students with challenging behaviors, need.

Before we get into learning specific strategies in this chapter, I want to provide a couple of small tricks you can do to foster a positive relationship with students who have challenging behaviors.

Recall the one-sentence intervention strategy (page 47). Try that. Write down things you notice about the student. You can add to your list as you go. Then, walk up to the student and say, "I notice that . . . ," stating what you notice. Students have a belief we don't notice them. When we take time to notice something about them, they are more likely to feel like we care about them and are then more likely to do what we ask. The intention is to show the student you see them.

When you use specific positive praise, you are giving the student attention (which is often what they want) but in a positive way rather than a negative way. Remember, it doesn't make sense to us, but students crave attention. They will get it in whatever form they can. We want to switch negative attention into positive attention. The more positives we can point out, the more positives we will see.

Another easy trick you can do with students who are difficult is to precorrect them. We assume students know what we expect them to do, but they don't always, particularly the challenging ones. If we tell them what we expect right before we expect it, they are more likely to do what we asked, and then we can offer them specific positive praise for doing what they have been asked. For example, say you have a student who never does their morning work or warm-up activity like you expect. You always find the student walking around the room. A way to provide precorrection is to remind them when they come into the room that they need to sit down and begin their morning work or warm-up activity: "Johnny, I know you will sit down and begin your warm-up activity. I can't wait to see you do it."

When Johnny sits down to begin his assignment, you immediately look at Johnny and explicitly thank him for beginning his morning work. This type of simple reminder sets students up for success, enabling us to arrange scenarios where we capture our students doing good things and have the opportunity to let them know we are proud of them and thankful for what they have done. The more you do this in your classroom, the more good things you will see, even with your students who struggle the most; it will just take them longer to get there.

In this section, I share the five specific strategies that are supported by research and that you can implement in your classroom right away: (1) choice, (2) positive peer reporting, (3) the Good Behavior Game, (4) a token economy, and (5) self-monitoring. These strategies can benefit all students, but they are extra helpful to students with challenging behaviors who the approaches detailed in previous chapters haven't reached.

Note that self-monitoring (or self-management, if you prefer) is much more specific to students with challenging behaviors and works well for students who are effective at a token economy. Note also that because this tier is focused on students where Tier 1 strategies haven't been effective, we are no longer focused on how to implement the strategies at the beginning of the school year versus in the middle of the year. These are all strategies to implement after the year has begun and you have had time to identify the students in need of them.

CHOICE

Choice is probably my favorite strategy because it is easy to implement and it is incredibly effective. It seems so simple, maybe almost too simple to actually work, but it truly does. And if you think about it, it makes sense. We tell students what to do from the moment they arrive at school until the moment they leave. For example, most of us have seating charts. Many students have assigned seats in each class, and some even have an assigned seat at lunch. Students can't use the restroom when they want to or even use their cell phone when they want to.

We may think, "Well, those are just expectations of students," which is true, but we can provide choice while maintaining expectations. Think about yourself in a professional setting, specifically a professional development session or a meeting called by your administration. We sit where we want to. We use the bathroom when we need to. Often, we even have our cell phones or computers out, sometimes engaging more deeply with them than the meeting at hand. In short, we have choices in a way our students typically do not.

Choice provides our students with options and makes them feel like they are in control. When students have a choice, they have feelings of motivation and independence (Nagro, Fraser, & Hooks, 2019). Choice can be used for all students, but it can be especially helpful for students with challenging behaviors just because of the fact they feel more in control.

Students like to feel like they are in control, particularly when they feel like they have no control, which is why choice can be so effective (Fay & Fay, 2016). Students with challenging behaviors feel like everyone around them is telling them what to do. They don't want to listen to anyone. They want to do what they want to do. When we give them choices, they feel like they have more control. We want them to have the control, but within the limits we set for them.

Using Choice in Primary and Secondary Grades

Choice is a strategy shown to be effective across all grade levels in any setting to not only decrease challenging behaviors but also increase academic engagement (Jolivette, Ennis, & Swoszowski, 2020). Whether you are teaching a primary or secondary grade, choice is beneficial and is based on students' preferences, so it fits to any grade. The important thing to remember about choice is that the options you give students must be equal in value. Saying to a student, "You can either complete your assignment or go to the office," is not an example of giving them two options that are equal in value, but giving a student the choice between two similar assignments is an example of this practice. Another important aspect of the choice strategy is that you, as the teacher, and the student have to agree on the choice options. You don't want to give the student an option you don't actually want them to choose.

Let's start by looking at how choice can be implemented in the classroom for all students across all grade levels. When you have choice options for all students, your students who struggle with their behavior are benefiting because they are given choices like everyone else. After sharing strategies for everyone, I will share how you can use choice to specifically target an individual student. The examples are not broken down specifically for primary versus secondary because the choice options work for any grade; however, the assignments themselves will be grade-level specific.

- Give your students a choice board of assignments needing to be completed. You may have one or two must-dos on the list, and then they pick a specific number of additional options to complete the work.
- Give your students a large set of problems, twenty for example, and tell them to pick a subset of those problems to complete (such as ten of the twenty).
- Have students choose the order in which they complete a set of multiple assignments or tasks.
- Have students choose the type (format) of assignment to complete (such as a paper, a video, or a poster). The content is still the same, but how they show what they know will be different.
- Give students options for a writing topic. All options should be geared toward ensuring students display the learning or skills intended of that assignment.
- Have students choose what to write with (type of pencil, marker, or pen) or on (different types of paper or on the computer).
- Have students choose what type of reinforcement they want to earn. Reinforcements can be anything students can earn. Examples of this may include free time, a homework pass, computer time, lunch with a friend or teacher, or a pencil.
- Allow students the choice of where to sit in the classroom (on the floor or at a different desk or table), but ensure it's clear that if there are disruptions, that choice is forfeited.

Within any of the options provided here, you give your students a choice of what and how to do tasks throughout the day. In essence, you are communicating, "It doesn't matter to me which problems you complete, as long as you complete them," or "It doesn't matter to me what you are writing on or with, as long as you complete the assignments." There are still clear boundaries in place, but there is flexibility within those boundaries. When you put the proverbial ball in your students' court, they are much more likely to do what you want them to do because of the control they think they have.

When thinking about a student who struggles with their behavior, providing the choices I included so far will help, but you may need to be more specific. First, it is important to determine the times of day, subject area, or assignment type the student is struggling the most with. You will want to observe the student to determine when the student would benefit best from choice.

Once you have observed the student and taken notes over when the student would benefit from more targeted choice options, you need to talk specifically with the student. When talking with the student, you need to consider cultural diversity (see the next section for more information on that). You also want to allow the student, within your own limits, to determine choice options the student wants to have. You and the student are also determining reinforcement ideas for the student to earn upon completion of the assignment. Let's look at an example:

> *Henry, a ninth grader, is not completing his independent work. He is talking to other students around him and just does not comply. His teacher, Mr. Sherman, is collecting data using event recording to determine how many times Henry does not work during independent time. He has also spoken with Henry about choice options for completing work during independent work time. Mr. Sherman and Henry decide to include a choice board. Henry can now pick three assignments he prefers in the order he wants to complete them, but he will have to complete two must-do tasks assigned by Mr. Sherman. Henry loves art, and he loves listening to music. Mr. Sherman and Henry agree that once Henry completes his choice board, he can draw while listening to music. Mr. Sherman collects data after implementing the choice strategy. Data show Henry is doing well with the choice strategy.*

Once a choice is made, it is important to meet with the student regularly and collect data to ensure the choice options are still effective. If issues remain, choice options can change as needed to better target the right kind of support the student needs to complete the tasks.

Diversifying for All Learners

The wonderful thing about the choice strategy is the fact that it is effective for all types of ability levels (Jolivette et al., 2020). Choice is most effective when you have developed a relationship with the students to know what their interests, strengths, and cultures are. Open communication and positive connections with students (and their families) ensure you are providing options that are meaningful to the students rather than creating options in isolation (Zolkoski et al., 2023). When developing choice options, you want to get to know not only the students but also their families. They can provide you with information on what students like and don't like. You can also learn about your students' preferred interaction styles. For example, some students are more reluctant to answer questions in a large-group setting. If you have a student whose native language is something other than English, consider providing choice options in the student's first language. Choice is naturally a strategy that is easy to diversify because it becomes the student's opportunity to choose options they most identify with. Keep in mind it is important to have regular check-ins with students to ensure you know if and when their preferences have changed.

POSITIVE PEER REPORTING

Students who struggle with their behavior often find themselves socially rejected by peers (Murphy & Zlomke, 2014). To counter this effect, try using positive peer reporting, also known as *tootling*, which is a *peer-mediated strategy*, meaning peers are taught to promote academic achievement and prosocial behavior in their classmates. As a concept, PPR dates back to 1976 when Tanya Grieger, James Kauffman, and Russell Grieger discovered rewarding kindergarteners for naming a peer who had done something nice correlated with observations during recess of cooperative play and decreased aggression (Murphy & Zlomke, 2014). In the 1990s, a similar intervention was used at a residential treatment center for youth, which is when the term *positive peer reporting* was first used (Lum et al., 2019). In simple terms, the work of Christopher H. Skinner, Tammy H. Cashwell, and Amy L. Skinner (2000) found tootling to be the opposite of tattling and is a twist on the expression "tooting your horn."

Tai A. Collins and colleagues (2020) conducted a meta-analytic review on PPR where they examined twenty-one studies to determine the impact of PPR on student behavior and found it is an effective strategy for improving disruptive behaviors, social behaviors, and academically engaged behaviors. Additional research demonstrates these findings are consistent across all grade levels. For example, Abigail M. Lambert, Daniel H. Tingstrom, Heather E. Sterling, Brad A. Dufrene, and Shauna Lynne (2015) find PPR to be an effective strategy in elementary school for decreasing classwide disruptive behaviors and increasing appropriate behaviors. Similarly, Todd Haydon, Alana Kennedy, Meredith Murphy, and Jason Boone (2023) find PPR to be an effective strategy for decreasing negative interactions among middle school peers who have EBDs. And John D. K. Lum and colleagues (2019) find classwide PPR to be effective with grade 9–12 students in decreasing off-task and disruptive behaviors while improving levels of student engagement. Let's look deeper at how to put this strategy to use.

Using PPR in Primary and Secondary Grades

PPR is an easy strategy to implement at any grade level and can be implemented in a variety of ways. The first step, no matter the age, is to introduce the concept of students reporting on the good behavior of others (Haydon et al., 2023). Rather than reporting on things they see their peers doing wrong, they are going to report what their peers are doing well. Students should know that doing so is the opposite of tattling. They also need to learn they will receive an opportunity to earn a reinforcement for reporting their peers' positive behaviors. (Think of the simple rewards we detailed in chapter 3, page 67, such as accumulation of points or tickets.)

The next step, which is something that should be thought about before introducing the strategy to students, is explaining your procedure for implementing PPR. Students need to know what positive behaviors are, how and when they should report positive behaviors, and the type and amount of reinforcement earned for reporting positive peer behaviors (Haydon et al., 2023). You want to make sure you think about how you want things to be done so you can clearly articulate that to the students. Students need to also know that you, as the teacher, will decide if the report is specific and genuine.

When considering positive behaviors, you want to think about the grade level you are teaching and the needs of your students. Positive comments may include sharing with a classmate, helping a friend, praising or complimenting others, volunteering, being honest, or asking for help.

The amount of time it takes to introduce and explain PPR depends on the age of the students and their skill level. For example, elementary students and even older students who significantly struggle with their behavior may need more explicit instruction and modeling. The teacher models PPR and provides various role-playing scenarios so students understand what it looks like to be specific when reporting positive behaviors.

To report positive behaviors, students should learn to look at their peer, smile, and report the positive thing the peer said or did (Haydon et al., 2023). For example, "Juan, I noticed that you helped Timmy by giving him a pencil to write with. You were being helpful!" After modeling, the students practice by taking turns providing positive statements to their peers. While students are practicing, the teacher walks around the room and provides specific feedback on what students are doing well and what changes need to be made. It may also be helpful to create and display a visual of the steps for reporting positive behavior so students can refer to it. Modeling and visual displays might also provide examples and nonexamples. An example of PPR may be "Sarah, you did a great job on your report in class today." A nonexample of PPR may be "Sarah, great job at not sucking when you did your report in class."

The teacher will need to determine when and how students will report positive behaviors. Reporting sessions are typically between five and ten minutes and should be conducted at a specific time of the day, like the end of a class period or school day (Haydon et al., 2023). In this way, reporting sessions become a part of everyday classroom procedures.

Students in upper elementary and secondary grades can write their PPR on a notecard. The notecards can be read during reporting time. The benefit of having a notecard or special reporting paper is that students can write down what they want to report at any time. There can be a spot in the classroom where students can get the notecard and drop the note in the reporting box.

Another option for reporting is to have the students raise their hand and report the positive behavior they witnessed from their classmate. A visual for how to report can help with this. Some teachers may find having students verbally report behaviors to be easier, especially in the early grades (K–2). When reporting is occurring, the teacher provides verbal praise to the reporter for sharing and the recipient for their positive behavior.

When thinking about the type of reinforcement system to implement with PPR, teachers need to think about the reinforcement system already in place (Haydon et al., 2023). If a ticket system or app system is currently being used, then continue with that system. The idea is to keep it simple rather than adding extras. When there are too many things, we can get overwhelmed and then don't implement with consistency.

You may also want to think about whether you will give individual points or tickets for positive peer reporting or design a group incentive. For an individual system, the reporter and student being reported on receive a ticket to be added to your current system (earn items from choice reinforcement board). In a group context, students work to earn points for the whole class to earn a larger reward, with the whole class choosing the reward to ensure buy-in.

Ultimately, determining the best type of reinforcement system is really up to each individual teacher based on what they feel is the easiest to implement consistently. But in any case, the final thing to decide on is how often peer reporting will be implemented in your class. For example, is this something you plan on doing daily, or will you randomly choose a specific class period or day you prefer to implement PPR? You may start out implementing PPR daily and then decide to choose specific days to implement. It will depend on how your students are doing with reporting. For example, you may find students are eager to begin but then stop reporting. At that time, you may tell your students you are going to pick a day of the week or a time of the day to report. Think about what works best for you and your students. If you choose a specific day or time of day, you will want to do so randomly, meaning you will change the day or the week and the time of the day at random versus it being the same every week. Varying the days and times of when PPR is implemented can help with students becoming bored.

After PPR is introduced and modeled, it is important to monitor the effectiveness of the intervention to know if it is working and what adjustments may need to be made. A simple frequency sheet can be used to count and total the number of times students report PPR each day as well as the type of statement being reported (Haydon et al., 2023). Figure 4.1 is an example of a PPR monitoring sheet. The sheet shows you if there are specific days or times of day where PPR is working well or not working well. You can also determine the number of positive statements. If you notice a specific group of students is having a difficult time with positive statements, you are able to work on it with the students. A goal can be created to improve positive statements, and a reward can be provided for accomplishing the goal.

Date	Date	Date	Date	Date
Day of Week	Day of Week	Day of Week	Day of Week	Day of Week
Time	Time	Time	Time	Time
Positive Statements	Positive Statements	Positive Statements	Positive Statements	Positive Statements
Neutral Statements	Neutral Statements	Neutral Statements	Neutral Statements	Neutral Statements
Negative Statements	Negative Statements	Negative Statements	Negative Statements	Negative Statements

FIGURE 4.1: Example of a positive peer reporting monitoring sheet.

*Visit **go.SolutionTree.com/behavior** for a free reproducible version of this figure.*

Although PPR is an evidence-based practice for increasing positive behaviors, there can be some challenges that you'll need a plan to handle. The first challenge is determining criteria for rewards. For example, when doing a group system, you need to think about how many tallies are required to earn the predetermined reward. You need to find a balance between it not being too easy to earn and being not so difficult that students become unmotivated, feeling like they will never earn the reward (Haydon et al., 2023).

Another challenge that can occur involves which students receive positive feedback from their peers. It is possible for students who struggle with their behavior to not get many positive reports as well as for those who are well liked to get most of the notes, which is contrary to the goals of this strategy. One way to help with this challenge is to set criteria where a student cannot report on the same student twice. Having a rule where students need to choose a different student each time helps ensure all students, including students who may struggle, will receive positive feedback. A student may also repeat a statement already shared. If this happens, the teacher can ask the student to share a different positive statement. If they are not able to do this, the teacher can offer a pass to avoid a power struggle with the student reporting.

It can be difficult to ensure long-term investment from students, but continually monitoring the effectiveness of PPR and making adjustments as you go will ensure it is implemented with fidelity. To help with students' long-term buy-in and effectiveness, it is important to ensure rewards are updated or alternated periodically. The rewards offered should also match the scale of achievement. For individual tickets or points, use your choice board with rewards being worth differing amounts (for example, a pencil versus lunch with the teacher). Group rewards would be a bigger deal (watching a movie, receiving free time, or issuing a homework pass). As we detail in chapter 3 (page 67), reward options need not (and probably shouldn't) have any monetary value.

Diversifying for All Learners

Prior to implementing PPR, it is important to understand your students' abilities to interact with their peers. Students with social skill deficits, challenging behaviors, or specific learning disabilities may need direct instruction on how to give appropriate praise to their peers (Haydon et al., 2023). Additionally, it is important to be aware of multicultural differences when teaching PPR. To best promote positive behaviors, it is important for teachers to model giving praise to students by using language that is both gender-neutral and free of stereotypes (Murphy & Zlomke, 2014). It is important to be inclusive of rewards and visual displays that not only reflect but also honor the various cultures and life experiences of the students in the class.

GOOD BEHAVIOR GAME

Disruptive behaviors interrupt a teacher's ability to teach and students' abilities to learn material being taught. Enter the Good Behavior Game, which is considered a classwide group contingency shown to be effective at reducing disruptive behavior (such as talking, out-of-seat, and off-task behaviors) while also promoting on-task behavior (Donaldson, Fisher, & Kahng, 2017; Flower, McKenna, Bunuan, Muething, & Vega, 2014; Groves & Austin, 2019). A classwide group contingency involves the entire class doing what has been asked (for example, raising your hand), and therefore, the entire class gets a reward (for example, free time).

The Good Behavior Game was first described by Harriet H. Barrish, Muriel Saunders, and Montrose M. Wolf (1969) as being an effective strategy for increasing prosocial behavior. It was initially used in a fourth-grade classroom where students were divided into two teams and asked to follow specific classroom rules. If students broke a rule, they received a mark on the board. Teams with fewer than six marks within a thirty-minute period of time won the game. If both teams had more than five marks, then the team with the least number of marks won the game and earned a special privilege. The researchers found a reduction in students out of their seat and inappropriate talking. To play the Good Behavior Game, specific rules are established, and students are put in teams. When teams follow the rules, they get a point, and whichever team has the most points earns a predetermined reward. Over the years, there have been variations in how the Good Behavior Game is implemented with some adding points for inappropriate behaviors instead of adding points for appropriate behaviors. Let's take a closer look at how you might implement this game.

Running the Good Behavior Game in Primary and Secondary Grades

In a review of the literature, Andrea Flower and colleagues (2014) find the Good Behavior Game to be effective at reducing challenging classroom behaviors in both primary grades and secondary grades, though how it works can vary based on grade level. For example, a kindergartener will not be able to follow a rule for the same length of time as a tenth-grade student. Fortunately, rules are easily adapted to the behavioral needs of students in the classroom.

The first step involves selecting at least one rule to be targeted (for example, raising your hand to talk). Again, the grade and ability of your students will determine how many rules should be established (Joslyn & Groves, 2023). Elementary students will need to start with one rule. Upper elementary students, however, may be able to handle more than one rule to play the game. Secondary students should be able to handle multiple rules when playing the game. With all that being said, you may have a group of students who struggle more than another. You will want to make adjustments to meet your students' needs to find the happy medium.

Next, you must determine the game's length of time (for example, twenty minutes). Here, too, it's important to find the sweet spot for your students, where time isn't so long that students can't be successful but is long enough for the game to be a challenge and something to work toward. For example, a kindergarten or first-grade class will need to begin playing the game with less time than an upper elementary class, while middle school and high school students will be able to go for a longer period of time and still be successful. However, you may have a class that struggles and, even though they are older, students who need to play for less time. The opposite can also be true where a younger group can play for a longer amount of time.

Next, with the help of the students in the class, decide on the reward students will earn (extra recess, free time, class privilege, and so on). To support this decision, it is important to collect baseline data about student behavior because it helps to know what behaviors to focus on, determine the point threshold, and monitor effectiveness. I suggest setting the point threshold based on the rate of problem behavior.

The next step is to determine the teams. The teams should be equally distributed where students who engage in the problem behavior are similarly distributed with students who engage in appropriate behaviors.

When you're ready to introduce the game to students, display the rules and teams where everyone can see them. For example, write information on the board or have a web- or computer-based platform where students are still able to view everything (Joslyn & Groves, 2023). Teach the rules of the game (ensure it's clear that lower scores are better if tallying for broken rules), communicating what behaviors are being targeted (be explicit about these and model them), who is on each team, and what rewards are available for the winners. Students should also know the length of time the game is followed. The time can be increased based on how well the students are doing, making data collection important.

Once the game begins, each time a rule is broken (or, alternatively, each time a rule is followed), the team gets a point (Joslyn & Groves, 2023). The teacher needs to deliver the point but also provide feedback by saying, "Team 1, remember to raise your hand when you want to answer a question." Once the time is up, the teacher announces the game is over, counts the points, and announces the winning team. The team with the least number of points wins, with the reward being given accordingly.

There are variations for implementing the Good Behavior Game you might want to consider. One variation is the Good Being Good Game, where instead of adding a point when students are not following designated rules, points are added when designated rules *are* followed. Response Cost is another variation where students receive a specific number of points to start with and lose a point for rules not being followed. The group with the most points at the end of the designated time wins the game. You could also try playing the game with a mystery win condition, where students don't know which rule they are being evaluated on until the end of the game. Change the criterion to win across days and settings. P. Raymond Joslyn and Emily Groves (2023) find all variations to be effective at reducing disruptive behaviors.

Diversifying for All Learners

As a group contingency strategy, the Good Behavior Game is a strategy that can be adapted for all learners. Most often, this game is used in general education classrooms, but it has been found to be effective in an extended range of educational settings (Flower et al., 2014). How the Good Behavior Game is taught depends on the students' targeted needs. The important thing to remember is the students need to feel successful. If the idea of "winning" the game does not feel achievable, then the students will not want to participate.

When putting students in groups, think about how students are grouped and be careful not to let any implicit bias cause disproportionality in your groupings, leading one group to be more successful than another. For example, if you have three students in your classroom with challenging behaviors, they need to be in different groups and not all in the same group. When you have students who have disabilities or for whom English is not a primary language, we need to ensure not only that students are explicitly taught but also that they are placed in groups where they can receive support from peers. Again, groups need to be equitable so students can feel successful.

You might have some concerns about negative peer interactions when targeting students who struggle with challenging behaviors; however, Emily A. Groves and Jennifer L. Austin (2019) find that the Good Behavior Game reduces not only disruptive behaviors but also negative peer interactions while increasing positive peer interactions.

TOKEN ECONOMY

A token economy is a strategy used at Tier 1 and Tier 2. Students earning positive reinforcement through the system you have created using tickets or an app to earn rewards is considered a token economy and a Tier 1 implementation of the strategy. It becomes a Tier 2 strategy when it is specific to an individual student. Consider that for some students who struggle with their behavior, a typical positive reinforcement system is not enough. It may be too broad for them or not immediate enough. A token economy can be made to be more immediate, specific to the individual needs of a student.

A token economy is one of my favorite strategies to implement because I used it as a classroom teacher without even knowing what it was called. The school I worked at used a schoolwide system where everyone used paper tickets, and we had a school store. Some of us had a classroom store where students would exchange their tickets for different items that cost different amounts of tickets such as pencils or lunch with the teacher. This is considered a token economy at Tier 1, but we also used an individualized token economy for students at Tier 2. A Tier 1 token economy is for all students whereas a Tier 2 token economy is specific to an individual student.

Not only did I see firsthand how effective the system can be, but research also supports its effectiveness at reducing challenging behaviors (Ivy, Meindl, Overley, & Robson, 2017). Research also supports the use of a token economy strategy at all levels for increasing academic achievement because it promotes on-task behaviors, task completion, and classroom participation (Ackerman, Samudre, & Allday, 2020).

Using a Token Economy in Primary and Secondary Grades

A token economy system can easily be customized for any grade. For example, the reinforcements used will be different depending on the grade level being taught. An individualized system is specifically based on the needs of the student. The sheet being used and the rewards being earned are also individualized. It will be important to ensure the student's interests are being considered at all levels.

For the purpose of this chapter and specifically this section, I will share the most important aspects to consider for using this strategy at Tier 2. First, determine the components of the system. For example, you must determine the scale of the token economy system, the challenging behaviors being targeted, the type of token being used (literal tokens, tally marks, tickets, and so on), how the tokens will be exchanged, and when the tokens will be exchanged. The next aspect to consider is how to incorporate your student's interests into your implementation. It is also important to consider influences of cultural and linguistic diversity. The system will need to be explicitly taught to the student to ensure the student understands all expectations.

When explicitly teaching the system to the student, be sure to review reinforcement ideas. For the token economy system to work effectively, it is critical to have reinforcements the student wants to work for. Although intrinsic motivation is where we want the student to be, the student will respond better to purposeful extrinsic motivators aligned to the goals the student is working toward. For example, we want students to do the work because they want to get a good grade or because they are supposed to, which is considered intrinsic motivation. However, not all students will respond to this, and they will need extrinsic motivation, too, which involves earning something they like for work completion.

When thinking about a recording sheet, such as the example in figure 4.2, you need to think about your student. For example, a primary student may like stickers or smiley faces, but a secondary student may prefer check marks or a plus or minus sign. Another aspect to consider is what the sheet will look like. You need to find a happy medium in making sure students feel successful but also a little bit challenged. Some students can have one-hour time blocks or subject period time blocks. However, some students need the tallies to come sooner and may need them to be in thirty-minute increments. The recording sheet can be a physical sheet the student carries with them throughout the day on a clipboard or in a folder. An electronic sheet can also be created.

Name:

Date:

Time	Following Directions	Completing Work	Keeping Hands and Feet to Self
8:00–9:00 a.m.	+	+	−
9:00–10:00 a.m.	+	+	+
10:00–11:00 a.m.	−	−	+
11:00 a.m.–12:00 p.m.	+	+	+
12:00–1:00 p.m.	+	−	+
1:00–2:00 p.m.	+	+	+
2:00–3:00 p.m.	+	+	+

What went well today?

What will I work on tomorrow?

FIGURE 4.2: Example of a token economy sheet.

*Visit **go.SolutionTree.com/behavior** for a free reproducible version of this figure.*

At the end of the day, the student and teacher discuss how the day went. It is important to talk about what improvements can be made for the next day, with the focus on the good that happened. It will be predetermined if there needs to be a specific percentage (for example, 80 percent positives) to earn an incentive or if each positive mark results in a number to be cashed in based on a menu of options. The idea is for the student to feel successful, so rather than focusing on the age, it is important to focus on what works best for the student.

The following are the specific steps for implementing an individualized token economy.

1. Determine the components of the system including the scale of the token economy system, the challenging behaviors being targeted, the type of token being used, and how and when the exchange occurs.
2. Consider the student's interests and cultural and linguistic needs when creating the system.
3. Create a reinforcement plan and rewards for the student to earn.
4. Explicitly teach the student how to use the token economy system.
5. Continually monitor to determine if the system is effective at changing the behaviors.

Other teachers working with the student, the student, and the student's parents or guardians should be involved when you are creating the token economy to ensure everyone is on the same page and the student's needs are being met.

Let's look at an example.

> Zach is a seventh-grade student who has a difficult time staying on task, which results in him not getting his work done. He also talks to others around him. Although the teacher, Mr. Maxwell, has an effective classroom-management plan where rules, procedures, incentives, and consequences are implemented with consistency, Zach is still having a difficult time in class. Mr. Maxwell decides to talk with Zach's other teachers to see if Zach is having a hard time in his other classes.
>
> Mr. Maxwell learns Zach has challenging behaviors in all his classes, so Mr. Maxwell decides to create an individualized token economy sheet for Zach. Mr. Maxwell meets with Zach and his parents to talk about the plan to determine what behaviors to focus on and learn more about his interests and what reinforcements he would like to earn. All those working with Zach meet to finalize the plan, and Zach is taught how the plan will work.

Everyone understands Zach will check in with Mr. Maxwell in the morning to get his tracking sheet. They decide he will focus on following directions, staying focused on his work, and staying quiet when working. The group decides to create one-hour blocks of time and use pluses and minuses to track Zach's behavior. Each teacher agrees to complete the form with Zach at the end of each class. At the end of the day, Zach will return to Mr. Maxwell's class to talk about how the day went and cash in for a reward. Each "plus" equals one point. Zach helps create a list of items he wants to earn and how much each item will cost. The form will go home with Zach to review with his parents.

Everyone feels confident in the plan created and decides to implement the plan the following day. They agree to meet in two weeks to look at the data sheets to see if Zach's behaviors improve and to make changes as necessary.

Diversifying for All Learners

A token economy system is great when thinking about diversifying for all learners because the system is individualized. It is important to be culturally responsive. The student's preferred language should be used when thinking about things such as defining expected behaviors and item choices. Communicating with families is also important. If the student's family does not speak English, we need to ensure a translator is present to ensure the family understands. Communication, whether in person or electronic, needs to be in the family's primary language. It is also critical for teachers to be conscientious in understanding their own belief system and the impact those beliefs have on the feelings or behaviors of students. These beliefs can be connected to our students' culture or a disability, for example. There are also times when we may be harder on boys than girls. As educators, it is critical to consider our own thoughts when thinking about our response to students' behaviors.

SELF-MONITORING

Self-monitoring is a self-management strategy where students learn to track their behavior using self-evaluation and self-recording (Hallahan et al., 2023). It's similar to a token economy system, except instead of the teacher evaluating the student, the student learns to evaluate their own behaviors and then record if and when the behavior occurs. Students need to be aware of their behaviors and able to control them for self-monitoring to be effective. Some students will be able to use self-monitoring after being taught because they have self-awareness. However, other students may benefit from learning self-awareness through an individualized token economy system before using self-monitoring.

Research finds self-monitoring to be effective at improving social behaviors and academic achievement (Yell, Meadows, Drasgow, & Shriner, 2013). Allison Leigh Bruhn, Suzanne Woods-Groves, Josephine Fernando, Taehoon Choi, and Leonard Troughton (2017) also conducted a systematic review of the literature spanning 2000–2017 to determine the effectiveness of self-monitoring for students with challenging behaviors. Bruhn and colleagues (2017) found forty-one different studies where self-monitoring resulted in improved behaviors and academic achievement, with specific gains in limiting off-task behavior, negative social interaction, and classroom disruption, while increasing positive social interactions, on-task behavior, and work completion. They also learned reinforcement is an essential component of self-monitoring.

Let's look at how it works.

Implementing Self-Monitoring in Primary and Secondary Grades

Self-monitoring is individualized, making it easily adaptable for students of any age in both general education and special education (Yell et al., 2013). Self-monitoring is based on specific behaviors of an individual student and will be different for each student. As stated, the student has to be aware of their behaviors in order for self-monitoring to work. Examples may include making bodily noises, not following directions, constantly requesting a drink or to use the restroom, not completing in-class assignments in a specific period of time, or not submitting homework assignments.

The first step in implementing self-monitoring is to create a goal. The goal is based on what behavior the student will demonstrate instead of the challenging behavior (Zolkoski et al., 2023). For example, a student who is not getting their work done will have a goal to submit their work on time. The goal should be person centered: "I will submit my work on time." Other examples can include "I will stay in my seat when doing independent work" or "I will raise my hand to ask for help." As the teacher, it is important to be supportive when meeting with the student to discuss the goals being created.

The next step involves developing a rating scale. The rating scale is age appropriate and is designed to help the student keep track of their behaviors (Zolkoski et al., 2023). No matter the student's age, the scale should be easy to complete and be in person-first language (for example, "I will listen when others are talking"). When deciding on the rating scale, the student and teacher need to determine how often the scale is reviewed.

A student in a primary grade may prefer a rating scale that includes smiley faces, and a student in a secondary grade may prefer a numbered rating scale. With that being said, it is important to not make generalizations, asking students what they prefer. Following are two examples of rating scales students can use.

- Emoji scale:
    + ☺ = "I did great!"
    + 😐 = "I did OK."
    + ☹ = "I didn't do very well."
- Number scale:
    + 2 = "I did great!"
    + 1 = "I did OK."
    + 0 = "I didn't do well making progress toward my goal."

The next step is to explicitly teach the student how to monitor their behavior and record their rating of their behavior on their sheet. The student should know exactly what the behavior is and how to perform the behavior (Zolkoski et al., 2023). Modeling should be a part of the teaching process. Examples and nonexamples should also be discussed. Part of the scoring procedure is the student's score and the teacher's score matching. The scoring can be based on only the student's rating, or the scoring sheet can have a space for the teacher to include a rating. If the form includes only the student's rating, the teacher can have their own form. When the scoring occurs and there is a disagreement on the rating, the student and teacher work together to come up with a mutually agreed-on score. To truly change a student's behaviors, it is important to have teachable discussions where the student and teacher are working together so the student can learn. Figure 4.3 is an example of a student-only rating, and figure 4.4 (page 122) is an example of a rating scale that includes a space for the teacher.

Name:				
Date:				
Goal	**Mathematics**	**Language Arts**	**Science**	**History**
I will follow the teacher's directions.	0 1 2	0 1 2	0 1 2	0 1 2
I will raise my hand if I have a question.	0 1 2	0 1 2	0 1 2	0 1 2
I will begin my work when it is given to me.	0 1 2	0 1 2	0 1 2	0 1 2

FIGURE 4.3: Example of a student-only self-monitoring sheet.

*Visit **go.SolutionTree.com/behavior** for a free reproducible version of this figure.*

Name:				
Date:				
Goal	**Mathematics**	**Language Arts**	**Science**	**History**
I will follow the teacher's directions.	Student Rating: 0 1 2 Teacher Rating: 0 1 2	Student Rating: 0 1 2 Teacher Rating: 0 1 2	Student Rating: 0 1 2 Teacher Rating: 0 1 2	Student Rating: 0 1 2 Teacher Rating: 0 1 2
I will raise my hand if I have a question.	Student Rating: 0 1 2 Teacher Rating: 0 1 2	Student Rating: 0 1 2 Teacher Rating: 0 1 2	Student Rating: 0 1 2 Teacher Rating: 0 1 2	Student Rating: 0 1 2 Teacher Rating: 0 1 2
I will begin my work when it is given to me.	Student Rating: 0 1 2 Teacher Rating: 0 1 2	Student Rating: 0 1 2 Teacher Rating: 0 1 2	Student Rating: 0 1 2 Teacher Rating: 0 1 2	Student Rating: 0 1 2 Teacher Rating: 0 1 2

FIGURE 4.4: Example of a student self-monitoring sheet with teacher ratings included.

Visit **go.SolutionTree.com/behavior** *for a free reproducible version of this figure.*

The next important step to remember is how the student will be reinforced for using the self-monitoring strategy. Research shows a significant influence on the effectiveness of self-monitoring when reinforcement is included (Davis et al., 2014). Students' motivation in the classroom is enhanced with the use of reinforcement. There is even more power in the effectiveness of the reinforcement when students choose their reinforcement. Reinforcements can be set up in a few ways, of course always while considering the needs of the student: when the student first attempts to use the self-monitoring checklist, when the student meets a predetermined goal, or when the student and teacher ratings match (Zolkoski et al., 2023). Students' interests need to be considered when creating a reinforcement sheet. Cultural and linguistic diversity also needs to be considered. We will talk more about considering the diversity of all learners in the next section.

Diversifying for All Learners

Because self-monitoring is individualized, it is inherently easy to be diversified for all learners. Although the teacher is involved in the whole process, the student is a part of all aspects of creating and implementing self-monitoring. What is great about self-monitoring is the fact the student has ownership over the strategy. It also allows the teacher to better understand how the student perceives their own abilities (Zolkoski et al., 2023).

When designing the self-monitoring checklist, the student should be a key contributor in knowing their own strengths, preferences, culture, language preference, and other unique characteristics (Zolkoski et al., 2023). Some students may want specific images of their favorite things (for example, character or sports person) while other students will want the checklist to be simple with nothing on it. There are also app-based checklists (for example, I-Connect or SCORE IT) that can be used for students who prefer technology over a paper form (Bruhn et al., 2017). The use of an app has been found to be successful at improving on-task behavior for students with ADHD or who have other learning disabilities (Wills & Mason, 2014). Communication throughout the process is essential when creating the student's self-monitoring checklist. It is also important to understand where and how the student wants their form to be located. For example, some students may not want others to know they have it while others may want to keep it on a clipboard or folder in their desk or backpack. The student will monitor their behavior throughout the day, but when, where, and how it is completed will depend on the student's preferences.

In the previous sections, you have been given some evidence-based strategies to support students with challenging behaviors. With consistency at Tier 1 and then at Tier 2, most students will be captured; however, there may be a student who needs even more support. These students will move to Tier 3.

Supports for Students at Tier 3

As you work with your students using strategies at the Tier 2 level, you will find most of them (possibly all of them) show decreasing need for continued support at this level. However, you may find that there are still a small number who continue to display challenging behavior beyond what you can accept in a well-functioning classroom. At Tier 3, it's time for more formal steps that include putting together a functional behavior assessment and supporting behavior intervention plan (BIP).

Let's take a look at each of these in turn.

FUNCTIONAL BEHAVIOR ASSESSMENT

Although we are always trying to understand why a student engages in challenging or disruptive behavior, when Tier 1 and Tier 2 efforts fail to achieve the outcomes necessary to address that need, a formal, purposeful, and individualized FBA can truly help us get to the core of the issue (Center on PBIS, n.d.b).

An FBA is designed to help a team of educators learn how to best support an individual student's needs (Center on PBIS, n.d.a). As a general education teacher or even a special education teacher, you are not solely responsible for completing an FBA; however, you are a part of the process. The team will differ depending on the student's needs. Additionally, not all school districts operate the same. A special education teacher or coordinator, a counselor or behavior specialist, an administrator, all teachers working with the student, the student, and the student's caregivers might all be part of the team (IRIS Center, 2025).

Although you, as the teacher, are likely not leading this team's efforts, I believe it is important for all teachers to understand how an FBA should be completed so you can ensure students' needs are getting met. There are entire books written about the FBA process, so think of this section as merely an introduction to the idea (for example, Cipani, 2018; O'Neill, Albin, Storey, Horner, & Sprague, 2015; Steege, Pratt, Wickerd, Guare, & Watson, 2019).

When completing an FBA, the team involved determines not only why behaviors continue to occur but what untried interventions are most likely to break the cycle and support the student's success. An FBA is explicit in identifying the *why* of a student's behavior to best replace negative behaviors with positive behaviors.

The steps of an FBA include the following.

1. Identify and define the target behaviors and replacement behavior.
2. Collect indirect data.
3. Create an initial hypothesis statement based on indirect data collected.
4. Collect direct data.
5. Formalize the hypothesis based on the direct data collected.

In this framework, the antecedent is what happens right before the behavior occurs, and the consequences are what happens directly after the target behavior (the challenging behavior to be changed). The replacement behavior is what we want the student to do instead of the challenging behavior.

It is important to be objective rather than subjective when behaviors are defined. For example, stating a student is aggressive is subjective. What does aggressive look like? Does the student hit or kick? Does the student say swear words? If so, what are the swear words? Avoid highly subjective (and deficit-based) labels like *lazy*. We all have different ideas of what "lazy" looks like, and it puts judgment on the student rather than a focus on the behavior. However, if we are specific in saying the student puts their head down and does not do their work, anyone on the team could observe the classroom and monitor each time the behavior occurs, coming away with the same observations.

Once the behaviors are objectively defined, indirect data collection begins. Typically, the behavior specialist is the person collecting indirect data, which is based on asking the opinion of others working with the student. The behavior specialist will have those educators working with the student fill out a questionnaire, complete a survey, or participate in an interview. This happens without the specialist directly observing the student. The student and their caregivers should also be interviewed when possible.

The behavior specialist takes all the indirect data and formulates a hypothesis, or a prediction for what is causing the behaviors to occur. The hypothesis statement includes the setting, events, antecedents, behavior, and consequences (IRIS Center, 2025). The function of a student's behavior can be to avoid, delay, or escape or to gain or access something.

After forming the initial hypothesis, it is important to directly observe the behaviors to determine if the hypothesis statement matches the actual behaviors being observed by the behavior specialist. Direct observation means exactly what it sounds like: a person is directly observing behaviors that are happening. The person can be a teacher, an administrator, or a behavior specialist. There are recording sheets that can be used including an interval recording, an event recording, a scatterplot, or an ABC Observation. Direct observations should include all types of observations over multiple days in all classes the student is in.

An interval recording involves breaking a specific period of time into intervals divided into small blocks of time (one minute, five minutes, ten minutes, and so on). If the defined behavior occurs in the block of time, a plus is added, but if the defined behavior does not occur, a minus is added. It's an easy-to-use format; however, although it tells you if a behavior occurs within a specific period of time, it does not tell you how many times the behavior occurs. Figure 4.5 is an example of an interval recording sheet.

Interval Recording Sheet
Student:
Date:
Observer:
Length of Interval:
Class/Teacher:
Start/Stop Times:
Target Behavior Defined:
Behavior Occurs: +
Behavior Does Not Occur: −

FIGURE 4.5: Example of an interval recording sheet.

continued ▶

Interval	Behavior
10	Example: +
20	+
30	–
40	

*Visit **go.SolutionTree.com/behavior** for a free reproducible version of this figure.*

An event recording, which is also easy to use, involves making a tally each time a behavior occurs so that a track record of the behavior's frequency within a specified period of time is established. Figure 4.6 is an example of an event recording sheet.

Event Recording Sheet	
Student:	
Date:	
Observer:	
Start/Stop Times:	
Class/Teacher:	
Target Behavior Defined:	
Add a tally mark each time the defined behavior occurs.	

Time	Tally	Total
Example: 8:00–8:20 a.m.	///////	7

FIGURE 4.6: Example of an event recording sheet.

*Visit **go.SolutionTree.com/behavior** for a free reproducible version of this figure.*

A scatterplot is like an event recording, but it shows an entire week at a time. A scatterplot can show you if there is a specific time of day or day of the week where the behavior is most likely to occur. Figure 4.7 is an example of a scatterplot recording sheet.

Scatterplot Recording Sheet

Student:

Date:

Observer:

Target Behavior Defined:

Activity	Start and Stop Time	Monday	Tuesday	Wednesday	Thursday	Friday	Total
Reading/Language Arts							
Mathematics							
Science							
Social Studies							
Recess							
Lunch							
Specials Music: Monday Physical Education: Tuesday/Wednesday/Friday Art: Thursday							

FIGURE 4.7: Example of a scatterplot recording sheet.

Visit go.SolutionTree.com/behavior for a free reproducible version of this figure.

The final example of a direct observation sheet is an ABC Observation. This is where the antecedent, behavior, and consequences are recorded. An ABC Observation is not easy to complete and cannot be done without proper training. What is beneficial about this type of data collection is that it provides a clear picture of what is happening. Rather than only looking at the behavior, the behavior specialist is seeing what is happening before the behavior and after the behavior. Figure 4.8 is an example of an ABC Observation sheet.

ABC Observation Sheet		
Student:		
Date:		
Observer:		
Time of Observation:		
Subject and Teacher:		
Antecedent	**Behavior**	**Consequence**
Example: Bell rings.	Student walks in room.	Teacher says, "Why are you late? Go sit down!"

FIGURE 4.8: Example of an ABC Observation recording sheet.

Visit **go.SolutionTree.com/behavior** *for a free reproducible version of this figure.*

After direct data are collected, the hypothesis statement is finalized. The final hypothesis statement will explain the function of the student's behaviors and replacement behaviors (IRIS Center, 2022). The final hypothesis statement helps ensure all interventions are logical and based on the final summary statement. It serves as the backbone for what comes next: the individualized BIP.

BEHAVIOR INTERVENTION PLAN

A BIP is designed based on the information learned from the FBA and includes strategies to prevent problem behaviors from occurring (Center on PBIS, n.d.b). The problem behaviors are prevented by addressing triggering antecedents, teaching replacement behaviors, and reinforcing the replacement behavior. As a teacher, it is important to understand the process even though you will not specifically oversee writing a BIP. The student's team, as detailed in the preceding section, creates a plan based on four FBA-based interventions (Center on PBIS, n.d.b).

1. Establish an intervention or support that directly changes the antecedent so it no longer triggers the problem behavior. The intervention is intended to prevent the problem behavior from occurring.

2. Determine the intervention or support that will directly teach replacement behaviors. Replacement behaviors are designed to serve the same function as the target behavior. For example, a student may get up from their seat and walk around the room rather than completing an academic task. The student can be taught to ask for a break or learn to sustain their attention through an assignment or activity until they can earn a short break.

3. Decide on an intervention or support that reinforces the replacement behavior. Often, the reinforcement can become more powerful, such as the student who is off task learning to stay on task for longer periods of time without needing to take a break. When the student stays on task for longer periods of time, the student can earn a longer break from the nonpreferred academic task (for example, rather than five minutes, the student can earn ten minutes).

4. Determine an intervention or support that prevents the target behavior from being reinforced. A student generally resorts to a challenging (target) behavior out of habit. It "serves" them in some way. So, the BIP is successful when the student's target behavior no longer serves the student. A plan should be created for redirecting the student to use the new replacement behaviors. The student's teachers can redirect the student when the first signs of off-task behavior occur and remind them to ask for a break.

Once the steps are followed, it is also important to decide on when, where, how, and by whom the BIP will be implemented. A contingency plan should be created in case of an emergency such as the student's behavior becoming more extreme than before. Data should be collected to determine the effectiveness of the plan. Steps for how progress is monitored and who is monitoring the student also need to be established. A fidelity checklist can help ensure the BIP is implemented in the way it was designed (Yell et al., 2013). The team will need to meet to determine the effectiveness of the BIP and determine if changes need to be made. See figure 4.9 (page 130) for an example of a checklist. This final step is an important one to complete to ensure the BIP is truly working the way it is intended. Our ultimate goal is to ensure all students' needs are being met and each student is successful.

Name:											
Grade/Classroom:											
Observer Name:											
Observer Date:											
Observation Start/End Time:											

Scoring: NO = not observed; 0 = not completed/error; 1 = minimally completed; 2 = mostly completed; 3 = fully completed
Student Response: 0 = negative response; 1 = no response; 2 = some positive response; 3 = mostly positive response; 4 = positive response

Intervention: Name each strategy being used when answering the following questions.	Adherence Score					Student Responsiveness					
Teacher implemented intervention as stated in BIP?	NO	0	1	2	3	0	1	2	3	4	
Teacher implemented antecedent strategies as stated in BIP?	NO	0	1	2	3	0	1	2	3	4	
Teacher implemented intervention during time stated in BIP?	NO	0	1	2	3	0	1	2	3	4	
Student was provided necessary prompts as outlined in BIP?	NO	0	1	2	3	0	1	2	3	4	
Student was provided opportunities to use replacement behavior?	NO	0	1	2	3	0	1	2	3	4	
Teacher delivers reinforcement as specified in BIP?	NO	0	1	2	3	0	1	2	3	4	
Reinforcement is provided based on BIP?	NO	0	1	2	3	0	1	2	3	4	

Source: Adapted from Florida's Positive Behavioral Interventions & Support Project, 2023.

FIGURE 4.9: Example of a fidelity checklist.

Concluding Thoughts

The intention of this chapter is to provide teachers with strategies to support students who need extra support with their behavior. It is important to know how to help students with challenging behaviors. There are simple things you learned from reading this chapter that can make a big difference for students. You have officially seen the whole multitiered process from beginning to end. Understanding the importance of establishing an effective classroom-management plan, knowing how to positively support students who need a little extra (just like we do when support involves academics), and having an idea of the FBA and BIP process is essential. Knowing the whole process can help you advocate for students with challenging behaviors, which ultimately helps them be successful in your classroom and beyond. You can be a protective factor for students with challenging behaviors. They will often be your hardest students, but the reward for their success is so much sweeter. Nothing is better than knowing you had a positive impact on the lives of your students—especially the students who needed you the most. Now, consider the following reproducible tool, "Reflective Thinking About Bias" (also available online at **go.SolutionTree.com/behavior**), as you confront your own biases to better support students.

Reflective Thinking About Bias

I invite you to reflect on the following questions to consider your own prejudices as you work to grow and critically think about how you can best support your students.

What assumptions do you have about people who are different than you? Please consider things like race, gender, religion, socioeconomic status, and so on.

How have the assumptions shaped your decisions? Specifically, have your assumptions influenced relationships with coworkers, students and their family members, or work choices?

Think about a time someone called you out by making an assumption or stereotype about you. How did it make you feel? How did you respond?

How have your biases limited your understanding of other individuals' perspectives or experiences?

What are some ways you can create a space for others to share their experiences?

How do you feel you will know if or when you've made progress on reducing your biases?

Learning, Behavior, and Your Classroom © 2025 Solution Tree Press • SolutionTree.com
Visit **go.SolutionTree.com/behavior** to download this free reproducible.

Voices From the Field

What do students who struggle with behavior need to be successful?

"Detention and suspension doesn't teach anyone anything."

—*A tenth-grade student*

"I decided to work when I realized my teacher cared about me."

—*An eleventh-grade student*

"I noticed my students who struggle with their behavior need more immediate rewards. They can't wait until the end of the six weeks. When I started being more purposeful with my students, they started doing better."

—*An elementary school teacher*

"My students like to earn things just like anyone. They are better at completing their work when they know they can earn something at the end."

—*A high school teacher*

"I like my chart [individual token economy] because it keeps me on track and helps me focus."

—*A fourth-grade student*

"When we focus on what students are doing right, we see more students making better choices."

—*A middle school principal*

"I love when my teacher gives me choices. It's better than being told what to do all the time."

—*A sixth-grade student*

CHAPTER 5

Promote Student Independence and Learning

Throughout this book, we have learned about the *why* of behavior, how to best build a positive environment and why it's important, and how to effectively establish classroom expectations and provide additional support to students who need it. In this chapter, we talk about how to promote student independence and learning.

Establishing and reinforcing classroom expectations is critical in managing your classroom. Once we have established the expectations, we need to think about how our *lessons* can truly support learning for *all* students. This chapter defines specific strategies you can implement when considering instruction that ensures you are meeting your students' needs in their growing independence. The chapter begins with a discussion of strategies for implementing best teaching practices to meet *all* students' needs. We talk about the learning process and then look at strategies for utilizing Bloom's taxonomy (Anderson & Krathwohl, 2001). Two ways to truly meet the needs of all learners is through differentiated instruction and UDL (CAST, n.d.e). Each section goes into detail on how exactly to differentiate instruction and utilize UDL. The chapter ends with a Concluding Thoughts section and a reproducible in which I ask you to reflect on your teaching.

Strategies for Implementing Best Practices for Teaching Academics

We think about teachers as the individuals responsible for giving students the material they need to learn. We may think this means standing in front of the classroom and teaching the material. Yes, as the teacher, we are responsible for providing instruction, but I want you to think about the role of a teacher as more of a facilitator. Ideally, we provide the information in a way that helps students become active and independent learners. We are there to support our students' learning. You can support this independence even when, initially, you must focus on your national, state, or district standards, which are the basis for everything you do. From these standards, there are a series of actions you take in order to plan your instruction. First, we'll look at assessing how to tackle teaching to these standards.

- Determine what your standards are by referring to your state guidelines or standards.
- Determine how your standards break down into specific objectives.
- Determine how to assess students' knowledge of the objectives, building back up to the broader standards.
- Determine the content of your lessons, including all instruction and activities.

In simple terms, and as illustrated in figure 5.1, your lesson content, assessments, objectives, and standards all need to be in alignment. When they are, you know that what you are teaching is based on the required standards being assessed.

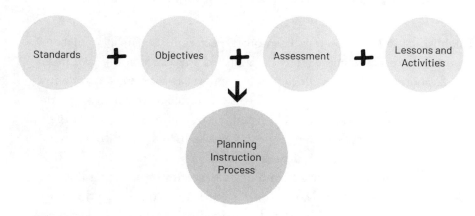

FIGURE 5.1: Planning instruction process.

The value in having a dedicated process for planning instruction is evident in that it becomes the road map to teaching and learning. Teachers have access to seemingly infinite resources for great individual lessons and activities on- and offline. Even sites like Instagram, TikTok, Pinterest, and Facebook can be valuable resources in this regard. But while lessons you encounter may be fun and engaging, the key question we must ask ourselves is, "Does this lesson match the assessment used to see if my students have mastered the standards?" If the answer is yes, then great! Implement it. If the answer is no, then you need to either find something else you can do or figure out how to make adjustments to the lesson you found that align it with your standards, objective, and assessments.

When we understand how we need to plan for our lessons, we next need to understand the learning process. We know teachers play a critical role in the learning process of students and that it's most effective when students are involved mentally, physically, and socially (Premana, Widiana, & Wibawa, 2023).

Ken Masters (2013) discusses the *Pyramid of Learning*, created by Edgar Dale, which demonstrates the importance of the student learning process by helping us determine the best mode for learning. It breaks down student retention of learning from low to high based on increasingly active learning activities in which students are active participants rather than passive activities in which they simply receive information.

- **Passive teaching methods:**
    + *Lecture*—5 percent retention
    + *Reading*—10 percent retention
    + *Audio and visual content*—20 percent retention
    + *Demonstration (modeling)*—30 percent retention
- **Participatory teaching methods:**
    + *Discussion group*—50 percent retention
    + *Practice by doing*—75 percent retention
    + *Teach others*—90 percent retention

Notice that lecture-based teaching methods actually provide the lowest rate of retention for students. Lecture, reading, video and audio, and demonstration are important tools to use, but they remain passive ways for students to learn. Inevitably, students are less excited about such learning because such lessons are entirely teacher centered. While we know that direct instruction has a valuable role in establishing student understanding about content (Simms, 2025), we want our students to retain as much information as possible, which means we also need to provide more participatory teaching methods where the students are actively involved in their learning.

When planning lectures, rather than focusing entirely on direct instruction the whole time, consider supplementing that instruction with activities where students interact with one another. For example, you are doing a whole-group introduction to a topic, but during the lecture, you stop and have students turn and talk to each other about the topic.

Another strategy to include during whole-group instruction is having students show what they know by answering questions you ask during the lesson. There are many ways for students to respond during your lesson. For example, students can write on whiteboards, say answers out loud in unison, engage in a four-square activity (move to corners of the room based on answer response), convey their understanding through a thumbs-up or thumbs-down, or rank their understanding from zero to five by holding up a fist or up to five fingers. In this example, you are lecturing, but students are also actively involved in what you are teaching.

In the strategies that follow—covering Bloom's taxonomy, differentiation, and UDL—we continue to tailor our approach to grade level, no matter the time of year, and are all about meeting all students' diverse needs. Best practices for teaching, no matter the grade, are based on student-centered lessons where we work to ensure all students are getting the information they need in an appropriate way.

BLOOM'S TAXONOMY

According to Dewa Nyoman Dede Premana and colleagues (2023), to improve student outcomes and achieve predetermined learning objectives, we need to improve the learning process we use in the classroom. One solution to best facilitate the delivery of knowledge to students is to develop activities that attract students' interests. Bloom's revised taxonomy (Anderson & Krathwohl, 2001) is a way to systematically support students' learning based on their state of cognitive development and can make it easier for students to learn, making the learning process more meaningful.

According to Northern Illinois University Center for Innovative Teaching and Learning (2020), Benjamin Bloom and other educators looked for ways to classify educational objectives, resulting in three learning domains.

1. The **cognitive domain** is based on knowledge and includes intellectual abilities both verbally and visually.
2. The **affective domain** is based on attitudes and includes values, beliefs, and feelings.
3. The **psychomotor domain** is based on skills and includes physical skill abilities.

Each of these domains requires students to use different sets of mental processing to achieve learning outcomes. The student learning process must be based on the learning objectives, and that process should be based on supporting the domains in which students process information.

Questioning students while we teach is a critical element of effective teaching because questions can be used to both teach and assess student understanding (Nappi, 2017). Judith S. Nappi (2017) believes questioning supports the development of critical thinking skills and should be embedded in instruction to support student success in the classroom. We need to remember the importance of purposefully designed questions where students make connections not only to their prior learning but also to the world around them. Students need to learn how to think critically and process new situations effectively. We can help our students with this by asking high-level-thinking questions. It is much easier to produce lower-level questions where we ask students to gather and recall information. However, lower-level questioning does not encourage students to engage in higher-level thinking.

Bloom and his colleagues created a framework with different levels of questioning teachers can use when developing questions for their students (Nappi, 2017). This framework provides a structured scaffold for asking questions where they become more challenging and allow for complex thinking. Teachers model more complex thinking and can guide students in becoming independent thinkers.

The original Bloom's taxonomy (Bloom, 1956) includes the following levels.

- **Knowledge:** Involves recalling information
- **Comprehension:** Involves understanding and remembering information given in written or verbal form
- **Application:** Involves applying what has been learned
- **Analysis:** Involves understanding the concepts of what has been learned; extends beyond knowledge and comprehension of information
- **Synthesis:** Involves creating something new from what has been learned
- **Evaluation:** Involves making judgments based on a deep understanding of information

This original framework was revised by Lorin Anderson and David Krathwohl (2001) to better fit outcome-based educational objectives. This revision renamed the two highest levels of the taxonomy from *synthesis* and *evaluation* to *evaluating* and *creating*. The revised taxonomy changed the nouns to verbs, as follows (Anderson & Krathwohl, 2001).

- **Remembering:** Involves recalling or recognizing information from memory; memory is used to recall definitions, facts, or lists. It can also

be used to recount information learned previously. Verbs to recall facts include *define*, *label*, *locate*, *list*, *memorize*, *name*, *record*, *state*, and *repeat*.
- **Understanding:** Involves comprehending information and grasping the meaning of various types of functions (written or graphic); verbs to comprehend information include *describe*, *explain*, *compare*, *contrast*, *observe*, *summarize*, *add*, *give*, and *predict*.
- **Applying:** Includes using information to solve problems by applying rules, concepts, or ideas; verbs to show using information to solve problems include *assign*, *construct*, *adapt*, *illustrate*, *express*, *modify*, *operate*, *sketch*, and *calculate*.
- **Analyzing:** Involves breaking information into parts to understand the relationship between them; verbs to show analysis of information include *compare*, *connect*, *analyze*, *differentiate*, *categorize*, *prioritize*, *diagram*, *estimate*, and *question*.
- **Evaluating:** Involves making judgments about the quality of information through critiquing or checking; peer evaluations or self-evaluations are examples of this level. Verbs to show evaluating information include *argue*, *measure*, *support*, *reframe*, *persuade*, *justify*, *appraise*, *critique*, and *convince*.
- **Creating:** Involves taking information to create something new; an example of this level includes project-based learning. Verbs to show creating include *negotiate*, *speculate*, *simulate*, *hypothesize*, *create*, *facilitate*, *adapt*, *role-play*, and *assemble*.

Let's look at how you can make effective use of these levels in your teaching.

Using Bloom's Taxonomy in Primary and Secondary Grades

Learning activities based on Bloom's taxonomy can generate curiosity and self-confidence while also improving students' ability to problem solve (Premana et al., 2023). The taxonomy in itself is based on the grade level and content area being taught. Student learning objectives are based on students' grade level. Questioning must therefore match the grade level and content area. The most important aspect of questioning is ensuring you have a wide variety of questions from all levels of Bloom's taxonomy. Activities and assessments, no matter the grade being taught, should move from basic skills to complex learning.

When lesson planning, first use the verbs from Bloom's taxonomy to create student learning objectives. Divide the categories into three sections: remembering and understanding, applying and analyzing, and evaluating and creating. It is helpful to create activities and questions for each learning level when planning to be best prepared to teach the lesson.

Table 5.1 includes each level of Bloom's taxonomy and examples of questions for each thinking level. Questions you create are based on and adapted to best fit the content and grade level you teach.

TABLE 5.1: Examples of Bloom's Taxonomy Questions

Level of Bloom's Taxonomy	Verbs	Questions
Remembering	Choose, define, recall, tell, label, name, match	What is . . . ? Where is . . . ? How is . . . ? Can you recall . . . ? Why did _____ happen?
Understanding	Explain, interpret, infer, illustrate, summarize, classify, compare, contrast, show, demonstrate	How would you summarize . . . ? How would you compare . . . ? What is the main idea of . . . ? What facts show . . . ? What is the best answer . . . ?
Applying	Apply, choose, develop, plan, organize, model, interview, select, solve, build	What examples can you find that . . . ? What approach would you use to . . . ? What facts would you select to show . . . ? What would the result be if . . . ? What other way would you plan to . . . ?
Analyzing	Analyze, classify, simplify, categorize, survey, divide, examine, conclude, assume, dissect	Why do you think . . . ? What inference can you make . . . ? Can you distinguish between . . . ? What ideas justify . . . ? What is the relationship between . . . ?
Evaluating	Agree, defend, determine, support, decide, influence, estimate, dispute, perceive, criticize	How would you justify . . . ? Why was it better that . . . ? What choice would you have made . . . ? What would you recommend . . . ? Can you assess the importance of . . . ?
Creating	Build, adapt, improve, propose, elaborate, create, solve, design, formulate	What would happen if . . . ? Can you invent . . . ? What way would you design . . . ? What facts can you compile . . . ? What if you could . . . ? What would you do if . . . ?

Source: Edupress, 2017.

Diversifying for All Learners

Bloom's taxonomy serves as a valuable tool for teachers to support students through multiple levels of questioning, all based on student readiness. For example, students learning English need access to grade-level content to help them become fully proficient in English and support their academic achievement (August, 2018). This same need for access to grade-level content is true of any other students you have who have exceptionalities. Although higher-level-thinking questions and activities are great, only using higher-level questioning and discussion does not support students' learning in an effective way.

As such, activities may need to be scaffolded to best support all needs. Bloom's taxonomy offers a framework for scaffolding instruction for students, considering both cognitive abilities and language proficiency levels. Scaffolding involves breaking up student learning into chunks and providing a tool or structure to support the student at each chunk (Alber, 2014). Scaffolding can include providing a sentence and question starters (Ferlazzo & Sypnieski, 2018) to support students during classroom discussions and activities. Visuals, gestures, and real-life examples also help students. Visual aids include graphic organizers, pictures, and charts. Preteaching vocabulary is another valuable strategy to support students with exceptionalities and students learning English. For example, you might provide students with pictures or other familiar and interesting contexts to introduce new words (Alber, 2014).

When asking questions, it is important to speak clearly and provide wait time for students to allow time to process information. While all learners need time to process information, especially when it's new, it is important to remember multilingual learners, in particular, are processing and thinking in two or more languages (Ferlazzo & Sypnieski, 2018). Wait time should be between three and five seconds. Allowing students time to preview text ahead of time is another strategy to support students. Peer-to-peer learning opportunities where students interact by speaking, listening, reading, and writing with peers support instruction and challenge students to engage at higher levels of proficiency (August, 2018).

The levels of Bloom's taxonomy help educators create meaningful and engaging learning experiences to simultaneously promote critical thinking skills and language development. When thinking of activities to utilize in the classroom, while considering the different levels of Bloom's taxonomy, using the various strategies discussed in this chapter truly provides the best supports for students.

DIFFERENTIATION

Classrooms are filled with students who are on different levels of instruction. When we think about the learners who come into our room, we do not have a classroom full of students who are on track to meet grade-level standards by the end of the school year; rather, we have some students who are extremely academically behind, some students who are somewhat academically behind, some students who are academically on track, some students who are academically ahead of their peers, and some who are academically far ahead of their peers. As an educator, the fact that we are responsible to ensure all students' academic needs are met can feel extremely overwhelming. How do we possibly ensure all students' needs are met when there are so many needs and so many are far behind academically?

Differentiation is a teaching approach for teachers to use as a starting point to meet all the diverse learning needs of students in the classroom (Tomlinson, 2014). Differentiated instruction is not a specific strategy; rather, it is a framework teachers use to implement a variety of instructional strategies and scaffolds such as utilizing effective classroom-management techniques, grouping students for instruction, assessing readiness of students, and teaching to students' proximal development zone (IRIS Center, 2022). Meeting a student at their current level of understanding means teaching to their zone of proximal development (Vygotsky, 1978).

The great thing about differentiating instruction is the fact differentiating supports English learners, learners with exceptionalities, and even students who are gifted. As we walk through this section, you will see how you are able to meet *all* your students' needs by effectively differentiating your instruction. Although the other chapters of the book have a specific section for diversifying for all learners, here we focus on diversifying throughout and more particularly on the content, process, and product of implementation rather than the grade level.

Much like Bloom's taxonomy, differentiated instruction can be used at any grade level and is truly designed to support all learners. According to the IRIS Center (2022), some evidence-based strategies for supporting students' needs through differentiation include providing a variety of instructional approaches, changing the design of assignments to suit student needs and goals, providing ongoing assessment to determine student readiness, adjusting instruction based on assessment results, providing various options for how students learn and demonstrate learning, working to make lessons both meaningful and engaging, and employing different grouping formats for instruction (small group, whole group, and independent learning).

In table 5.2 (page 142), you see the difference between a traditional classroom and a classroom where the teacher utilizes differentiated instruction.

TABLE 5.2: A Traditional Classroom Versus a Differentiated Classroom

Traditional Classroom Instruction	Differentiated Classroom Instruction
Instruction is teacher centered.	Instruction is student centered.
There is one learning format that is generally whole group.	There are a variety of formats for learning (whole group, small group, and independent).
When grouping occurs, it is based on achievement level (high, medium, or low).	Flexible grouping is based on students' learning needs and interests.
Instruction is generally provided in one way—lecture.	Instruction is provided in several ways (hands-on learning activities, modeling, lecture, and so on).
Instruction is aligned with grade-level standards.	Content is based on grade-level standards, but instructional tasks are designed to support students' needs.
Information is presented based on a single textbook.	Information is presented using a variety of sources (computer-based resources, textbooks from more than one grade level, and so on).
All students have the same assignments.	Students have a voice in how they complete the assignments they do.
Summative assessment is used to determine what students have learned.	Formative assessment as well as summative assessment is used throughout to guide instruction.
Learning is assessed at the end of a unit and typically involves a written test.	Students may be given a written test at the end of a unit; however, students also have several options for demonstrating their learning (video, models, reports, and so on).
Fair means all students work on the same tasks.	*Fair* means students work on a task to meet their needs. It may be the same task or different from the task assigned to their peers so long as it achieves learning of the grade-level objectives and standards.
Success is based on grades and mastery of course material.	Success is based on the academic growth of an individual student through the acquisition of grade-level objectives and standards.

There can be a misconception that teachers must individually tailor instruction to every student. How else will you meet all the needs of the students in your classroom? However, when differentiating instruction, you are differentiating for groups of students rather than each individual student (IRIS Center, 2022). What is challenging is that students' needs vary across content areas, within content areas (a student may be proficient with addition but struggle with division), and across the school year. Ongoing assessment and flexible grouping are two important strategies to support differentiated instruction.

First, let's examine more closely what the most common forms of assessment look like through the lens of differentiation.

- **Preassessment:** Use this assessment to determine students' interests and understanding of the content that is about to be taught. This initial assessment can help the teacher assign student groups. A preassessment may include a unit pretest, teacher observation, or a KWL (what I *know*, what I *want* to know, what I *learned*) chart.
- **Formative assessment:** This assessment form occurs throughout the lesson or unit and is used to determine whether students understand the material. Formative assessment should be used to help design meaningful lessons and help the teacher assign students to different groups. Work samples, small-group and whole-group discussions, exit tickets, and answering questions on a dry-erase board are examples of formative assessment.
- **Summative assessment:** This form of assessment occurs at the end of a lesson or unit. A summative assessment helps determine if students learned the standard. Chapter or unit tests, projects, demonstrations, and presentations are all forms of summative assessment.

Assessments allow for flexible grouping, which helps ensure all students' needs are met. Grouping ideas include whole group, small group (four to six students), peer pairs, and independent study (IRIS Center, 2022). Small groups may be homogeneous where students are grouped based on having similar needs to focus on specific skills or content. Heterogeneous grouping is based on putting students in groups with differing learning needs. In heterogeneous grouping, students bring their own unique strengths and knowledge to the group. Flexible grouping gives students the opportunity to work with classmates who are similar and different in both interests and skills.

Another way to differentiate to best meet student needs is to consider instructional elements. There are three instructional elements to consider when differentiating: content, process, and product.

1. **Content:** The knowledge and skills the students need to master
2. **Process:** The activities students use to master the content being taught
3. **Product:** The method students use to show they mastered the content being taught

Formative assessment helps teachers see where students are in mastering the content being taught. Data from the preassessment and formative assessments are used to create a plan for students who have not mastered the content but then also to create enrichment activities for those who have already mastered the content or master it quickly (IRIS Center, 2022). In the following sections, as noted earlier, we'll show how to think about differentiating instruction not based on grade level but based on content, process, and product.

Differentiate Content

Differentiating content still means all students are learning the same concept or skill, but the curriculum used to teach the skill may be different (IRIS Center, 2022). For example, content can vary in difficulty. Students may be in skill-based groups (lower proficiency, medium proficiency, or higher proficiency). In the lower-proficiency group, the teacher supports the student through the entire lesson. Students then work in pairs to complete the assignment pertaining to what they learned with the teacher. In the medium-proficiency group, the teacher works with the students but then gives them time to work in pairs to complete an assignment that also involves more difficult work. The higher-proficiency group clarifies any questions students may have. The students work in pairs to complete an assignment with various levels of difficulty. Bloom's taxonomy is used to ensure higher-order-thinking questions and activities are utilized.

Content can also be differentiated through materials provided. For example, provide a range of learning resources based on the readiness level and interests of students. This might involve a range of materials, such as textbooks, internet resources, audiobooks, videos, and computer games. Content should be presented in many ways (say it, show it, and model it). When content is presented in multiple ways, students develop a deeper understanding of concepts (IRIS Center, 2022). Scaffolding may be necessary for some students. For example, vocabulary may need to be pretaught. During lessons, it is important to address unfamiliar words and monitor comprehension. Graphic organizers and mental imagery (drawing a picture) can support learning.

Differentiate Process

In addition to differentiating based on content, the way students make sense of a specific topic or skill varies, which means teachers need to vary the activities (the process) students use to master the skills or concepts being taught (IRIS Center, 2022). When differentiating based on process, consider students' interests and readiness level, including the length of time students have to complete a task, stations, graphic organizers, manipulatives, and jigsaw activities.

Let's look at some of these processes and tools more closely.

- **Graphic organizers** are simple and can be flexible in nature when you allow students the opportunity to decide on the type of graphic organizer. The amount of information students are expected to fill in can also be differentiated. KWL charts, flow charts, Venn diagrams, and word webs are examples of graphic organizers. The Frayer Model, which is used to help students learn new words or concepts, is also another example of a graphic organizer (IRIS Center, 2022). For example, a word is written in the middle of the organizer (four boxes). One box has the definition of the word. Another box has characteristics of the word. The last two boxes have examples and nonexamples.
- **Manipulatives** can take difficult abstract concepts and make them more concrete with objects. For example, fractions can be difficult, but when slices of pizza or pie are used as examples, it can be easier to understand.
- **Jigsaw activities** (Jigsaw Classroom, n.d.) are an effective cooperative learning strategy. To do a jigsaw activity, the teacher divides the students up into groups of four to six. The groups should be heterogeneous. One person from each group is designated as the leader. Next, the lesson is divided into sections based on the number of students in the group. One student from each group is assigned a section of the lesson. Students are assigned based on interest or readiness level. The next step involves giving students time to read over and study their content. Then, students move into their "expert" groups, where students have time to talk about the content they learned and think about how they will present information to their home-base group. Once students return to their home-base group, each student reports their findings. The leader of each group is responsible for making sure each group member is given time to present their information and participate in discussions. During this time, the teacher is walking around the room to monitor student progress and answer questions. Students are then assessed to determine their understanding of the concept or skill.
- **Learning stations** can also be referred to as *stations*, *centers*, or *small groups*. Although learning centers are most often used in elementary school, they can easily be implemented in secondary classrooms as a way for students to be actively involved in the learning process. There are several ways to incorporate stations into the classroom, and they involve a lot of planning and preparation. When you plan on the front end, you become the facilitator while students are working. Students need to know exactly what the expectations are for each station.

As stations are a bit more complicated than these other processes, let's put a little extra focus on how to implement them effectively. In grades K–2, it is important to start by modeling your expectations for each station. You may even have to practice what those expectations look like. Students in grades 3–5 and secondary grades probably don't need specific modeling of expectations; however, they will need for you to explain what your expectations are, and your expectations should be in written form so students know what to do and avoid interrupting you with questions.

When first beginning stations, no matter the age of your students, it is important to walk around the room to monitor what students are doing and provide positive reinforcement for students who are meeting your expectations. The process of introducing stations and monitoring will be different depending on the grade level being taught. I would like to provide a friendly reminder that we cannot assume students will know what we expect if we don't tell them, no matter what age they are. Students need to understand what your expectations are, and you need to be consistent with reinforcing your expectations.

While students are working at their station, the teacher is working with small groups of students. Small groups may be homogeneous (same learning levels) or heterogeneous (different learning levels). The teacher table is where you are instructing students. What you would be doing as a whole group becomes what is done in the small group. Students who are in the high-readiness group will likely not need the same amount of instructional time as students who are at a lower readiness level. The topic may be better with heterogeneous groups so students can learn from one another. It really depends on what is being taught. Literacy groups and mathematics groups are generally homogeneous groups. However, science and social studies make it easier to have heterogeneous groups.

The teacher table can be a station rotation, or students can be called to the teacher table while the other students are working independently. Time is a factor, particularly when the teacher table is a part of the station rotation. When thinking about time management, we must consider the transition time for students to move between stations. When planning, always account for the transition time and the instructional time. If you plan on working with each group for fifteen minutes, plan on at least seventeen minutes to allow time for the transition. Additionally, when the teacher table is a part of the station rotation, you will probably only want three to four stations because of time.

Stations can be organized where students are physically moving from one area in the room to another area of the room when the station is complete. Stations can also be organized where students have folders with a choice board. There are some items that they "must do" and other items they can choose from. We talk more about ideas for products in the next section. You may also decide to have materials for stations in one specific place in your classroom, and students have the ability to sit where they would like when completing their tasks.

Station ideas will look different based on grade level and content area. For example, in a secondary classroom, stations may be based on breaking up a unit into sections. Each portion of the unit is a station. Poetry stations can be designed to represent different types of poetry. Each type of poetry is a station. Social studies may be based on a specific country or even a person, and activities are based on what students need to learn about the given topic. Note-taking can be done as a station rather than as a whole-group lesson. Guided notes can be used as a way to ensure students are completing the tasks and learning material. In a primary classroom, stations can be based on subject area. For example, during language arts, stations may include vocabulary or word study, the computer, writing, activities to support the weekly reading, or activities to support grammar, and then the teacher table is where guided reading happens. In kindergarten through second grade, students are typically learning to read. However, as students get older or their reading level increases, they are reading to learn. All students should participate in guided reading lessons. Bloom's taxonomy and the level of books being read will help ensure all students' needs are met. There may be some stations where students are required to complete daily activities (for example, mathematics facts, vocabulary, or computer) while other station work is based on deciding when to complete it.

When and how students complete their work is up to each individual teacher. Typically, I like having stations go for a week. Students learn about the stations on Monday and have until Friday to complete them. It is an incentive to have students complete their stations by Thursday so they can have free choice on Friday. Students must have work to turn in. You will see as follows how to differentiate products to ensure all students are engaged in learning.

Differentiate Product

Teachers are also able to differentiate the product, or the way students are assessed to determine if they understand the concepts and skills during and at the end of a unit. There are many ways students can demonstrate their knowledge (videos, reports, presentations, and so on). It is important to have a clear set of expectations for students to follow and a rubric that can be used no matter the product being assessed. The assignment needs to be challenging but not so difficult students are not able to complete it on their own. It is also helpful to create activities that reflect real-world application and options for visual, auditory, and kinesthetic (hands-on activities) learning (IRIS Center, 2022).

You can tier completed products, based on Bloom's taxonomy, so that what students are asked to complete is based on their level of readiness. Consider creating a choice board to involve student voice in this differentiation, providing a few options that they "must do" along with other options that they can choose from. Choices need to be challenging and require about the same amount of time to complete (IRIS Center, 2022).

Another example of a strategy to use for differentiating products is based on a version of tic-tac-toe (IRIS Center, 2022). The teacher creates activities that address the key concepts and skills being learned in a specific unit. For example, students must choose three product options to form a vertical, horizontal, or diagonal line. Another option is letting students choose one activity from each row or column. More than one version of tic-tac-toe can be created, based on student readiness level. Choice examples may include a video, poster, written report, demonstration, song, PowerPoint presentation, or debate. A choice board may be a list of items, a bingo board, or even a dinner menu. A dinner menu would include an appetizer, an entrée, side dishes, and a dessert. There can be variations on what are requirements to complete versus activities to choose from.

A final way to provide options for a product is called RAFT (role, audience, format, and topic; IRIS Center, 2022). Students pick an option from each column, or students may be asked to choose one specific column. The options should be based on the topic area. Bloom's taxonomy will be helpful in differentiating the products based on student readiness.

Sometimes teachers are at a school where tests are created by district curriculum specialists, and sometimes teachers are at a school where they create tests. It is important to remember, when creating a test, a variety of question types should be utilized—for example, multiple choice, matching, labeling of maps, ordering items or events, fill in the blank, true/false, and essays. Questions should be asked in simple language with as few words as possible and avoid negatives (IRIS Center, 2022). It is important to ensure questions are based on the grade-level content, and there should be criteria stated (for example, length of an essay) so students understand your expectations.

UNIVERSAL DESIGN FOR LEARNING

UDL is a framework used for designing and delivering instruction in the classroom to optimize teaching and improve student learning to address students' diverse needs (CAST, n.d.e). UDL has specific guidelines to be used as tools for implementation, which you can learn more about at the CAST website (www.cast.org/impact/universal-design-for-learning-udl).

Although you will notice similarities between what we just learned about with differentiated instruction and what we are about to learn about with UDL, there are differences. Both are approaches to maximizing learning for all students by offering more than one way to learn content and demonstrate learning (IRIS Center, 2022). The difference between the two is when and how changes are made to address students' needs. Instruction is differentiated during instruction when teachers notice the needs of students, and changes are made to the curriculum. On the other hand, UDL occurs when designing curriculum and builds options into the curriculum.

Classrooms are increasingly diverse, and a one-size-fits-all model is not effective to meeting all students' needs. Matthew James Capp (2017) conducted a meta-analysis of the literature between 2013 and 2016 to determine the effectiveness of UDL. Results of the analysis find UDL to be an effective teaching method for improving the learning process for all students. Similarly, Margaret E. King-Sears and colleagues (2023) find a positive impact on academic achievement of prekindergarteners to adults with the use of UDL when compared to a classroom not using UDL practices.

According to CAST (n.d.d), UDL has three primary principles.

1. **Provide multiple means of engagement:** When providing multiple means of engagement, students are activating the affective networks of the brain, which involve the *why* of learning.
2. **Provide multiple means of representation:** When providing multiple means of representation, students engage the recognition networks, which involve the *what* of learning.
3. **Provide multiple means of action and expression:** When providing multiple means of action and expression, students are activating the strategic networks, which involve the *how* of learning.

What follows is a breakdown of each principle that includes guidelines and checkpoints for each. All the information derives from the CAST website because CAST has grown the field of UDL through research, development, and partnership.

Multiple Means of Engagement

Providing multiple means of engagement is a critical element to learning. We must remember our students differ significantly in ways they can be motivated and engaged. Neurology, culture, background, and personal relevance are some examples of sources that influence individual differences (CAST, n.d.b). Some students prefer spontaneity and novelty, and the idea of routine feels boring and causes disengagement. On the other hand, some students prefer a strict routine because spontaneity or novelty is frightening. Some of our students enjoy working in groups with their peers while others prefer to work alone.

There are three guidelines to support engagement, each with a series of considerations for teachers to factor into their lesson planning and approach to the classroom environment (CAST, n.d.b).

1. **Welcoming interests and identities:** The design options for this guideline involve ensuring student autonomy and choice, optimizing relevance and authenticity, nurturing a sense of joy and play, and addressing biases, threats, and distractions.
2. **Sustaining effort and persistence:** The design options for this guideline include clarifying goals, optimizing challenges and supports, fostering collaboration, ensuring a sense of belonging, and providing feedback.
3. **Emotional capacity:** The design options for this guideline are focused on students acquiring self-regulation skills, like recognizing their own expectations, beliefs, and motivations; developing an awareness of themselves and others; promoting reflection; and cultivating empathy.

Multiple Means of Representation

Students are different in the way they perceive and comprehend information presented to them. For example, students may have learning disabilities or cultural and language differences. How students approach the content will be different (CAST, n.d.c). We all have preferences in how we grasp information. Some students prefer written or visual representation while other students prefer auditory representation. Learning and the transfer of learning happen when multiple means of representation are used because students are better able to make connections. Providing options for representing information is crucial because there is not one means of representation that is optimal for all students.

There are three guidelines to support representation, each with a series of considerations for teachers to factor into their lesson planning and approach to classroom environment (CAST, n.d.c).

1. **Equality in perception:** The design options need to include equal perception to reduce barriers to learning by providing information in more than one modality (for example, touch or seeing) and in different formats (for example, larger font or louder sound).
2. **Linguistic and nonlinguistic representation:** The design options for language and symbols need to take into account the importance of clarifying vocabulary and symbols and clarifying syntax and structure.

Lesson design should support decoding of text, mathematical notations, and symbols and promote understanding across languages.
3. **Comprehension through useable knowledge:** The design options promote future decision making and include activating or providing background knowledge, supporting processing and visualization, and highlighting patterns and big ideas. The idea is to maximize generalization.

Multiple Means of Action and Expression

Students are different in the way they navigate their learning environment and express what they know (CAST, n.d.a). For example, students with ADHD can have difficulties with their organizational ability or time management skills. Students with language barriers, whether due to a language disorder or being English learners, will approach learning differently. Some students may be able to understand and express themselves verbally while others express themselves in written text. There is not one means of action or expression that is optimal for all learners, which is why it is extremely important to provide options for action and expression.

There are three guidelines for supporting multiple means of action and expression: physical action, expression and communication, and executive functions (CAST, n.d.a).

1. **Physical action:** The design options include varying methods to respond and navigate while also optimizing access to assistive technology and tools.
2. **Expression and communication:** The design options include using multiple media to communicate, using numerous tools for construction and comprehension, and building fluencies with graduated levels of support.
3. **Executive functions:** The design options include guidance for appropriate goal setting, support for planning and strategy development, facilitating management of information and resources, and enhancing capacity for progress monitoring.

Concluding Thoughts

When thinking about all the different levels of instruction our students are at, we must think about how students retain the most information when we think about how instruction is delivered. Lecture-based whole-group instruction is not how students retain information. Knowing this means we must adjust how we teach. When I visit with teachers, the biggest concern in making a change to move away from whole-group lessons is feeling like teachers are not in control of the students.

We often feel like we are in more control when we are presenting the material to the students. However, if we step back and look around, we can notice what is really happening. Yes, the teacher is providing the information, but all students are not receiving the information. Some students are focusing on what is being taught, some students are talking to the person next to them, and some students may be reading a book or doing something completely different. We feel like we are in control, but we really aren't. What does this mean? How can we make a change? I hope you feel empowered to use the strategies you've learned from chapter 5 to support the academic needs of your students.

Reading this chapter may have provoked many different feelings. One feeling might be excitement because you have strategies and tools to use in best supporting all learners. We know it is important to meet the needs of our students, but we may not know how or even where to begin looking. This chapter provides you with the tools you need to begin implementing strategies right away in your classroom. Others may feel overwhelmed with all the information provided in this chapter. There is a lot of information, and you may think there is no possible way to do it all. My hope is that you can see how each of the strategies really complements the others. Don't think you have to change everything you are doing all at one time. Pick one area you would like to focus on. Pick one lesson or subject area in which you would like to try to implement what you've learned from the chapter. Start small. Make a plan for yourself and then execute the plan. There will be a lot of planning on the front end, and at times, you may feel frustrated or like things are not working. I challenge you to stay the course. Once you get the hang of it, add something else. I found for myself and in working with others that it starts out hard because it's new. However, it gets easier and is actually easier in the long run because students who are actively engaged in the learning don't typically have challenging behaviors. Once you get the hang of it, you won't want to teach any other way. You need to give yourself time to let the plan work. Be reflective when trying something you haven't tried before. Ask yourself what went well and why. Then, think about what didn't go well and reflect on why. You may find you didn't plan as well as you thought you had. Sometimes, you feel like you have thought of everything but realize in the moment you forgot something. It is OK. Be reflective and adjust. Now, consider the reproducible tool, "Thinking About Differentiating Instruction" (also available online at **go.SolutionTree.com/behavior**), as you make your plan for differentiating instruction.

Thinking About Differentiating Instruction

It can be difficult to want to try new things when teaching. The following are some reflective questions you can ask yourself.

What goal do you have regarding differentiating your instruction?

What steps can you take to achieve your goal?

What resources will be needed?

Describe potential obstacles that may arise. How do you believe you can overcome the obstacles?

Learning, Behavior, and Your Classroom © 2025 Solution Tree Press • SolutionTree.com
Visit **go.SolutionTree.com/behavior** to download this free reproducible.

How did it go as you worked to achieve your goal? What challenges did you face, and what steps can be taken to improve?

Where do you want to see yourself in planning to best differentiate instruction one month from now and three months from now? How will you assess yourself?

Voices From the Field

How does learning meet your needs or the needs of your students?

> "Today my pre-advanced placement English teacher had us rotate through stations to learn about different types of poetry. I loved it because I didn't have to listen to my teacher talk the entire class period."

—A ninth-grade student

> "My students love Nearpod. We have a lot of content to cover, and Nearpod is a fun way to deliver the content. For example, students can watch YouTube videos based on the topic, turn and talk to one another, and take guided notes. It allows me to not just stand in front of the class and lecture at them."

—An eighth-grade social studies teacher

> "My students love stations, and we use them regularly. One station is the computer, another station is where they take notes, they do independent work at a third station, and they also come to my teacher table."

—An algebra teacher

> "It is my expectation that my teachers differentiate instruction by doing small groups. We have teachers who are all in with small groups and others who need more encouragement. My teachers who need more encouragement go and watch my teachers who are doing it well. Data show the success of small groups."

—A middle school principal

> "I had one teacher who wanted to try stations. She saw success with it within the first week. Her students were more engaged in the learning and did better on their end-of-week assessment. The students love it. I will say you must have control over your classroom."

—An elementary school principal

"My favorite classes are the ones where my teachers let us work in small groups and do stations. I feel more independent, and I like that."

—*A seventh-grade student*

"In one of my master's level classes I learned about using small groups to differentiate instruction. I decided I would try it. I will say it was a lot of work on the front end. I had to do a lot of planning and preparing. I realized some things I needed to change immediately, but after the first week I realized how successful it really was. My students did much better on their vocabulary tests. The test they had over the story-of-the-week was much better, too. I decided to implement stations in mathematics, too, because my students and I love it so much."

—*A fifth-grade teacher*

CHAPTER 6
Practice Self-Care

We all have different ideas on what it means to engage in self-care. I think about various things that can be what I call bucket fillers. Bucket fillers are the things we do for ourselves, or others do for us, that fill our buckets and make us feel good. Stress is a bucket depleter. It empties our bucket and causes us to feel burned out and overall exhausted. What I find to be a bucket filler isn't going to be the same for you, and vice versa.

I thought it best to conclude this book by providing reminders of the importance of taking care of yourself. Teachers innately give so much of themselves to their classroom and students. Teaching is hard and can be a thankless job. It is vital to take care of yourself because, believe it or not, you as the teacher are the center of the classroom and the management of the room. When we don't take care of ourselves, we can get into habits we know are not best for ourselves or for our management of the classroom. This is a brief chapter, but it is important. As educators, we are in the business of taking care of others. It's just what we do, and we don't think twice about it. Sometimes we forget to take care of ourselves. We give to the point of having nothing left in us to give. It is way easier said than done, but you have to take care of yourself so you can be your best self when taking care of those around you. Teacher burnout is a real thing and something to ensure you work to mitigate for yourself.

Teacher burnout is defined as a condition where a teacher has drained both personal and professional resources needed to do the job (Walker,

2021). Although burnout is common among all professions, teachers typically see higher levels of burnout. A study by Alliance for Excellent Education reports that 40–50 percent of new teachers leave the profession within their first five years of teaching (Thompson, 2019). Another poll finds that 44 percent of educators in K–12 education states always or often feeling burned out, which outpaces all other industries nationally (Marken & Agrawal, 2022). According to a Gallup poll written by Stephanie Marken and Sangeeta Agrawal (2022), the COVID-19 pandemic only exacerbated already existing challenges in the teaching profession. While poor well-being and an adverse working environment are associated with teachers' intentions to leave the profession, supportive school environments are linked to a decreased likelihood to leave the profession and better well-being (Walker, 2021).

The teaching profession is not an easy one. We step into the role of a teacher to make a difference in the lives of our students, and we know it will be difficult, but I don't think we realize how difficult until we do it. We can take important steps to take care of ourselves to prevent burnout and stay in the profession we felt called to be a part of. Specifically, I provide tips to remember and then will discuss strategies for self-care including exercise, mindfulness, and finding your joy.

Tips to Remember for Taking Care of Yourself

One big thing we can do for ourselves is to set healthy boundaries (Thompson, 2019). I have to admit I am not always good at this one. If we find ourselves saying yes to too many things, we cause ourselves stress. As teachers, we often work long into the evening and often on weekends. We become workaholics. To prevent this happening, we can set boundaries and stop working at a specific time in the evening. We can limit or eliminate working on the weekends. You may be thinking this isn't possible. But as the adage goes, sometimes it's better to work smarter (or more efficiently) than harder.

Another thing you can do for yourself is to take some time off when you are feeling overwhelmed. We often feel teaching is not just a job; it's our identity. I feel this for myself. Teaching is who I am. However, an important part of self-care is taking breaks when necessary to manage stress (Thompson, 2019). Those breaks might come in little five- or ten-minute bursts. You might find it's time for a personal day, maybe one that sets up a long weekend. Whatever the case or context, you will find when you take a break, you feel more rejuvenated and ready to teach.

Charmain Jackman (2022) found three things to support emotional well-being: *reflect*, *release*, and *recharge*. Self-reflection allows us the opportunity to foster emotional wellness and is an excellent way to avoid unhealthy patterns and live fulfilling lives. Daily, you can ask yourself what a challenge was. You can also ask yourself what a joyful moment was. Think of someone who helped you and let them know you are thankful for them.

While release is also important, it can be difficult. We often hold on to the feelings of frustration, grief, regret, or inadequacy. It is important to release our feelings by taking a few minutes to consider how you are feeling and identify emotions, thoughts, and behaviors you need to release. Create a list to capture your feelings and then release them by tearing up the paper, crushing it up into a ball, or shredding it. Once you have gone through the ritual of releasing your regrets, notice how you feel. Often, people feel a sense of relief or like a weight has been lifted off them.

Finally, recharging is vital. According to Lindsay Thompson (2019), the top three barriers people feel prevent them from practicing self-care are consistency, fatigue, and time. We are often too tired or feel like we don't have enough time, or we just don't engage in the self-care activities regularly. One way to prioritize yourself is to think about self-care in small bite-sized activities. Self-care doesn't have to take hours to find the benefits. Engaging in activities you enjoy for small amounts of time helps to build consistency, which promotes a more long-standing change. To begin, think about one habit you want to change. Think about how you've practiced the habit in the past and what helped you stay consistent. Think about an activity you can do each day for five minutes. Is there a person you want to do the activity with? Where do you want to do the activity, and when will you do it? The third thing you can do to help yourself recharge is to create a visual cue. What is something you can do to help increase the likelihood of you doing the activity and reaching your goal? Maybe you need to set an alarm or put your workout clothes out the night before. Think about the habit you want to change and then five visual cues you can include to support your habit of choice. But first, you *have* to prioritize yourself at times in order to recharge. We often feel guilty for focusing on ourselves, but remember, you deserve to feel rested and peace of mind. Ask yourself, "What do I want to invite into my life? What brings me joy?"

We all view self-care differently. I love watching movies with my family and spending time with my friends. These things fill my bucket. There are times when I think to myself, "There is no way I have time for lunch or dinner," but after the fact, I realize I feel so much better. I also love a good massage or getting a pedicure. I work to exercise regularly. I know it makes a difference for me. It has taken me a long time to realize that taking time for me makes me better at what I am doing. Stop and take care of yourself so you can take care of your students.

Strategies for Implementing Self-Care

We know self-care is important, but where do we begin? The idea of self-care for one person isn't going to be self-care for another. The trick is finding something you enjoy and making the time for yourself so you can be the best version of you. However, I think that exercising, being mindful, and finding those things that give you joy are particularly helpful forms of self-care.

EXERCISE

Exercise is one of my favorite things to do. I feel better when I exercise. There are so many different forms of exercise to enjoy! Maybe a gym membership is for you. Gyms often have classes to choose from, machines and different equipment to use to lift weights, and various types of treadmills. For some people, there is a need to physically go somewhere to be motivated to exercise. Some people have friends or coworkers they go with. There are also different types of gyms. There are yoga studios, Pilates studios, boxing gyms, CrossFit, and so many more. Other people don't feel comfortable working out at a place and prefer to work out from home. What is great about working out from home is the simple fact you are at home. There are many platforms to access workouts and equipment that can be purchased. There is also the great outdoors where all you need is a pair of tennis shoes for walking or running. The important thing is the movement itself. Find what works for you, and give yourself permission to do it!

Exercise can be a wonderful outlet and helps you stay mentally and physically fit. Teachers are less stressed when they don't bring work home and find "me" time to go on a walk alone or read (Haydon, Stevens, & Leko, 2018). Having time away is stress reducing.

Todd Haydon, Doug Stevens, and Melinda M. Leko (2018) conducted a study involving teacher stress and protective factors. Efforts to support health and well-being served as a protective factor against stress. Teachers who exercised a few times a week or were involved in coaching, outside school activities, or their own children's activities were better able to manage stress and had less overall stress. Brandis M. Ansley and colleagues (2021) find similar results when examining teacher burnout and teacher efficacy. Physical exercise increased coping strategies and reduced stress and burnout. There are many types of physical exercise you can do. The important thing is that you enjoy what you are doing. If you don't enjoy it, you won't do it.

According to the National Institutes of Health (2021), there are four types of exercise, including endurance, strength, balance, and flexibility, spread across a huge variety of individual activities.

Find what you love. Switch things up so you don't get bored. You may be thinking you don't have time, but remember to keep it bite-size. Start with sessions of ten to fifteen minutes. From that baseline, can you get to thirty minutes? Forty-five minutes? I find that there are times when I can only do twenty or thirty minutes, but there are other times when I can stretch up to an hour. Find a person who can help hold you accountable. It can be a person you work out with or a person you check in with. I love seeing teachers and administrators working out together right after school. It gets the workout done and creates a sense of community within your school.

MINDFULNESS

Mindfulness involves being aware of what is happening in the present moment within oneself in a nonjudgmental way with curiosity and acceptance (Kabat-Zinn, 1990). When practicing mindfulness, you are fully present to what is happening in the here and now without hanging on to the past or worrying about what will happen in the future. Mindfulness is considered a healthy coping mechanism, much like physical exercise, and mitigates stress and burnout (Ansley et al., 2021). Other studies further show mindfulness-based interventions are associated with self-reported increases in job satisfaction and general wellness while decreasing occupational stress (Ansley et al., 2021; de Carvalho et al., 2021; Jennings et al., 2017). John Meiklejohn and colleagues (2012) find practicing mindfulness can increase a sense of self-efficacy, well-being, ability to effectively manage classroom behaviors, and capacity to foster supportive student relationships.

Teachers benefit from mindfulness, and students can benefit, too. Mindfulness can be integrated into the classroom and is considered an innovative practice aligned with SEL (Zolkoski & Lewis-Chiu, 2019). CASEL (n.d.d) supports mindfulness as a universal intervention for the classroom. With that said, before thinking about implementing mindfulness in your classroom, you need to have an established practice for yourself.

To begin, think about bite-size pieces again. You can sit mindfully for a few minutes daily. To do this, you practice focusing your attention to your breath (Zolkoski & Lewis-Chiu, 2019). When you notice your mind beginning to wander, gently bring your attention back to the breath. It is helpful to find a spot to sit comfortably in a chair. You may close your eyes or keep them open, whichever you feel most comfortable with. Then, take a breath in and slowly let your breath out. You are simply focusing on your breath, noticing when you breathe in and out. I will share two of my favorite mindfulness exercises, and then I will share my resources for teachers who want to begin practicing. There are also mindfulness apps you can put on your phone to be guided through the process.

Mindful breathing involves lying on your back or sitting in a chair where your legs are flat on the floor and your arms are at your sides. If you like, close your eyes. Notice your back touching the floor or chair. Notice your shoulders, back, arms, hands, and legs. Next, notice what it feels like to breathe in and out. There isn't a right or wrong way to breathe. Pay attention to your in-breath. Try to notice when you start to breathe in and then notice the feeling of your in-breath all the way until the first moment you breathe out. You may notice it's hard to focus on your breath. You may find it helpful to say "in" each time you breathe in. Practice this for a few minutes. When you are ready, open your eyes, take a final breath, and notice how you feel. Try to do this daily for a few minutes and see how you feel.

My other favorite mindfulness practice is called thought watching. I like it because I find my mind wandering a lot. To begin, you do the same thing as you do in mindful breathing. Find a comfortable spot and then bring your attention to your breath. Notice your breath in your belly and settle into the quiet. Then, you begin watching your thoughts go by just like you watch people on a sidewalk go by. Notice when a thought comes and then watch the thought pass by. You may notice thoughts have personalities like we do, but rather than following the thought, notice the thought and let the thought go. If you find yourself focusing on the thought, be sure to congratulate yourself because you noticed it. Return your attention back to your breath and, when your attention is stable, begin watching your thoughts again. You may also notice some thoughts are alone, and others travel in groups, but just keep breathing and noticing. When you are ready, take a final deep breath and open your eyes. Notice how you feel. Do you feel more relaxed? Remember, practicing mindfulness takes time and consistency. Following are resources for you to learn more.

- Mindful Teachers: www.mindfulteachers.org
- Mindfulness in Schools Project: https://mindfulnessinschools.org
- Mindfulness by Greater Good Science Center: https://greatergood.berkeley.edu/topic/mindfulness
- *Happy Teachers Change the World* by Thich Nhat Hanh and Katherine Weare (2017)
- *Mindfulness for Teachers: Simple Skills for Peace and Productivity in the Classroom* by Patricia A. Jennings (2015)

FIND YOUR JOY

We can easily lose our joy, or our passion, when we forget to take care of ourselves. It can become easy to focus on the negative. We have to switch our mindset. At the end of the day, before you go home, take a few minutes, and think of the positive things that happened during the day. Even on the hard days, I can come up with positive things. Remind yourself why you got into teaching in the first place. Why did you become an educator? Since even before I became a teacher, I knew it was going to be hard. I am one who has always wanted to be a teacher. I played teacher in my bedroom. I wanted to become a teacher to make a positive impact on students' lives. My passion and joy come from helping others, but if I am not careful, I lose the passion because I do all the things we learned about that cause stress. One way to not lose the joy and passion is to create a routine for yourself. When you create a routine for work and home, it's easier to separate the two.

Patricia Phelps and Tammy Benson (2012) conducted a study to find commonalities among teachers who have sustained their passion for teaching. They believe that finding the commonalities can be used to encourage teachers to maintain and model an enthusiastic passion for education. Passion is a driving force for career success and can prevent burnout. Teachers were interviewed, and the authors found several commonalities and themes among the teachers. One theme was having a positive attitude. Talk to others who are positive and avoid those who are negative. Although everyone has negative days, being around people who are positive can help. One teacher interviewed said teaching is too difficult to not have your heart in the job. It also becomes easier to maintain your passion and positive attitude when you realize the positive impact you are making on the students and world in general. The teachers also talked about accepting change, which can be difficult but is necessary. When we accept change and view it as a learning opportunity, we are more likely to have a positive outlook. Professional development through collaboration is another way to keep your passion. The last commonality involves, not surprisingly at all, relationships. Relationships, relationships, relationships! Each teacher talked extensively about the importance of having strong relationships with parents and students.

Liying Cui (2022) conducted a review of the literature to determine the role of teacher-student relationships when predicting teachers' enthusiasm, occupational well-being, and emotional exhaustion. Cui (2022) found maintaining positive relationships between students and teachers is crucial. Positive relationships increased professional well-being of educators. Positive relationships with students also helped teachers avoid burnout and emotional exhaustion while increasing work engagement. Teachers' passion is associated with enhancing student participation and motivation, which positively impacts students' success in school.

Concluding Thoughts

I cannot emphasize enough the importance of self-care. Trust me; I know it is easier said than done, but it is just so very important. It is not selfish to take time for yourself. It is necessary. You will be your best self when you take even just a little time for yourself. Find your joy, whatever that is. Maybe it's something I have shared in this chapter or something entirely different. Give yourself permission to do it, and if that feels like too much, then let me give you permission to take time for yourself! Remember, a depleted bucket doesn't do anyone any good.

Voices From the Field

What do you do to support your own self-care?

"Shopping with all the extra coffee stops and a nice dinner. 😵 It can get messy sometimes if it's been a rough time at school."

–A fourth-grade teacher

"Full skincare routine (because during most days I'm too tired to do it all) and lying in the bathtub eating fruit and watching Netflix. 😋"

–An eighth-grade teacher

"I like to go out and do something in nature and hang out with my family!"

–A Kindergarten teacher

"Nothing, I'm a mom. 😋 Only slightly kidding. 😄 Girls' nights, reading books, book club, and I don't get to do it often, but I love going to the movies."

–A seventh-grade teacher

"I try to spend time ALONE. It's hard as a teacher, a wife, and a mom (especially when that mom guilt kicks in), but if I have a chance to truly decompress and think through ALL the things, I find myself recharged."

–A tenth-grade teacher

"I actually use my personal days. I didn't use them in the past, but I was really starting to feel overwhelmed and wasn't in a good place mentally. I take the kids to school, and then I get back in bed to read and watch TV."

–A first-grade teacher

Epilogue

I believe teaching is one of the hardest jobs but is also one of the most rewarding jobs. It is often a thankless job. Seeing the lightbulb moments your students have when they realize they have figured something out, seeing your students work and work at something to finally get it, or capturing a hard-to-capture student is everything. You may not get a thank-you, but the moments just described and so many more are why we teach. We make a difference. We get to decide if the difference we are going to make will be positive or negative. I don't believe any of us got into the field of teaching to negatively impact students. Sometimes, we may lose sight of our *why*.

Chapter 1 (page 7) set the foundation for better understanding our students and where they are coming from. My hope with this book is for you to have everything you need not only to be an effective educator, but to feel like an effective educator. It starts with understanding behavior. Understanding brain development and the *why* of behavior is crucial for truly having empathy for our students.

We learned in chapter 2 (page 35) how important building a positive learning environment is. Building a positive environment and positive relationships with students and families impacts not only your students and their academic success but also your overall well-being. Remember to work to create positive connections with all your students, particularly the students who may be a little more difficult to love. Your success and your students' success rely on these positive relationships. Social-emotional competence where SEL strategies are utilized in the classroom supports not only healthy relationships with students and colleagues but also the implementation of evidence-based instructional strategies while decreasing teacher burnout and increasing coping strategies (Ansley et al., 2021).

Without a structure of consistently establishing and reinforcing your classroom-management plan, as you learned about in chapter 3 (page 67), you cannot effectively get to the teaching and student learning. Your ability to teach is greatly impacted by your ability to effectively manage your class. It also impacts your stress and creates burnout. Consistency in all aspects is vital. If you are starting in the middle of the year, remember it is going to be more difficult. Students have been positively reinforced for their negative behaviors, which makes it harder to establish expectations. Consistency with your plan will be everything for you and the success of you and your students.

Even when you have the best classroom-management plan, there will be students who struggle with their behavior. In chapter 4 (page 101), I hope you find the strategies to support students at Tier 2 give you confidence in being able to effectively manage students who struggle. Don't forget that even with the best classroom management, students will still struggle. Some of your students will need more support, and they will need you to believe in them. Some of them will need you to believe in them more than they believe in themselves. I hope if or when you have a student who moves to Tier 3, you will feel more confident in what the process is supposed to look like.

Chapter 5 (page 133) is a lot. There is so much information packed into one chapter. It may feel overwhelming. Take the chapter one bit at a time. Pick an area you want to focus on and get good at that. You will find the other strategies are easier to implement. Self-reflection will be critical when trying new things. Think about what worked well and didn't go well. Reflect on why something went well or didn't go well. The self-reflection piece will be important in your growth and success. I personally love small groups because of how successful they have been for my teaching and teachers I have supported. I also love allowing students the opportunity to choose the type of product they are going to complete to show what they know.

I cannot emphasize enough the importance of chapter 6 (page 157) and taking care of yourself so you can be the best version of you for your students. Your mind and body will thank you. Your students will thank you, and most importantly, you will thank you. You will be a better you and will be able to do all the things you have learned about in this book. Self-care can help us remember our *why* even on the hard days. Think about what brings you joy and fills your bucket. You can't be effective for anyone if you have nothing left to give. The best thing you can do is take care of yourself so you are able to give your best to others.

I want to end this book with my favorite quotes that empower me, and I hope they empower you, too!

My teacher thought I was smarter than I was—so I was. —Six-year-old student

Let that quote sink in. Your students will meet you where you set your expectations. Be sure to set them high!

Every child is one adult away from being a success story. —Josh Shipp

Again, let that quote sink in. How powerful is that? You can and will be a student's success story. They will make you work for it, but goodness, it will be worth it.

References and Resources

Ackerman, K. B., Samudre, M., & Allday, R. A. (2020). Practical components for getting the most from a token economy. *Teaching Exceptional Children, 52*(4), 242–249. https://doi.org/10.1177/0040059919892022

Acosta, J., Chinman, M., Ebener, P., Malone, P. S., Phillips, A., & Wilks, A. (2019). Understanding the relationship between perceived school climate and bullying: A mediator analysis. *Journal of School Violence, 18*(2), 200–215. https://doi.org/10.1080/15388220.2018.1453820

Adichie, C. N. (2009, July). *The danger of a single story* [Video file]. TED Conferences. Accessed at www.ted.com/talks/chimamanda_ngozi_adichie_the_danger_of_a_single_story?language=en on March 21, 2025.

Agency for Healthcare Research and Quality. (2022). *National healthcare quality and disparities report.* Accessed at www.ncbi.nlm.nih.gov/books/NBK587182/pdf/Bookshelf_NBK587182.pdf on July 26, 2024.

Alber, R. (2014). *6 scaffolding strategies to use with your students: Support every student by breaking learning up into chunks and providing a concrete structure for each.* Accessed at www.edutopia.org/blog/scaffolding-lessons-six-strategies-rebecca-alber on July 26, 2024.

American Psychological Association. (2022). *How to help children and teens manage their stress.* Accessed at www.apa.org/topics/children/stress on July 26, 2024.

Anderson, L. W., & Krathwohl, D. R. (Eds.). (2001). *A taxonomy for learning, teaching, and assessing: A revision of Bloom's taxonomy of educational objectives.* New York: Longman.

Ansley, B. M., Houchins, D. E., Varjas, K., Roach, A., Patterson, D., & Hendrick, R. (2021). The impact of an online stress intervention on burnout and teacher efficacy. *Teaching and Teacher Education, 98,* 1–11. https://doi.org/10.1016/j.tate.2020.103251

August, D. (2018). Educating English language learners: A review of the latest research. *American Educator, 42*(3), 4–9, 38–39.

Barrish, H. H., Saunders, M., & Wolf, M. M. (1969). Good Behavior Game: Effects of individual contingencies for group consequences on disruptive behavior in a classroom. *Journal of Applied Behavior Analysis, 2,* 119–124. http://dx.doi.org/10.1901/jaba.1969.2-119

Bear, G. G., Yang, C., Mantz, L. S., & Harris, A. B. (2017). School-wide practices associated with school climate in elementary, middle, and high schools. *Teaching and Teacher Education, 63,* 372–383. http://dx.doi.org/10.1016/j.tate.2017.01.012

Benner, A. D., Boyle, A. E., & Sadler, S. (2016). Parental involvement and adolescents' educational success: The roles of prior achievement and socioeconomic status. *Journal of Youth and Adolescence, 45,* 1053–1064. https://doi.org/10.1007/s10964-016-0431-4

Bloom, B. S. (Ed.). (1956). *Taxonomy of educational objectives: The classification of educational goals; Handbook I: Cognitive domain.* New York: Longmans.

Bos, M. G. N., Wierenga, L. M., Blankenstein, N. E., Schreuders, E., Tamnes, C. K., & Crone, E. A. (2018). Longitudinal structural brain development and externalizing behavior in adolescence. *Journal of Child Psychology and Psychiatry, 59*(10), 1061–1072. https://doi.org/10.1111/jcpp.12972

Bruhn, A. L., Woods-Groves, S., Fernando, J., Choi, T., & Troughton, L. (2017). Evaluating technology-based self-monitoring as a Tier 2 intervention across middle school settings. *Behavioral Disorders*, *42*(3), 119–131. https://doi.org/10.1177/0198742917691534

Burdick-Will, J. (2018). Neighborhood violence, peer effects, and academic achievement in Chicago. *Sociology of Education*, *91*(3), 205–223. https://doi.org/10.1177/0038040718779063

Capp, M. J. (2017). The effectiveness of Universal Design for Learning: A meta-analysis of literature between 2013 and 2016. *International Journal of Inclusive Education*, *21*(8), 791–807. https://doi.org/10.1080/13603116.2017.1325074

CAST. (n.d.a). *Design multiple means of action and expression.* Accessed at https://udlguidelines.cast.org/action-expression on September 30, 2024.

CAST. (n.d.b). *Design multiple means of engagement.* Accessed at https://udlguidelines.cast.org/engagement on September 30, 2024.

CAST. (n.d.c). *Design multiple means of representation.* Accessed at https://udlguidelines.cast.org/representation on September 30, 2024.

CAST. (n.d.d). *The UDL guidelines.* Accessed at https://udlguidelines.cast.org on July 26, 2024.

CAST. (n.d.e). *Universal Design for Learning.* Accessed at www.cast.org/impact/universal-design-for-learning-udl on July 26, 2024.

Center on PBIS. (n.d.a). *Tier 3.* Accessed at www.pbis.org/pbis/tier-3 on July 26, 2024.

Center on PBIS. (n.d.b). *What is PBIS?* Accessed at www.pbis.org/pbis/what-is-pbis on July 26, 2024.

Centers for Disease Control and Prevention. (2021). *About the CDC-Kaiser ACE study.* Accessed at www.cdc.gov/violenceprevention/aces/about.html on July 26, 2024.

Centers for Disease Control and Prevention. (2023a). *Data and statistics on children's mental health.* Accessed at www.cdc.gov/childrensmentalhealth/data.html on July 26, 2024.

Centers for Disease Control and Prevention. (2023b). *Suicide data and statistics.* Accessed at www.cdc.gov/suicide/suicide-data-statistics.html on July 26, 2024.

Choose Love Movement. (n.d.). *Education*. Accessed at https://choose lovemovement.org/education on March 17, 2025.on July 26, 2024.

Cipani, E. (2018). *Functional behavioral assessment, diagnosis, and treatment: A complete system for education and mental health settings* (3rd ed.). New York: Springer.

Cohen, R. K., Opatosky, D. K., Savage, J., Stevens, S. O., & Darrah, E. P. (2021). *The metacognitive student: How to teach academic, social, and emotional intelligence in every content area*. Bloomington, IN: Solution Tree Press.

Collaborative for Academic, Social, and Emotional Learning. (n.d.a). *Connect your criteria*. Accessed at https://pg.casel.org/connect-your-criteria on July 26, 2024.

Collaborative for Academic, Social, and Emotional Learning. (n.d.b). *Fundamentals of SEL*. Accessed at https://casel.org/fundamentals-of-sel on July 26, 2024.

Collaborative for Academic, Social, and Emotional Learning. (n.d.c). *How does SEL support educational equity and excellence?* Accessed at https://casel.org/fundamentals-of-sel/how-does-sel-support-educational-equity-and-excellence on July 26, 2024.

Collaborative for Academic, Social, and Emotional Learning. (n.d.d). *Program guide*. Accessed at https://pg.casel.org on July 26, 2024.

Collaborative for Academic, Social, and Emotional Learning. (n.d.e). *What does the research say? Hundreds of independent studies confirm: SEL benefits students*. Accessed at https://casel.org/fundamentals-of-sel/what-does-the-research-say on July 26, 2024.

Collins, T. A., Drevon, D. D., Brown, A. M., Villarreal, J. N., Newman, C. L., & Endres, B. (2020). Say something nice: A meta-analytic review of peer reporting interventions. *Journal of School Psychology, 83*, 89–103. https://doi.org/10.1016/j.jsp.2020.10.002

Conscious Discipline. (n.d.a). *The Conscious Discipline brain state model*. Accessed at https://consciousdiscipline.com/methodology/brain-state-model on July 26, 2024.

Conscious Discipline. (n.d.b). *Conscious Discipline methodology*. Accessed at https://consciousdiscipline.com/methodology on July 26, 2024.

Conscious Discipline. (n.d.c). *Creating the school family.* Accessed at https://consciousdiscipline.com/methodology/school-family on July 26, 2024.

Conscious Discipline. (n.d.d). *Seven powers for conscious adults.* Accessed at https://consciousdiscipline.com/methodology/seven-powers on July 26, 2024.

Conscious Discipline. (n.d.e). *Seven skills of discipline.* Accessed at https://consciousdiscipline.com/methodology/seven-skills on July 26, 2024.

Cook, C. R., Fiat, A., Larson, M., Daikos, C., Slemrod, T., Holland, E. A., et al. (2018). Positive greetings at the door: Evaluation of a low-cost, high-yield proactive classroom management strategy. *Journal of Positive Behavior Interventions, 20*(3), 149–159. https://doi.org/10.1177/1098300717753831

Cook, C. R., Grady, E. A., Long, A. C., Renshaw, T., Codding, R. S., Fiat, A., et al. (2017). Evaluating the impact of increasing general education teachers' ratio of positive-to-negative interactions on students' classroom behavior. *Journal of Positive Behavior Interventions, 19*(2), 67–77. https://doi.org/10.1177/1098300716679137

Coward, I. G. (2018). Adolescent stress: Causes, consequences, and communication as an interventional model. *Canadian Journal of Family and Youth, 10*(1), 25–51. https://doi.org/10.29173/cjfy29341

Cui, L. (2022). The role of teacher-student relationships in predicting teachers' occupational wellbeing, emotional exhaustion, and enthusiasm. *Frontiers in Psychology, 13*, 1–7. https://doi.org/10.3389/fpsyg.2022.896813

Daily, S. M., Mann, M. J., Kristjansson, A. L., Smith, M. L., & Zullig, K. J. (2019). School climate and academic achievement in middle and high school students. *Journal of School Health, 89*(3), 173–180.

Davis, T. N., Dacus, S., Bankhead, J., Haupert, M., Fuentes, L., Zoch, T., et al. (2014). A comparison of self-monitoring with and without reinforcement to improve on-task classroom behavior. *Journal of School Counseling, 12*(12), 1–23.

de Carvalho, J. S., Oliveira, S., Roberto, M. S., Gonçalves, C., Bárbara, J. M., de Castro, A. F., et al. (2021). Effects of a mindfulness-based intervention for teachers: A study on teacher and student outcomes. *Mindfulness, 12*, 1719–1732. https://doi.org/10.1007/s12671-021-01635-3

DK Publishing. (2020). *How the brain works: The facts visually explained.* New York: Author.

Donaldson, J. M., Fisher, A. B., & Kahng, S. (2017). Effects of the Good Behavior Game on individual student behavior. *Behavior Analysis: Research and Practice, 17*(3), 207–216. http://dx.doi.org/10.1037/bar0000016

Durlak, J. A., Mahoney, J. L., & Boyle, A. E. (2022). What we know, and what we need to find out about universal, school-based social and emotional learning programs for children and adolescents: A review of meta-analyses and directions for future research. *Psychological Bulletin, 148*(11–12), 765–782. https://doi.org/10.1037/bul0000383

Edupress. (2017). *Quick flip questions for the revised Bloom's taxonomy.* Garden Grove, CA: Teacher Created Resources.

Farmer, T. W., Reinke, W., & Brooks, D. S. (2014). Managing classrooms and challenging behavior: Theoretical considerations and critical issues. *Journal of Emotional and Behavioral Disorders, 22*(2), 67–73. https://doi.org/10.1177/1063426614522693

Fay, J., & Fay, C. (2016). *Teaching with love and logic: Taking control of the classroom* (2nd ed.). Golden, CO: Love and Logic Institute.

Felitti, V. J. (2002). The relation between adverse childhood experiences and adult health: Turning gold into lead. *Permanente Journal, 6*(1), 44–47. https://doi.org/10.7812/tpp/02.994

Felitti, V. J. (2019). Origins of the ACE study. *American Journal of Preventative Medicine, 56*(6), 787–789. https://doi.org/10.1016/j.amepre.2019.02.011

Ferlazzo, L., & Sypnieski, K. H. (2018). Teaching English language learners: Tips from the classroom. *American Educator, 42*(3), 12–16, 38–39.

Florida's Positive Behavioral Interventions & Support Project. (2023). *Fidelity of tiered interventions.* Accessed at https://apbs.org/wp-content/uploads/2023/04/K03-Fidelity-of-Tiered-Interventions-Final_3.23.23.pdf on December 2, 2024.

Flower, A., McKenna, J. W., Bunuan, R. L., Muething, C. S., & Vega, R. (2014). Effects of the Good Behavior Game on challenging behaviors in school setting. *Review of Educational Research, 84*(4), 546–571. https://doi.org/10.3102/0034654314536781

Friend, M., & Cook, L. (2012). *Interactions: Collaborative skills for school professionals* (7th ed.). Indianapolis, IN: Pearson.

Gladden, R. M., Vivolo-Kantor, A. M., Hamburger, M. E., & Lumpkin, C. D. (2014). *Bullying surveillance among youths: Uniform definitions for public health and recommended data elements, version 1.0*. Atlanta, GA: Centers for Disease Control and Prevention. Accessed at https://files.eric.ed.gov/fulltext/ED575477.pdf on December 27, 2024.

Gonzalez, L. M., Borders, L. D., Hines, E. M., Villalba, J. A., & Henderson, A. (2013). Parental involvement in children's education: Considerations for school counselors working with Latino immigrant families. *Professional School Counseling, 16*(3), 185–193.

Gorski, P. C. (2018). *Reaching and teaching students in poverty: Strategies for erasing the opportunity gap*. New York: Teachers College Press.

Greenberg, M. T. (2023, March 6). *Evidence for social and emotional learning in schools* [Report]. Accessed at https://learningpolicyinstitute.org/product/evidence-social-emotional-learning-schools-report on January 12, 2025.

Grenny, J., Patterson, K., McMillan, R., Switzler, A., & Gregory, E. (2023). *Crucial conversations: Tools for talking when stakes are high* (3rd ed.). New York: McGraw Hill.

Grieger, T., Kauffman, J. M., & Grieger, R. M. (1976). Effects of peer reporting on cooperative play and aggression of kindergarten children. *Journal of School Psychology, 14*(4), 307–313. https://doi.org/10.1016/0022-4405(76)90027-3

Groves, E. A., & Austin, J. L. (2019). Does the Good Behavior Game evoke negative peer pressure? Analyses in primary and secondary classrooms. *Journal of Applied Behavior Analysis, 52*(1), 3–16. https://doi.org/10.1002/jaba.513

Hallahan, D. P., Pullen, P. C., & Kauffman, J. M. (2023). *Exceptional learners: An introduction to special education* (15th ed.). Indianapolis, IN: Pearson.

Hallahan, D. P., Pullen, P. C., Kauffman, J. M., & Badar, J. (2020, February 28). Exceptional learners. In G. Noblit (Ed.), *Oxford research encyclopedia of education*. Oxford, England: Oxford University Press. https://doi.org/10.1093/acrefore/9780190264093.013.926

Hanh, T. N., & Weare, K. (2017). *Happy teachers change the world: A guide for cultivating mindfulness in education*. Berkeley, CA: Parallax Press.

Haydon, T., Kennedy, A., Murphy, M., & Boone, J. (2023). Positive peer reporting for middle school students with emotional and behavioral disorders. *Intervention in School and Clinic, 58*(4), 273–279. https://doi.org/10.1177/10534512221093784

Haydon, T., Stevens, D., & Leko, M. M. (2018). Teacher stress: Sources, effects, and protective factors. *Journal of Special Education Leadership, 31*(2), 99–107.

Huang, F. L., & Cornell, D. G. (2021). Teacher support for zero tolerance is associated with higher suspension rates and lower feelings of safety. *School Psychology Review, 50*(2–3), 388–405. https://doi.org/10.1080/2372966X.2020.1832865

Hutton, L. (n.d.). *10 ways to get community support for your school.* Accessed at www.familyeducation.com/school-learning/parental-involvement/10-ways-get-community-support-your-school on July 26, 2024.

IRIS Center. (2022). *Differentiated instruction: Maximizing the learning of all students.* Accessed at https://iris.peabody.vanderbilt.edu/module/di/#content on July 26, 2024.

IRIS Center. (2025). *Functional behavioral assessment: Identifying the reasons for problem behavior and developing a behavior plan.* Accessed at https://iris.peabody.vanderbilt.edu/module/fba/#content on March 18, 2025.

Ivy, J. W., Meindl, J. N., Overley, E., & Robson, K. M. (2017). Token economy: A systematic review of procedural descriptions. *Behavior Modification, 41*(5), 708–737. https://doi.org/10.1177/0145445517699559

Jackman, C. (2022, June 1). *The 3 R's for teacher self-care: Reflect. Release. Recharge* [Blog post]. Accessed at www.pbs.org/education/blog/the-3-rs-for-teacher-self-care-reflect-release-recharge on July 26, 2024.

Jennings, P. A. (2015). *Mindfulness for teachers: Simple skills for peace and productivity in the classroom.* New York: Norton.

Jennings, P. A., Brown, J. L., Frank, J. L., Doyle, S., Oh, Y., Davis, R., et al. (2017). Impacts of the CARE for Teachers program on teachers' social and emotional competence and classroom interactions. *Journal of Educational Psychology, 109*(7), 1010–1028. https://doi.org/10.1037/edu0000187

Jigsaw Classroom. (n.d.). *The jigsaw classroom.* Accessed at www.jigsaw.org/#overview on December 1, 2024.

Jolivette, K., Ennis, R. P., & Swoszowski, N. C. (2020). Choice-making at Tier 2: Linking and adapting choice by type and function. *Preventing School Failure: Alternative Education for Children and Youth*, *64*(1), 37–47. https://doi.org/10.1080/1045988X.2019.1653256

Joslyn, P. R., & Groves, E. A. (2023). The Good Behavior Game. In J. L. Matson (Ed.), *Handbook of applied behavior analysis: Integrating research into practice* (pp. 905–928). New York: Springer.

Kabat-Zinn, J. (1990). *Full catastrophe living: Using the wisdom of your body and mind to face stress, pain, and illness*. New York: Bantam Dell.

Katz, K. (1999). *The colors of us*. New York: Holt.

King-Sears, M. E., Stefanidis, A., Evmenova, A. S., Rao, K., Mergen, R. L., Owen, L. S., & Strimel, M. M. (2023). Achievement of learners receiving UDL instruction: A meta-analysis. *Teaching and Teacher Education*, *122*, Article 103956. https://doi.org/10.1016/j.tate.2022.103956

Knowles, C., Murray, C., & Gau, J. (2024). Measuring teacher-student relationships among children with emotional and behavioral problems. *School Psychology International*, *45*(6), 699–723. https://doi.org/10.1177/01430343241248759

Lambert, A. M., Tingstrom, D. H., Sterling, H. E., Dufrene, B. A., & Lynne, S. (2015). Effects of tootling on classwide disruptive and appropriate behavior of upper-elementary students. *Behavior Modification*, *39*(3), 413–430.

Lodi, E., Perrella, L., Lepri, G. L., Scarpa, M. L., & Patrizi, P. (2022). Use of restorative justice and restorative practices at school: A systematic literature review. *International Journal of Environmental Research and Public Health*, *19*(1). https://doi.org/10.3390/ijerph19010096

Lum, J. D. K., Radley, K. C., Tingstrom, D. H., Dufrene, B. A., Olmi, D. J., & Wright, S. J. (2019). Tootling with a randomized independent group contingency to improve high school classwide behavior. *Journal of Positive Behavior Interventions*, *21*(2), 93–105. https://doi.org/10.1177/1098300718792663

Luthar, S. S., Barkin, S. H., & Crossman, E. J. (2013). "I can, therefore I must": Fragility in the upper-middle classes. *Development and Psychopathology*, *25*(402), 1529–1549. https://doi.org/10.1017/S0954579413000758

Marken, S., & Agrawal, S. (2022, June 13). *K–12 workers have highest burnout rate in U.S.* Accessed at https://news.gallup.com/poll/393500/workers-highest-burnout-rate.aspx on July 26, 2024.

Maslow, A. H. (1943). A theory of human motivation. *Psychological Review, 50*(4), 370–396.

Maslow, A. H. (1962). *Toward a psychology of being.* New York: D. Van Nostrand.

Maslow, A. H. (1970a). *Motivation and personality.* New York: Harper & Row.

Maslow, A. H. (1970b). *Religions, values and peak experiences.* New York: Penguin.

Maslow, A. H. (1987). *Motivation and personality* (3rd ed.). Indianapolis, IN: Pearson.

Masters, K. (2013). Edgar Dale's *Pyramid of Learning* in medical education: A literature review. *Medical Teacher, 35*(11), e1584–e1593. https://doi.org/10.3109/0142159X.2013.800636

McCormick, R. (2017). Does access to green space impact the mental well-being of children: A systematic review. *Journal of Pediatric Nursing, 37,* 3–7. https://doi.org/10.1016/j.pedn.2017.08.027

Meiklejohn, J., Phillips, C., Freedman, M. L., Griffin, M. L., Biegel, G., Roach, A., et al. (2012). Integrating mindfulness training into K–12 education: Fostering the resilience of teachers and students. *Mindfulness, 3,* 291–307.

Mihalas, S., Morse, W. C., Allsopp, D. H., & McHatton, P. A. (2009). Cultivating caring relationships between teachers and secondary students with emotional and behavioral disorders: Implications for research and practice. *Remedial and Special Education, 30*(2), 108–125. https://doi.org/10.1177/0741932508315950

Mills, K. L., & Tamnes, C. K. (2014). Methods and considerations for longitudinal structural brain imaging analysis across development. *Developmental Cognitive Neuroscience, 9,* 172–190. http://dx.doi.org/10.1016/j.dcn.2014.04.004

Mischel, J., & Kitsantas, A. (2020). Middle school students' perceptions of school climate, bullying prevalence, and social support and coping. *Social Psychology of Education, 23*(1), 51–72. https://doi.org/10.1007/s11218-019-09522-5

Murphy, J., & Zlomke, K. (2014). Positive peer reporting in the classroom: A review of intervention procedures. *Behavior Analysis in Practice, 7*(2), 126–137. https://doi.org/10.1007/s40617-014-0025-0

Myers, D., Freeman, J., Simonsen, B., & Sugai, G. (2017). Classroom management with exceptional learners. *Teaching Exceptional Children, 49*(4), 223–230. https://doi.org/10.1177/0040059916685064

Nagro, S. A., Fraser, D. W., & Hooks, S. D. (2019). Lesson planning with engagement in mind: Proactive classroom management strategies for curriculum instruction. *Intervention in School and Clinic, 54*(3), 131–140. https://doi.org/10.1177/1053451218767905

Nappi, J. S. (2017). The importance of questioning in developing critical thinking skills. *The Delta Kappa Gamma Bulletin: International Journal for Professional Educators, 84*(1), 30–41. Accessed at www.dkg.is/static/files/skjol_landsamband/bulletin_grein_jona.pdf on July 26, 2024.

National Alliance on Mental Illness. (2023). *Mental health by the numbers.* Accessed at www.nami.org/mhstats on July 26, 2024.

National Association of People Against Bullying. (n.d.). *Bullying in the news.* Accessed at https://www.napab.org/bullying-in-the-newson on February 11, 2025.

National Congress of American Indians. (2016, June 23). *Dr. Vincent Felitti: Reflections on the Adverse Childhood Experiences (ACE) Study* [Video file]. Accessed at www.youtube.com/watch?v=-ns8ko9-ljU&t=311s on July 26, 2024.

National Institute of Health. (2025). *Infographic: Four types of exercise and physical activity.* Accessed at https://www.nia.nih.gov/health/exercise-and-physical-activity/three-types-exercise-and-physical-activity on February 11, 2025.

National Institute of Mental Health. (2022). *Coping with traumatic events.* Accessed at www.nimh.nih.gov/health/topics/coping-with-traumatic-events on July 26, 2024.

National Institute of Neurological Disorders and Stroke. (2023, March 17). *Brain basics: Know your brain.* Accessed at www.ninds.nih.gov/health-information/public-education/brain-basics/brain-basics-know-your-brain on July 26, 2024.

Northern Illinois University Center for Innovative Teaching and Learning. (2020). *Bloom's Taxonomy.* Accessed at https://www.niu.edu/citl/resources/guides/instructional-guide/blooms-taxonomy.shtml on February 11, 2025.

O'Neill, R. E., Albin, R. W., Storey, K., Horner, R. H., & Sprague, J. R. (2015). *Functional assessment and program development for problem behavior: A practical handbook* (3rd ed.). Boston: Cengage Learning.

Owens, J., & McLanahan, S. S. (2020). Unpacking the drivers of racial disparities in school suspension and expulsion. *Social Forces, 98*(4), 1548–1577. https://doi.org/10.1093/sf/soz095

Ozer, E. J., Lavi, I., Douglas, L., & Wolf, J. P. (2017). Protective factors for youth exposed to violence in their communities: A review of family, school, and community moderators. *Journal of Clinical Child & Adolescent Psychology, 46*(3), 353–378. https://doi.org/10.1080/15374416.2015.1046178

Perfect, M. M., Turley, M. R., Carlson, J. S., Yohanna, J., & Saint Gilles, M. P. (2016). School-related outcomes of traumatic event exposure and traumatic stress symptoms in students: A systematic review of research from 1990 to 2015. *School Mental Health, 8,* 7–43. https://doi.org/10.1007/s12310-016-9175-2

Phelps, P. H., & Benson, T. R. (2012). Teachers with a passion for the profession. *Action in Teacher Education, 34*(1), 65–76. https://doi.org/10.1080/01626620.2012.642289

Physiopedia. (n.d.). *Limbic system.* Accessed at www.physio-pedia.com/Limbic_System?utm_source=physiopedia&utm_medium=search&utm_campaign=ongoing_internal on July 26, 2024.

Premana, D. N. D., Widiana, I. W., & Wibawa, I. M. C. (2023). Improving conceptual knowledge in elementary school students with revised Bloom's taxonomy-oriented learning activities. *Thinking Skills and Creativity Journal, 6*(1), 9–18. https://doi.org/10.23887/tscj.v6i1.57454

Reyes, M. R., Brackett, M. A., Rivers, S. E., White, M. & Salovey, P. (2012). Classroom emotional climate, student engagement, and academic achievement. *Journal of Educational Psychology, 104*(3), 700–712. https://doi.org/10.1037/a0027268

Rimm-Kaufman, S., & Sandilos, L. (2015). *Improving students' relationships with teachers to provide essential supports for learning: Applications of psychological science to teaching and learning modules.* Accessed at www.apa.org/education-career/k12/relationships on July 26, 2024.

Romm, K. F., Barry, C. M., & Alvis, L. M. (2020). How the rich get riskier: Parenting and higher-SES emerging adults' risk behaviors. *Journal of Adult Development, 27*(4), 281–293. https://doi.org/10.1007/s10804-020-09345-1

Sawyer, M. (2015). Bridges: Connecting with families to facilitate and enhance involvement. *Teaching Exceptional Children, 47*(3), 172–179.

Schwartz, K. (2016). *I wish my teacher knew: How one question can change everything for our kids.* Boston: Da Capo Lifelong Books.

Scott, T. M. (2017). *Teaching behavior: Managing classrooms through effective instruction.* Thousand Oaks, CA: Corwin.

Sheybani, M. (2019). The relationship between EFL learners' willingness to communicate (WTC) and their teacher immediacy attributes: A structural equation modelling. *Cogent Psychology, 6*(1), Article 1607051. https://doi.org/10.1080/23311908.2019.1607051

Simms, J. A. (2025). *Where learning happens: Leveraging working memory and attention in the classroom.* Bloomington, IN: Marzano Resources.

Skiba, R. J. (2000). *Zero tolerance, zero evidence: An analysis of school disciplinary practice.* Bloomington, IN: Indiana Education Policy Center.

Skinner, C. H., Cashwell, T. H., & Skinner, A. L. (2000). Increasing tootling: The effects of a peer-monitored group contingency program on students' reports of peers' prosocial behaviors. *Psychology in the Schools, 37*(3), 263–270. https://doi.org/10.1002/(SICI)1520-6807(200005)37:3<263::AID-PITS6>3.0.CO;2-C

Slagt, M., Dubas, J. S., Deković, M., & van Aken, M. A. G. (2016). Differences in sensitivity to parenting depending on child temperament: A meta-analysis. *Psychological Bulletin, 142*(10), 1068–1110. https://doi.org/10.1037/bul0000061

Smale-Jacobse, A. E., Meijer, A., Helms-Lorenz, M., & Maulana, R. (2019). Differentiated instruction in secondary education: A systematic review of research evidence. *Frontiers in Psychology, 10.* https://doi.org/10.3389/fpsyg.2019.02366

Smith, D., Fisher, D., & Frey, N. (2015). *Better than carrots or sticks: Restorative practices for positive classroom management.* Arlington, VA: ASCD.

Smith, D., Fisher, D., & Frey, N. (2017). *Managing your classroom with restorative practices.* Arlington, VA: ASCD.

Society for Neuroscience. (2018). *BrainFacts: A primer on the brain and nervous system.* Accessed at www.brainfacts.org/-/media/Brainfacts2/Brain Facts-Book/Brain-Facts-PDF-with-links.pdf on July 26, 2024.

Sprick, J., Sprick, R., Edwards, J., & Coughlin, C. (2021). *CHAMPS: A proactive and positive approach to classroom management* (3rd ed.). Eugene, OR: Ancora.

Steege, M. W., Pratt, J. L., Wickerd, G., Guare, R., & Watson, T. S. (2019). *Conducting school-based functional behavioral assessments: A practitioner's guide* (3rd ed.). New York: Guilford Press.

Steiner, E. D., Doan, S., Woo, A., Gittens, A. D., Lawrence, R. A., Berdie, L., et al. (2022). *Restoring teacher and principal well-being is an essential step for rebuilding schools: Findings from the State of the American Teacher and State of the American Principal surveys.* Accessed at www.rand.org/pubs/research_reports/RRA1108-4.html on July 26, 2024.

Substance Abuse and Mental Health Services Administration. (2022). *Trauma and violence.* Accessed at www.samhsa.gov/trauma-violence on July 26, 2024.

Thatcher, T. (2019, February 4). *Can emotional trauma cause brain damage?* Accessed at https://highlandspringsclinic.org/can-emotional-trauma-cause-brain-damage on July 26, 2024.

Thomas, M. S., Crosby, S., & Vanderhaar, J. (2019). Trauma-informed practices in schools across two decades: An interdisciplinary review of research. *Review of Research in Education, 43*(1), 422–452. https://doi.org/10.3102/0091732X18821123

Thompson, L. (2019, January 20). Importance of self-care as a teacher. *NEA Today.* Accessed at www.nea.org/professional-excellence/student-engagement/tools-tips/importance-self-care-teacher on January 14, 2025.

Tomlinson, C. A. (2014). *The differentiated classroom: Responding to the needs of all learners* (2nd ed.). Arlington, VA: ASCD.

U.S. Department of Health and Human Services. (2021, March 30). *Why some youth bully.* Accessed at www.stopbullying.gov/bullying/why-some-youth-bully on July 26, 2024.

U.S. Department of Health and Human Services. (2024, October 7). *What is bullying.* Accessed at www.stopbullying.gov/bullying/what-is-bullying on November 30, 2024.

U.S. Department of Health and Human Services. (2025, February 3). *Effects of bullying.* Accessed at www.stopbullying.gov/bullying/effects on March 18, 2025.

Vijayakumar, N., Op de Macks, Z., Shirtcliff, E. A., & Pfeifer, J. H. (2018). Puberty and the human brain: Insights into adolescent development. *Neuroscience & Biobehavioral Reviews, 92,* 417–436. https://doi.org/10.1016/j.neubiorev.2018.06.004

Vygotsky, L. S. (1978). *Mind in society: The development of higher psychological processes.* Cambridge, MA: Harvard University Press.

Walker, T. (2021, November 12). Getting serious about teacher burnout. *NEA Today.* Accessed at www.nea.org/nea-today/all-news-articles/getting-serious-about-teacher-burnout on July 26, 2024.

White, R., & Renk, K. (2012). Externalizing behavior problems during adolescence: An ecological perspective. *Journal of Child and Family Studies, 21,* 158–171. https://doi.org/10.1007/s10826-011-9459-y

Wills, H. P., & Mason, B. A. (2014). Implementation of a self-monitoring application to improve on-task behavior: A high-school pilot study. *Journal of Behavioral Education, 23,* 421–434. https://doi.org/10.1007/s10864-014-9204-x

Wong, H. K., & Wong, R. T. (2018). *The first days of school: How to be an effective teacher* (5th ed.). Mountain View, CA: Wong.

World Health Organization. (2022, June 8). *Mental disorders.* Accessed at www.who.int/news-room/fact-sheets/detail/mental-disorders on July 26, 2024.

Yell, M. L., Meadows, N. B., Drasgow, E., & Shriner, J. G. (2013). *Evidence-based practices for educating students with emotional and behavioral disorders* (2nd ed.). Indianapolis, IN: Pearson.

Zolkoski, S. M. (2019). The importance of teacher-student relationships for students with emotional and behavioral disorders. *Preventing School Failure: Alternative Education for Children and Youth, 63*(3), 236–241. https://doi.org/10.1080/1045988X.2019.1579165

Zolkoski, S. M., Bullock, L. M., & Gable, R. A. (2016). Factors associated with student resilience: Perspectives of graduates of alternative education programs. *Preventing School Failure, 60*(3), 231–243. https://doi.org/10.1080/1045988X.2015.1101677

Zolkoski, S. M., & Lewis-Chiu, C. (2019). Alternative approaches: Implementing mindfulness practices in the classroom to improve challenging behaviors. *Beyond Behavior, 28*(1), 46–54. https://doi.org/10.1177/1074295619832943

Zolkoski, S. M., Lewis Chiu, C., & Lusk, M. E. (2023). *Motivated to learn: Decreasing challenging student behaviors and increasing academic engagement*. Bloomington, IN: Solution Tree Press.

Zolkoski, S. M., Sayman, D. M., & Lewis-Chiu, C. G. (2018). Considerations in promoting parent and family involvement. *Diversity, Social Justice, and the Educational Leader, 2*(2).

Index

A

ABC Observations, 125, 128
academic achievement, 30, 31, 32, 36
  Bloom's taxonomy and, 140
  bullying and, 27
  classroom environment and, 40, 46, 70
  expectations and, 82, 97
  nonverbal teacher behaviors and, 46
  parental involvement and, 20
  positive peer reporting and, 108
  self-monitoring and, 120
  social and emotional learning and, 54, 59, 63
  token economies and, 116
  UDL and, 149
accommodations, 52, 92
ACEs. *See* adverse childhood experiences (ACEs)
Acosta, J., 17
action, multiple means of, 149, 151
ADHD. *See* attention deficit hyperactivity disorder (ADHD)
adolescence, brain development in, 8–9

adverse childhood experiences (ACEs), 21–24. *See also* trauma
aesthetic needs, 28
affective domain, 136–137
Agency for Healthcare Research and Quality (AHRQ), 24–25
Agrawal, S., 158
AHRQ. *See* Agency for Healthcare Research and Quality (AHRQ)
Alliance for Excellent Education, 158
Allsopp, D. H., 40
American Psychological Association (APA), 26
amygdala, 10, 11, 23–24, 27. *See also* brain development
analysis, 137
Anderson, L., 137
anxiety, 14, 20, 23, 26, 36
APA. *See* American Psychological Association (APA)
application, of knowledge, 137, 139
apps
  family engagement and, 94–95
  positive reinforcement using, 83
arrival procedures, 77–78

185

assessment, 142–144
　differentiation and, 147–149
assumptions, 85, 102–103
attention deficit hyperactivity
　　disorder (ADHD), 151
　access to nature and, 19
　brain development and, 14
　classroom arrangement and, 49
attention getters, 77
attitude, positive, 163
Austin, J. L., 115
authenticity, 39, 58, 73, 82, 150

B

Barrish, H. H., 113
behavior
　assumptions about, 102–103
　brain development and, 8–27
　as communication, 13
　expectations and boundaries on, 69
　internal and external factors
　　influencing, 14–26
　labeling, 31–32
　positive peer reporting on, 102, 108–112
　trauma and, 20–25
　understanding, 3, 7–34, 165
behavior intervention plans, 128–130
belonging
　bullying and, 17
　need for, 28
　stress and, 70
Benson, T., 163
biases, 15
　socioeconomic status and, 19–20
　token economies and, 119
biological factors, 14
BIP. *See* behavior intervention plans
Bloom, B., 136
Bloom's taxonomy, 32, 136–140, 147, 148
books, brain development and exposure to, 20
Boone, J., 108
boundaries, 30–31, 67–100
　self-care and, 158
　strategies for communicating and
　　reinforcing, 69–92
Boyle, A., 54
brain development, 5, 165
　in adults vs. adolescents, 10
　basics of, 8–13
　biological factors in, 14
　community and, 19–20
　consequences and, 87–88
　home environment and, 18–19
　how behavior is linked to, 9–12
　internal and external factors
　　influencing, 14–26
　peer influence and, 16–18
　rules and, 75–76
　stress and, 26–27
　trauma and, 20–25
brain state model, 56
breathing, mindful, 161–162
Bruhn, A. L., 120
bucket fillers, 157
"Building a Positive Classroom
　　Environment," 63, 64
bullying, 17–18
　stress from, 26–27
burnout, 2, 32, 157–158

C

Capp, M. J., 149
caring, 40, 44, 46, 53
　assumptions vs., 102–103
　community and, 19
　social and emotional learning and, 58
　teacher-student relationships and, 40–48
CASEL. *See* Collaborative for Academic, Social,
　　and Emotional Learning (CASEL)
Cashwell, T. H., 108
CAST, 148, 149
cell phone procedures, 78
Centers for Disease Control (CDC), 37
change, accepting, 163
check-ins
　class meetings, restorative
　　practices and, 60–61
　feelings, 42
checklists
　fidelity, 129, 130
　self-monitoring, 123
Chinman, M., 17
Choi, T., 120
choice, 31, 102, 104–108
choice boards, 148

Choose Love Movement, 56
circle meetings, 60–61
citizenship, 36
class discrimination, 19–20
class discussion procedures, 78
class meetings, 60–61. *See also* meetings
classroom arrangements, 5, 48–52
classroom environment.
    See positive classroom environment
"Classroom Expectations"
    reproducible, 97, 98–99
classroom management, 2, 3, 166
    expectations and boundaries in, 67–100
    importance and difficulty of, 67–68
    positive classroom environment and, 35–66
    supporting students with effective, 29–32
climate, school, 17
clumsiness, growth spurts and, 9
cognitive abilities
    Bloom's taxonomy and, 136–140
    trauma and, 21
cognitive domain, 136–137
cognitive needs, 28
collaboration, 163
Collaborative for Academic, Social, and
    Emotional Learning
    (CASEL), 53, 55–56, 58–59
Collins, T. A., 108
The Colors of Us (Katz), 59
communication
    about consequences, 87
    behavior as, 13
    of expectations and
        boundaries, 30–31, 69–92
    expression and, 151
    with families, 44, 92–95
    self-monitoring and, 123
communities
    brain development and, 19–20
    classroom, restorative practices for, 59–62
comprehension, 137, 151
conflict management, restorative
    practices for, 59–62
congenital defects, 14
Conscious Discipline, 56
consequences, 31, 71, 84–92
    brain development and, 11
consistency, 29–32

consequences and, 91
expectations and, 70
in positive reinforcement, 82
social and emotional learning and, 57
in Tier 1 supports, 101
content, 143–144
contingencies, classwide group, 102, 113–115
contingency plans, 129
contracts, class behavior
    consequences and, 91
    rules in, 72
control, 102, 104–108
Cook, C. R., 42, 46
coping strategies, 37, 161–162
cortisol, 27
COVID-19 pandemic, 1, 2, 158
    mental health and, 25
creating, Bloom's taxonomy on, 137–139
creativity, 36
Cui, L., 163
cultural self-awareness, 93
curriculum
    content differentiation with, 144
    social and emotional learning and, 58–59

D

Dailos, C., 42, 46
Dale, E., 135
data collection, 124–125
decision making, social and emotional
    learning and, 53–54
defensiveness, 39
depression, 25, 37
differentiated instruction, 32, 133, 141–148
    content and, 144
    process and, 144–147
    product and, 147–149
    traditional classrooms vs., 142
    Universal Design for Learning
        and, 32, 133, 148–151
direct observation, 125–128
discipline, seven skills for, 56.
    See also positive reinforcement
dismissal procedures, 78
diversification
    Bloom's taxonomy and, 140
    choice strategy and, 107–108

consequences and, 92
Good Behavior Game and, 115
positive classroom environment and, 46–48, 52
positive peer reporting and, 112
positive reinforcement and, 84
procedures and, 81
restorative practices and, 62
rules and, 75
self-monitoring and, 122–123
social and emotional learning and, 58–59
token economies and, 119

diversity
choice and, 107
family involvement and, 92–93
lesson for supporting, 59
self-monitoring and, 122

Douglas, L., 19
Dufrene, B. A., 108
Durlak, J., 54

E

early childhood, brain development in, 8
EBDs. *See* emotional and behavioral disorders (EBDs)
Ebener, P., 17
emoji rating scale, 121
emotional and behavioral disorders (EBDs), 3, 14
brain development and, 14
teacher-student relationships and, 40
emotional capacity, 150

emotions
brain development and, 11
bullying and, 18
competencies related to, 53–54
feelings check-ins and, 42

empathy
consequences and, 87
families and, 96–97
reflecting on showing, 33, 34
restorative practices and, 60–61
teacher-student relationships and, 40
understanding student needs and, 27

engagement
of families, 93–95
providing multiple means of, 149–150

teacher preparation and, 49

environment
brain development and, 8
bullying and, 17–18
home, 18–19
positive, 5, 30, 35–66
punitive consequences and, 82
safe, 15–16
student needs and, 28

equality in perception, 150
equity, and referrals for challenging behavior, 15
esteem needs, 28
evaluation, knowledge and, 137, 138, 139
event recordings, 126
executive functions, 12, 151
exercise, 160–161

expectations, 17, 67–100, 133
assumptions and, 102–103
consequences supporting, 71, 84–92
ensuring student understanding of, 81
of families, 20
perspectives on, 100
positive reinforcement of, 70, 81–84
precorrection and, 104
procedures supporting, 70, 76–81
restorative practices and, 60–61
rules to support, 70, 71–76
social and emotional learning and, 58–59
strategies for communicating and reinforcing, 69–92
students' need for, 28
supporting students with, 30–31

explicit instruction, of procedures, 76–80
expression, multiple means of, 149, 151
extracurricular activities, 43, 46

F

families
authentic partnerships with, 58
choice and, 107–108
class behavior contracts and, 72
communication of expectations and, 30
consequences and, 90
creating the school, 56
difficult situations with, 95–97
home environment, brain development, and, 18–19

parental involvement and, 19–20, 92–93
positive classroom environment and, 44
strategies for engaging with, 92–97
stress and, 26
Fay, C., 47, 96
Fay, J., 96
FBA. *See* functional behavior assessments
feelings check-ins, 42
Fernando, J., 120
Fiat, A., 42, 46
fidelity checklists, 129, 130
fight or flight, 20, 24
Fisher, D., 38–39
flexible grouping, 142–144
formative assessments, 143
Frayer Model, 145
Freedman, M. L., 161
Frey, N., 38–39
functional behavior assessments, 30, 31–32, 123–128

G

Gau, J., 40
Giegel, G., 161
Gladden, R. M., 17
goals, self-monitoring and, 120
Good Behavior Game, 31, 102, 113–115
Good Being Good Game, 114–115
Google Voice, 44
Gorski, P. C., 19
graphic organizers, 145
Greenberg, M. T., 36
greeting students, 42, 45
Grieger, T., 108
Grieger, R., 108
Griffin, M. L., 161
Groves, E. A., 115
growth mindset, 73
growth spurts, 9
guided notes, 147
guided reading, 147

H

Hallahan, D. P., 14
Hamburger, M. E., 17
Haydon, T., 108, 160

health, 37. *See also* mental health
help, asking for, 79, 80
hierarchy of needs, 27–28, 30, 47–48, 54
hippocampus, 10, 11–12, 23–24, 27. *See also* brain development
Holland, E. A., 42, 46
homework, rules on, 72
hypervigilance, 20

I

impulsivity, 11
independence, 5, 32, 133–156
choice and, 105–108
instructional elements, 143–144
intentionally inviting teachers, 38–40
intentionally uninviting teachers, 38–39
interest inventories, 42–43, 45–46, 47
interests, student
engagement and, 150
self-monitoring and, 122
teachers' interest in, 42–43, 45–46
token economies and, 116–117
interval recordings, 125–126
IRIS Center, 141

J

Jackman, C., 158–159
Jesse Lewis Choose Love Movement, 56
jigsaw activities, 145
Joslyn, P. R., 115
joy, finding your, 162–163

K

Karathwohl, D., 137
Kauffman, J. M., 14
Kaufman, J., 108
Kennedy, A., 108
King-Sears, M. E., 149
Kitsantas, A., 17
knowledge, 137
Knowles, C., 40

L

Lambert, D. H., 108
language, 151

Bloom's taxonomy and, 140
brain development and, 20
choice and, 107–108
rules and, 71, 72, 75
social and emotional learning and, 55, 57
Larson, M., 42, 46
late work policies, 72
Lavi, I., 19
learning
Bloom's taxonomy and, 136–140
brain's capacity for, 9
differentiation for, 141–148
hippocampus and, 11–12
process in, 135
promoting, 133–156
social and emotional, 53–59
learning disabilities, brain development and, 14
learning objectives, 138–139
learning stations, 145–147
lecture-based teaching, 135–136
Leko, M. M., 160
lesson planning, 5, 52, 133, 134–135
Lewis, J., 56
Lewis Chiu, C., 3–4, 101
limbic system, 11
linguistic representation, 150–151
love, need for, 28
Love and Logic (Fay), 47
low birth weight, 14
Lumpkin, C. D., 17
Lusk, M. E., 3–4, 101
Lynne, S., 108

M

Mahoney, J., 54
Malone, P. S., 17
manipulatives, 145
Marken, S., 158
Maslow, A., 27–28, 30, 47–48, 54
Master, K., 135
materials
content differentiation with, 144
how to access, 50
preparing daily, 48–49
McHatton, P. A., 40
meetings, restorative practices and, 60–61
Meiklejohn, J., 161

memory, 11–12
mental health
access to care for, 37
classroom environment and, 36–38
depression and, 25, 37
families and, 95–96
trauma and, 24–25
Mihalas, S., 40
mindfulness, 161–162
mindset
growth, 73
of helping, 75–76
Mischel, J., 17
modeling
positive peer reporting, 111
procedures, 76–80
self-monitoring and, 121
social and emotional learning, 55
monitoring
positive peer reporting, 111, 112
self-, 31, 102, 119–123
Morse, W. C., 40
Motivated to Learn: Decreasing Challenging Student Behaviors and Increasing Academic Engagement (Zolloski, Lewis Chiu, & Lusk), 3–4, 101
motivation
choice and, 105–108
expectations and, 81–82
nonverbal teacher behaviors and, 46
MTSS. *See* multitiered systems of support (MTSS)
multitiered systems of support (MTSS), 29
Murphy, M., 108
Murray, C., 40

N

names, learning student, 41–42, 45
NAMI. *See* National Alliance on Mental Illness (NAMI)
National Alliance on Mental Illness (NAMI), 36–37
National Institutes of Health, 160
nature, 19
needs
behavior in communicating, 13
Maslow's hierarchy of, 27–28, 47–48, 54
positive classroom environment and, 30

questioning, 103
teachers' responsibility for meeting, 16–17
understanding student, 27–29
negative punishment, 86
negative reinforcement, 86
neglect, 18–19
neurological differences, 14
neurotransmitters, 14
newsletters, 44
nonlinguistic representation, 150–151
nonverbal communication, positive classroom environment and, 46
Northern Illinois University Center for Innovative Teaching and Learning, 136
note-taking, 147

O

observation
   ABC, 128
   direct, 125–128
one-sentence intervention, 47, 103
organization, positive classroom environment and, 51
overstimulation
   classroom arrangement and, 49
   positive classroom environment and, 52
Ozer, E., 19

P

parenting styles, 18–19
parietal lobe, 10, 11. *See also* brain development
participatory teaching methods, 135
passion, finding your, 162–163
passive teaching methods, 135
PBIS. *See* positive behavioral interventions and supports (PBIS)
peer-mediated strategies, 108
peers
   brain development and, 16–18
   stress and, 26–27
peer-to-peer learning, 140
pencil-sharpening procedures, 79, 80
perception, equality in, 150
perspectives, 5
   on expectations, 100
   on learning and independence, 155–156
   on self-care, 164

social and emotional learning and, 55, 57
   on supports, 132
   what do you like about your teacher?, 65–66
Phelps, P., 163
Phillips, A., 17
Phillips, C., 161
physical action, 151
physiological needs, 28
poetry stations, 147
positive behavioral interventions and supports (PBIS), 29
positive classroom environment, 5, 30, 35–66, 165–166
   beginning vs. middle of the year, 44–46
   classroom arrangements and, 48–52
   research on, 36–38
   restorative practices for, 59–62
   social and emotional learning and, 53–59
   strategies for, 38–62
   teacher-student relationships and, 40–48
positive peer reporting, 31, 102, 108–112
positive punishment, 85–86
positive reinforcement, 31, 68
   choice in, 106
   definition of, 85–86
   positive peer reporting and, 110
   self-monitoring and, 122
   to support expectations, 70, 81–84
   token economies and, 116–117
positivity, 25
poverty, 19–20
power of proximity, 86–87, 88
praise, specific positive, 103
preassessment, 143
precorrection, 104
predictability, 30–31
prefrontal cortex, 10, 11, 23–24. *See also* brain development
Premana, D. N. D., 136
preteaching vocabulary, 140
preventative actions, 4
preventative reinforcement, 68
primary grades
   Bloom's taxonomy in, 138–139
   choice in, 105–107
   classroom arrangements for, 49–50
   consequences in, 87–91
   examples of rules for, 73–74

expectations in, 82–84
Good Behavior Game in, 113–115
learning stations in, 147
maintaining rules in, 71–72
positive peer reporting in, 108–112
positive reinforcement in, 82–84
procedures supporting
    expectations in, 76–80
restorative practices in, 60–61
self-monitoring in, 120–122
showing care in, 41–44
social and emotional learning in, 54–57
token economies in, 116–119
privacy, 44
proactivity, 4, 51, 68
problem solving, 36
procedures
    expectations supported by, 70, 76–81
    primary and secondary grades, 76–80
process, 143–144
product, 143–144, 147–148
professional development, 163
proximity, power of, 86–87, 88
psychomotor domain, 136–137
puberty, brain development and, 9, 11
Pullen, P. C., 14
punishment, 69. *See also* consequences
    negative, 86
    positive, 85–86
    school climate and, 82
purpose, 61, 165
Pyramid of Learning (Dale), 135

Q

questions and questioning
    about behavior, 103
    Bloom's taxonomy and, 137–140
    diversification and, 140
    positive classroom environment and, 39
    restorative practices and, 62
    "What do I wish my teacher knew?," 47–48

R

RAFT (role, audience, format, topic), 148
rating scales, for self-monitoring, 120–122
reactive management, 39
readiness levels, 144–145
recharging, self-care and, 158–159
"Reflecting on Showing Empathy," 33, 34
reflection, 166
    on biases, 130–131
    on positive classroom environment, 51
    self-care and, 158–159
    on showing empathy, 33, 34
"Reflective Thinking About Bias," 130–131
relationships
    building positive, with students, 40–48
    with families, 92–97
    restorative practices and, 60–61
    skills for, 53–54
    social and emotional learning and, 58–59
    strategies for fostering, 103–104
    teacher self-care and, 163
    in Tier 1 interventions, 69
    Tier 2 supports and, 102–103
    whole child focus and, 36
release, self-care and, 158–159
relevance, 54–55
remembering, 137–138, 139
representation, multiple
    means of, 149, 150–151
reproducibles
    "Building a Positive Classroom
        Environment," 63, 64
    "Classroom Expectations," 97, 98–99
    "Reflecting on Showing Empathy," 33, 34
    "Reflective Thinking About Bias," 130–131
    "Thinking About Differentiating
        Instruction," 152, 153–154
research
    on positive classroom environment, 36–39
    on positive peer reporting, 108
    on self-care, 158
    on self-monitoring, 120
resilience, 32, 40
respect, 36, 87
Response Cost, 115
response to intervention (RTI), 29
responsibility
    for meeting students' needs, 16–17
    restorative practices and, 60–61
restorative practices, 59–62
restroom procedures, 77, 79–80
rewards

Good Behavior Game and, 114
   for positive peer reporting, 112
   positive reinforcement and, 83
risk taking
   brain development and, 16–17
   family expectations and, 20
risk taking, brain development and, 9, 11
Roach, A., 161
RTI. *See* response to intervention (RTI)
rules
   adaptable, 72
   beginning vs. midyear, 73–75
   expectations supported by, 70, 71–76
   Good Behavior Game and, 113–115
   must-have, 71–72

S

safety, 15–16
   classroom arrangements and, 48
   community, 19–20
   need for, 28
   social and emotional learning and, 59
Saunders, M., 113
scaffolding, 137–138, 140
scatterplots, 126–127
schools
   climate in, 17
   as factor in student behavior, 15–16
   stress from, 26
seat work procedures, 78–79, 80
seating arrangements
   choice in, 106
   learning student names and, 41–42
   positive learning environment and, 50, 52
secondary grades
   Bloom's taxonomy in, 138–139
   choice in, 105–107
   classroom arrangements for, 49–50
   consequences in, 87–91
   expectations in, 82–84
   Good Behavior Game in, 113–115
   maintaining rules in, 71–72
   positive peer reporting in, 108–112
   positive reinforcement in, 82–84
   procedures supporting expectations in, 76–80
   restorative practices in, 60–61

   self-monitoring in, 120–122
   showing care in, 41–44
   social and emotional learning in, 54–57
   token economies in, 116–119
SEL. *See* social and emotional learning (SEL)
self-actualization, need for, 28
self-awareness, 53–54, 93
self-care, 5, 32, 157–164, 166–167
   strategies for, 160–163
self-management, 53–54, 104
self-monitoring, 31, 102, 119–123
self-regulation, trauma and, 21
sensory disorders, classroom arrangement and, 49, 52
seven powers of conscious adults, 56
Sheybani, M., 46
Shipp, J., 167
Sideline, 44
Skinner, A. L., 108
Skinner, C. H., 108
Slemrod, T., 42, 46
small groups, 145–147
Smith, D., 38–39
social and emotional learning (SEL), 53–59, 161
social awareness, 53–54
social competence, 15
   core competencies for, 53–54
   self-monitoring and, 120
social media, 44, 94–95
social studies, 147
socioeconomic status, 19–20, 93
standards, 134
Sterling, H. E., 108
Stevens, D., 160
strategies, 4, 5
   for additional support, 102–123
   best practices for teaching academics, 134–151
   choice, 102, 104–108
   for engaging with families, 92–97
   for expectations and boundaries, 69–92
   for positive classroom environment, 38–62
   for self-care, 160–163
stress
   brain development and, 26–27
   chronic, 26, 27
   nature and, 19

self-care and, 157–164
short-term, 26
signs of, 27
of teaching, 2
trauma and, 21–25
structure, 17, 29–32, 70
student work, displaying, 49
substance abuse
    mental health and, 37
    prenatal exposure to and brain development, 14
    trauma and, 22
success, giving students tools for, 12
suicidal behaviors, 37
    bullying and, 18
    trauma and, 24–25
summative assessments, 143
supplies, procedures for, 80
support, 13
    classroom management as, 29–32
    multitiered, 29–32
    Tier 1, 29–30, 68–69, 101, 115–116
    Tier 2, 26–32, 68–69, 101–132, 166
    Tier 3, 29–32, 123–130
survival, 24
synthesis, 137

T

teachers
    clothing of, 39
    as factor in student behavior, 15–16
    family relationships with, 93–95
    letting students get to know, 43
    mental health and, 25
    in positive classroom environment, 38–39
    relationships of with students, 40–48
    self-care for, 5, 32, 157–164
    what do you like about your teacher?, 65–66
teaching
    best practices in, 32, 134–151
    purpose and, 3
    rewards and challenges of, 2
technology, rules on using, 72
temperament, 14, 15
temporal lobe, 11–12.
    See also brain development

"Thinking About Differentiating Instruction," 152, 153–154
Thompson, L., 159
thought watching, 162
tickets, positive reinforcement using, 83
tic-tac-toe, 148
Tier 1 supports, 29–30, 68–69
    consistency with, 101
    token economies, 115–116
Tier 2 supports, 29, 30, 31–32, 68–69, 101–132, 166
    choice, 102, 104–108
    Good Behavior Game, 102, 113–115
    positive peer reporting, 102, 108–112
    self-monitoring, 102, 119–123
    strategies for, 102–123
Tier 3 supports, 29, 30, 31–32, 68–69, 123–130
    behavior intervention plans, 128–130
    functional behavior assessment, 123–128
time and time management
    for restorative practices, 61–62
    for social and emotional learning, 56–57
time off, 158
token economies, 31, 102, 115–119
tootling. *See* positive peer reporting
transcendence, need for, 28
trauma
    brain development, behavior, and, 20–25
    definition of, 21
    families and, 95–96
treasure boxes, positive reinforcement using, 83
Troughton, L., 120

U

understanding, 138, 139
unintentionally inviting teachers, 38–39
unintentionally uninviting teachers, 38–39
Universal Design for Learning (UDL), 32, 133, 148–151
University of Texas at Tyler, 3
U.S. Department of Health and Human Services, 17–18

V

ventral striatum, 10, 11.
    See also brain development

verbal warnings, 88
violence
    bullying and, 18
    socioeconomic status and, 19–20
visual aids, 140
Vivolo-Kantor, A. M., 17
vocabulary, preteaching, 140
Voices from the Field, 5
    on expectations, 100
    on learning and independence, 155–156
    on self-care, 164
    on supports, 132
    what do you like about your teacher?, 65–66

W
well-being, 158–159
"What do I wish my teacher knew?," 47–48
whole child concept, 56, 63
    classroom environment and, 36–38
    social and emotional learning and, 54
whole-group instruction, 136
Wibawa, I. M. C., 136
Widiana, I. W., 136
Wilks, A., 17
win-win process, with difficult families, 96–97
Wolf, J. P., 19
Wolf, M. M., 113
Wong, H. K., 76
Wong, R. T., 76
Woods-Groves, S., 120

Z
Zolkoski, S. M., 3–4, 101
zone of proximal development, 141

Motivated to Learn
Staci M. Zolkoski, Calli Lewis Chiu, and Mandy E. Lusk

In *Motivated to Learn*, you will gain evidence-based approaches for engaging students and equipping them to better focus in the classroom. With this book's straightforward strategies, you can learn to motivate all your students to actively participate in learning.

BKG037

The Purpose-Driven Classroom
Daniel L. Vollrath

In *The Purpose-Driven Classroom*, author Daniel L. Vollrath uses dispositional teaching to address productivity and promote positive habits. He presents seven productive behaviors that general education teachers can teach to all students across all content areas.

BKG050

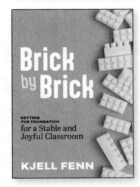

Brick by Brick
Kjell Fenn

Using research-supported strategies, author Kjell Fenn guides new teachers through four pillars of successful teaching: planning, structure, engagement, and confidence. Learn how to design assessments, craft lesson plans, and find the structure for students and teachers to experience joy in the classroom.

BKG214

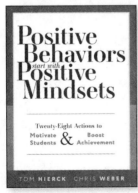

Positive Behaviors Start With Positive Mindsets
Tom Hierck and Chris Weber

Using 28 measures, teachers can proactively plan, introduce new ideas, and strengthen existing practices to ensure that all students develop positive mindsets and productive behaviors. Learn why fostering four positive mindsets is critical to student success in school and life.

BKG107

Solution Tree | Press
a division of Solution Tree

Visit SolutionTree.com or call 800.733.6786 to order.

Quality team learning **from authors you trust**

Global PD Teams is the first-ever **online professional development resource designed to support your entire faculty on your learning journey.** This convenient tool offers daily access to videos, mini-courses, eBooks, articles, and more packed with insights and research-backed strategies you can use immediately.

 GET STARTED
SolutionTree.com/**GlobalPDTeams**
800.733.6786